Big Ideas in Outdoor Primary Science

Big Ideas in Outdoor Primary Science takes a fresh approach to learning science in outdoor contexts. It combines new thinking in science teaching using big ideas, with our growing need to look after our planet, and encourages children to learn from what scientists have to say about issues which will impact their lives today and in the future.

The book offers primary teachers the subject and pedagogical knowledge, as well as the confidence they need, to integrate the seeds of big ideas into their curriculum. To this end, it provides models of good practice which exemplify how primary-aged children can work towards understanding some of science's big ideas and engage with important issues related to wildlife conservation.

The easy-to-use book covers topics such as:

- Interdependence
- Adaptation
- Inheritance
- Following in Darwin's footsteps
- Protecting ecosystems

Full of ideas for outside learning, this book is a comprehensive, valuable and essential resource for all teachers of primary science.

Peter Loxley taught in both primary and secondary schools for many years, including in the UK, Australia and Jamaica. Peter was previously Subject Leader of Science Education at the University of Northampton, UK.

Big Ideas in Outdoor Primary Science

Understanding and Enjoying the Natural World

Peter Loxley

LONDON AND NEW YORK

First published 2021

by Routledge
2 Park Square, Milton Park, Abingdon, Oxon OX14 4RN

and by Routledge
52 Vanderbilt Avenue, New York, NY 10017

Routledge is an imprint of the Taylor & Francis Group, an informa business

© 2021 Peter Loxley

The right of Peter Loxley to be identified as author of this work has been asserted by him in accordance with sections 77 and 78 of the Copyright, Designs and Patents Act 1988.

All rights reserved. No part of this book may be reprinted or reproduced or utilised in any form or by any electronic, mechanical, or other means, now known or hereafter invented, including photocopying and recording, or in any information storage or retrieval system, without permission in writing from the publishers.

Trademark notice: Product or corporate names may be trademarks or registered trademarks, and are used only for identification and explanation without intent to infringe.

British Library Cataloguing-in-Publication Data
A catalogue record for this book is available from the British Library

Library of Congress Cataloging-in-Publication Data
A catalog record has been requested for this book

ISBN: 9780367178338 (hbk)
ISBN: 9780367178345 (pbk)
ISBN: 9780429057953 (ebk)

Typeset in Frutiger
by Apex CoVantage, LLC

CONTENTS

	Preface	viii
	Acknowledgements	ix
1.	**Big idea thinking**	1
2.	**Outdoor learning**	6
	Benefits of outdoor learning	6
	Regular diet of outside learning	6
	Science learning	7
	Outdoor learning fosters an affection for nature	7
	Gardening can help save the natural world	8
	Connecting inside and outside learning	8
	Technology for outdoor learning	9
	Parks and community gardens	9
	Woodlands and nature reserves	10
	Support from experts	11
3.	**Working towards big ideas**	14
	Introduction	14
	Subject knowledge	14
	Models of good practice	15
	Indicators of good practice	16
4.	**Interdependence**	23
	Part 1: Subject knowledge	**24**
	Learning through experience	24
	Thinking and talking with scientific ideas	24
	Germination and photosynthesis	24
	Why we need to 'feed' plants	25
	Interdependence	25
	Ecosystems	26

Contents

Competition for resources	26
Biodiversity	28
Part 2: Working towards the big idea	**28**
Models of good practice	28
Topic: Food provided by plants	28
Topic: The producers	36
Topic: Ecosystems	47

5. Adaptation — 65

Part 1: Subject knowledge — 66

Learning from experience	66
Thinking and talking with scientific ideas	66
Woodland habitats	66
Adaptation and evolution	67
Darwin's theory of natural selection	68
The tree of life	69
Biodiversity and classification	70

Part 2: Working towards the big idea — 70

Models of good practice	70
Topic: Habitats	70
Topic: Adaptation	79
Topic: Adaptation and Evolution	89

6. Inheritance — 107

Part 1: Subject knowledge — 108

Learning from first-hand experience	108
Thinking and talking with scientific ideas	108
Pollination, fertilisation and seed dispersal	109
Inheritance and diversity	110
Selective breeding of plants	111
Asexual reproduction	111

Part 2: Working towards the big idea — 112

Models of good practice	112
Topic: Variety and growth	112
Topic: Life cycles of plants	119
Topic: Inheritance and evolution	130

Contents

7. Following in Darwin's footsteps — 144

Part 1: Subject knowledge — 145

Introduction — 145
Darwin the family man — 145
Darwin the gentleman scientist — 146
Darwin's theory of evolution — 146
Jean-Baptiste Lamarck's theory of evolution — 148
Darwin's correspondents — 148
Darwin's scientific women — 149

Part 2: Working towards the big idea — 150

Models of good practice — 150
    Topic: Finding things out — 150
    Topic: Scientific explanations — 154
    Topic: Darwin's science — 162

8. Protecting ecosystems — 178

Part 1: Subject knowledge — 179

Loss of biodiversity — 179
Farming, food and climate change — 180
What has biodiversity ever done for us? — 180
Ecosystem services — 181
Wildlife conservation — 182
Garden habitats — 182
Citizen science — 184

Part 2: Working towards the big idea — 185

Models of good practice — 185
    Topic: Wildlife guardians — 185
    Topic: Homes for bees — 192
    Topic: Protecting ecosystems — 200

Index — 213

PREFACE

Much of the elementary scientific knowledge taught in primary schools serves as the basis for more complex learning in later years. However, this does not mean that the ideas learnt by primary-aged children cannot be used outside the classroom to help them make sense of their experiences and to respond to issues which affect them. By working towards understanding big scientific ideas, children can develop informed ways of thinking about issues related to their own wellbeing, and also the wellbeing of the natural world. In the words of the inspirational Greta Thunberg: 'I want people to unite behind the science . . . I'm not the one who's saying these things. I am not the one we should be listening to . . . I say we need to listen to the scientists' (Greta Thunberg, 2019).

ACKNOWLEDGEMENTS

I would like to thank Routledge for publishing the book and for the support they have provided.

I would like to say a very special thank you to my wife, Anna, for the valuable contributions she made to the book. Although her ideas are never referenced, you can be sure they feature prominently in every page. I would also like to thank her for providing many of the images which help bring the ideas alive.

CHAPTER 1
BIG IDEA THINKING

Scientific ideas are created by communities of scientists to help explain and predict how the natural world works. The world is very complex, and hence science has a lot of ideas to help explain it. When ideas are combined they produce bigger, more powerful ideas which can be used to explain a progressively wider range of events and related phenomena, and hence a more comprehensive picture of the way the world works. The bigger the idea the more explanatory power it has.

The optimistic aim of this book is not just for children to learn scientific ideas but to learn to adopt them as their own so they can think with them when they are experiencing and talking about the natural world. This requires children to understand science not as a series of separate facts, but as a way of seeing and thinking about the living world.

To be useful, scientific ideas need to provide understanding which can influence our thinking about aspects of the natural world in which we have an interest. For example, imagine sitting in a garden surrounded by a wide variety of different kinds and colours of flowering plants. What first catches your eye are the plants with the brightest flowers, such as the double-stemmed red roses and the tall purple foxgloves. Past your ear flies a lone bumblebee. You feel compelled to keep an eye on it as it makes a 'bee line' for the nearest foxglove. As you watch the bee moving from flower to flower, you now notice that there are quite a lot of other bees in the garden who are also attracted to the foxgloves. As you continue to watch the bumblebee it flies away from the foxgloves, straight past the bright red roses and lands none too securely on a verbena with small, delicate purple/pink flowers. As the sun comes out from behind a cloud, a butterfly flutters past your ear and you start to wonder whether these flying insects are attracted to your perfume. What you have noticed is that none of the bees or butterflies seem attracted to the sweet smelling red roses, which puzzles you and you wonder why.

In a garden there are lots of things happening which can be explained with the help of scientific ideas. For example, it is not surprising that bees are not attracted to the red rose, as scientists have discovered that bees cannot see the colour red and to the bee the rose looks much like the surrounding green foliage. However, bees are highly attracted to shades of purple, blue and yellow and look out for plants with flat, single blossoms which are easiest to access. The colour of the flower makes them stand out, but it is the stuff inside the flower that they are really after. Bees are looking for ways to get at the pollen and nectar, and certain plants have evolved in ways which make it easy for bees to get what they want. Although we can only see them with an ultraviolet camera, there are markings (guides) inside some flowers which direct bees to the nectar and pollen. Once inside the flower the bees unwittingly pollinate the plant and help it to reproduce. As they say, a win-win situation for both parties!

Charles Darwin described *pollination* as an act of contrivance, by which the plant uses its flowers as devices to attract pollinators. The flower is a device which provides benefits for both the plant and the pollinator. Knowing what colour flowers attract bees is a small idea, which is useful information for gardeners. However, it is of limited use when trying to make sense of what is really going on between plants and bees. Thinking of the flower as a device for *reproduction* is

Chapter 1 **Big idea thinking**

a bigger idea because it not only enables us to picture in our minds what is going on between plants and bees, but also what is going on between all the other types of pollinators and their preferred plants. We can now start to think of the structure of any flower and how it suits the types of pollinators it attracts.

Interdependence is an even bigger idea which can be witnessed in the behaviour of the bee and flower. Both the bee and the plant are dependent on each other for their survival. Without the plant the bee would have no food, while the plant cannot reproduce without the help of the bee. It is not only the bees and flowering plants which depend on each other – the idea of interdependence can be witnessed through the interconnected behaviours of all the living things in the garden and throughout the living world. With the idea of interdependence underpinning our thinking we can now start to see the garden as an *ecosystem* in which interdependent organisms are living together in particular environmental conditions.

A stable ecosystem generally contains primary producers (plants) capable of harvesting energy from the sun. Plants use the energy to produce and store food through the process called photosynthesis. When animals eat the plants, the energy is passed through the food chain by primary consumers (herbivores) and secondary consumers (carnivores). Primary consumers such as caterpillars feed directly on the plant, while secondary consumers get their share of the energy by consuming the caterpillars. Decomposers (bacteria and fungi) work at the bottom of the food chain, feeding on waste products and dead plant and animal tissue. The decomposers recycle organic materials back into the soil so new plants can grow. Animals such as worms, slugs and snails break down dead leaves and other organic material, helping to make the job of the decomposers a bit easier. The relationship amongst plants and animals can be represented as food chains and food webs which show how energy is passed along from the primary producer to the different types of consumers.

In an ecosystem some animals will be dependent on plants to provide for their other needs, as well as for food. For example, trees and other plants release the vital oxygen animals need to survive. Trees also provide shelter and nesting sites for birds and small mammals as well as homes for bees, beetles and other invertebrates. Understanding how living things depend on each other for their survival helps children to think and talk about their experiences of the natural world in new ways. Ideas such as interdependence and ecosystems can excite children's minds and move their imaginations. No longer will they see a tree as just something to climb; when looked at through scientific eyes they can see the vital role it plays in supporting the biodiversity of the ecosystem. By understanding ecosystems, children are able to visualise the bigger picture of how living things are connected and the effect destroying vegetation can have on animal populations.

Further understanding of ecosystems comes from ideas such as *adaptation* and *inheritance*. Adaptation is the way living things change over time to suit their environment. Adaptation to their environment happens because of the small differences that occur in offspring as a result of reproduction. Over generations, the small changes accumulate so that living things become progressively better suited for a particular way of life. Eventually they can become so well adapted to a way of life that they cannot survive in any other way. Imagine what this means to birds and other woodland animals when a woodland is cleared to make way for urban development. Where do they go? Where else can they find similar habitats? As ever more woodlands are destroyed, gardens and green spaces in the towns become their only refuge. By understanding the science, children appreciate the reasons why nature is in such serious trouble and become aware of the potentially devastating consequences unnatural changes to the environment can have for wildlife. By adopting the big ideas as their own, children are able to develop informed arguments about the need to protect the natural environment and decide for themselves how to act.

Inheritance and adaptation also underpin our understanding of *evolution*. Evolution through natural selection is the process that has created the remarkable diversity of wildlife which enriches our lives and is essential for our health and wellbeing. By learning about evolution children are able to see the bigger picture of how life developed on earth and are able to make sense of their place on the evolutionary 'tree of life'. By looking back at their common ancestors children learn to see the living world with new eyes and are able to see themselves as part of nature, rather than just an observer.

Working towards understanding big ideas such as interdependence, inheritance and adaptation can be used to inform children's thinking about issues related to their own wellbeing, as well as the wellbeing of the natural world. The activities and projects set out in this book support the progressive development of these scientific ideas, which can influence the way children relate to the natural world.

Knot garden   Physic garden   Dyer's garden

Living wall   Greenhouse   Park   Sunken garden

Poisons garden   Perfume garden   Darwin's garden

Wardian case   Conservatory   **Skip garden**

Garden barge   Discovery garden   Zen garden

Window box   Hydroponic chamber   Bog garden

School garden   Pocket park   Allotment

Floating garden   Apothecary's garden   Field

Glasshouse   **Urban garden**   Propagator

Nature reserve   Culinary garden   Herb garden

Cloche   Orchard   **Arid garden**   Vineyard

Wildflower garden   Gravel garden   Patio garden

Garden of Remembrance   Brown roof   Wildlife corridor

Medicinal garden   Botanic garden   Hothouse

Treehouse   Pond garden   Alpine garden   Orangery

Healing garden   **Edible garden**   Organic garden

Community garden   Prison garden   **Bottle garden**

Secret garden   Solander box   Linnaeus' garden

CHAPTER 2
OUTDOOR LEARNING

Benefits of outdoor learning

There is wide-ranging evidence for the benefits of learning outside the classroom in natural environments. A large-scale study carried out by Plymouth University (2016) found that learning outdoors can have positive impacts for both children and their teachers.

> The message is clear – getting children outdoors is fantastic for their health, wellbeing and learning and can set them on a pathway to happy, healthy and environmentally sustainable life styles.
>
> (Natural Connections, Martin Gilchrist, 2017)

Evidence shows that giving children well-managed opportunities to discover, learn about and experience the living world is highly beneficial in a number of ways. In addition to enhancing their health, wellbeing and educational outcomes, learning in natural environments can have positive effects on children's resilience, self-esteem, communication skills, team work and behaviour.

The Plymouth University results are consistent with other studies which suggest teachers particularly value outside learning because it inspires creativity, supports conceptual learning and makes the curriculum come alive for children. There is also substantial evidence for the positive impact outside learning has on children's attitudes to learning. Schools and teachers consistently report that outdoor learning enthused and motivated children, resulting in greater engagement with learning.

Learning outdoors offers diverse experiences that encourage active engagement with stimulating settings that not only help develop children's scientific knowledge and skills, but also aid their personal and social development. Children who sometimes struggle in the confines of the classroom can flourish outdoors where they have greater freedom and have the opportunity to learn in different ways. Children benefit because the range of locations and experiences afforded by the outdoor environment are far wider and more comprehensive than those available in the classroom (Loxley et al., 2018).

Regular diet of outside learning

Outdoor learning is considered to be a key aspect of a child's education in the early years. However, as children get older, they go outside to learn less frequently. There are justifiable reasons, including the ever-increasing transport costs, issues relating to health and safety and lack of time to cover a prescribed curriculum. However, children do not cease to benefit from outdoor experiences just because they are a few years older. Just as children need a balanced diet of food and exercise to grow healthy bodies, their minds need to be nourished by regular interactions with nature to help them develop healthy attitudes to the living world. Like doctors who recommend five portions or more of fruit a day, conservationists recommend five sessions with nature every term.

Science learning

Much of the research into outdoor learning is qualitative, with outcomes based on comments from children and teachers. Therefore claims for the impact outside learning has on attainment in core subjects such as science is often subjective and can vary significantly between different studies. This means that we should not presume that all the educational advantages discussed in the research literature are solely due to working in an outdoor context. For example, although gardening can have positive effects on children's attitude to learning, there is little evidence to suggest that it can inherently increase children's attainment in science without the sessions being specifically designed to enhance scientific skills and understanding.

Teachers who took part in research sponsored by the Royal Horticultural Society (2010), identified learning outcomes which were not necessarily related to the physical act of gardening, but resulted from using gardening as a tool or context for science learning. They reported that working in the garden provided a wide range of opportunities for children to become active and independent learners. Working outside enabled more investigative work in which children took greater control of their own learning and in which the teacher's role became more facilitative. The range of strategies teachers used was broader than was possible in the classroom, involving children moving about, touching, feeling, exploring and observing for themselves. In particular, teachers involved in the research reported that when using gardening as a teaching tool, children become more active in seeking knowledge and solving problems and generally more ready to learn. They also found that gardening helped enhance science skills and attainment.

With regard to conceptual development, research suggests that outdoor learning is most effective when supplemented with focussed classroom learning, providing children with information and ideas which help them appreciate and make sense of their outdoor experiences. Whether learning inside or outside the classroom, it is the teacher's job to organise and assist children's learning.

Outdoor learning fosters an affection for nature

The *State of Nature 2019* report reveals that 41% of UK species have declined over recent decades and 15% are threatened with extinction. This suggests that the UK is amongst the most nature-depleted countries in the world. Of the 218 countries assessed for 'biodiversity intactness', the UK is ranked 189, a consequence of centuries of industrialisation, urbanisation and over-exploitation of our natural resources (Chris Packham).

The decline in wildlife is shocking, and yet somehow we have grown to accept the devastation as a normal part of our modern, technological lives. For most people nature is not part of their lives. It is out there somewhere, a place to be visited when they are not so busy doing something else. An unpublished survey carried out in 2017 by the Wildlife Trusts found a third of adults were unable to identify a barn owl and three quarters unable to identify an ash tree. Two-thirds of the people surveyed felt that they had 'lost touch with nature'. Another research study carried out by the Royal Society for the Protection of Birds (RSPB) found only one in five British children to be 'positively connected to nature'.

There is considerable evidence that concern for the living world is based on an affection for nature that only develops from contact with it. Children are more likely to want to save what they love, but are unlikely to love what they cannot name or do not see. By confining learning to the classroom, schools are denying children opportunities to engage positively, and develop an affection for the natural world. Only by experiencing the wonder of the natural world will children grow to love it.

> Nature needs to be seen as a vital part of everyday life – shaping mental and physical health, play, friendship, imagination – rather than as something hived off and distant, to be visited occasionally on a school trip or family outing, or existing as a specialist subset of science.
>
> (A Peoples Manifesto for Wildlife, 2018)

Outdoor learning can help make nature a part of children's lives and help them develop an affection for the wildlife which is part of it. To get to know the living world children need regular contact with it. The *Peoples Manifesto for Wildlife* recommends that children spend at least one day a fortnight learning outdoors in natural environments. This is a big ask for primary schools who struggle with limited resources and an over-prescribed curriculum. The most easily accessible outdoor learning areas available are usually the school grounds, and therefore schools need to make the most of them. Turning the school grounds into a nature reserve by growing plants that attract wildlife is an easy and inexpensive way of creating an outdoor context for children to interact with nature, and at the same time making their science learning more relevant to their lives.

Gardening can help save the natural world

School gardens provide children with opportunities to get close to nature and to take action to help save the natural world. According to the Royal Horticultural Society (RHS), the benefits of gardens go far beyond the pleasure they provide for their owners. No matter where they live, people in cities benefit from greening up the environment. Although each garden is small, added together the positive effect on biodiversity and the associated ecosystem services can be significant. Collectively, gardens play a crucial role in improving air quality, reducing flooding, moderating climate change, supporting wildlife and promoting healthy life styles.

Schools can play their part in protecting wildlife by ensuring that every available space in the school grounds contains plants. Planting shrubs, trees and hedges can provide food and shelter for birds and insects. Growing flowering plants provides pollen and nectar for the insect pollinators, which in turn attract birds which feed on the insects and their larvae. If space is limited plants can be grown in containers or up against walls or fences that have space for climbing plants. Whatever space is available, it is important to grow as many different types of plants as possible.

Connecting inside and outside learning

A school garden that plans for wildness and provides openness, diversity and opportunities for exploration and investigation allows children to become immersed in discovery learning. School gardens should be very different from those designed for adults who often prefer neat and tidy, well-ordered settings. Discovery gardens are much freer, with wild spaces which excite children's imaginations with their surprising diversity of plants and hiding places for small animals.

Ideally, a school garden should be designed so that learning outdoors can be integrated with learning in the classroom. The design should enable children to visualise the garden as part of the classroom, with children able to move freely between the inside and outside spaces. Discovery gardens should flow from one habitat area to the next, with plants and features that stimulate children's senses and foster their curiosity about the natural world. Also, don't forget somewhere for children to sit quietly to listen and watch, as well as places for them to work in their outside classroom. Refer to Chapter 8 for more information about how children can help turn the school grounds into a wildlife garden.

Technology for outdoor learning

Wildlife cameras enable children to watch live video of birds visiting feeders and nesting boxes all year around. Nesting boxes with a wired-in webcam enable children to watch video of eggs hatching, chicks growing and birds feeding their young. Cameras can also be set up to capture video of animals that are active after dark such as hedgehogs, foxes and bats. You may also want to fit a camera with a red mason bee box to watch the female arranging her nest and laying her eggs in spring and early summer.

Smart phone identification apps are very useful, especially for identifying trees, wildflowers and invertebrates. Some of the conservation trusts and citizen science project websites provide free identification apps. For example, a bug identification app can be downloaded free from the Open Air Laboratories (OPAL) website.

Easy-to-use digital cameras capable of taking high-quality images are invaluable for recording wildlife. The images can be used back in the classroom to identify and study small animals and plants. They can also be used to create classroom displays and to illustrate the findings from wildlife surveys and other studies which are published on the school website, on a blogging platform or in the school's science magazine. Binoculars are also essential for fieldwork, especially for spotting birds, flying insects and small mammals and exploring the canopy of trees. Use low, single magnification binoculars which are easy for children to use. Visit the RSPB website for advice.

Parks and community gardens

The local park is a valuable resource for outside learning and might be within walking distance from your school. Children like parks which are fun to explore and contain a wide variety of plants and animals. Due to an abundance of trees and other plants, parks play their part in improving local air quality and supporting wildlife, as well as promoting healthy life styles. Through regular visits children can get to know the ecology of their local park and how it changes from season to season.

If your school grounds have limited space, why not consider taking on a council allotment? This could be organised and managed with the help of parents and other adult volunteers. Otherwise, seek out a local community garden scheme and find out how the school can contribute and use the garden for science learning. Social Farms and Gardens is an organisation which supports thousands of grass root community garden projects across the UK.

Chapter 2 **Outdoor learning**

Woodlands and nature reserves

Woodlands are exciting places for children to explore. In spring, they find the floor carpeted in bluebells and the air alive with birdsong. Summer is the time of year when dragonflies zip about above the water and butterflies and bees flit between brightly coloured flowers. Autumn is the time when living things start to slow down and signs of change are everywhere in preparation for winter. Trees and bushes change the colour of their leaves from vibrant greens to stunning browns and oranges, and birds eat their fill of the abundant red and purple berries before the tough winter months. Winter is a challenging time for all animals. Some get through by hibernating, while others survive on food they hid away in summer. Birds survive on insects and worms which live in the soil and leaf litter. Where there are trees and shrubs, there are always plenty of minibeasts no matter what time of the year.

Nature reserves are protected habitats for certain animals or plants, or sometimes both. Nature reserves vary; they might be an area of ancient wood or an area of wetland which is home to rare migrating birds. Reserves include coastal areas, rivers, grassland, heathland, moorland, marine habitats, mountain areas and farmland. There are lots of nature reserves in the UK which are run by a variety of conservation trusts. Most of the trusts provide resources for schools which help children to explore, appreciate and enjoy the natural world. They also provide opportunities for children to support their conservation work by taking part in award schemes, volunteering and becoming citizen scientists. Chapter 8 provides detailed information about how schools can access the resources offered by the various conservation trusts.

Those schools in towns and cities might be forgiven for thinking that wildlife reserves are places which are only found in the countryside. Nothing could be further from the truth, as many of the Wildlife Trusts' nature reserves are in urban areas. In recent years, a wide range of initiatives have created wildlife sites in cities and towns across the country. If you work in an urban school, visit your local wildlife trust website to discover the wildlife sites in your town or city.

Support from experts

We can all do with a bit of support when involved in outside learning. However much we prepare for a visit to a woodland or other nature reserve, it is always useful to have an expert on hand to provide advice and insights which can fire children's imaginations.

Support from experts is an important part of primary science education, as they provide role models to which children can aspire. Children look forward to meeting new people, who often bring with them exciting new resources, experiences and ideas. STEM (science, technology, engineering and mathematics) ambassadors are volunteers who have been trained to support the teaching of the STEM subjects in schools. Amongst these ambassadors are expert gardeners, ecologists and conservationists who are able to actively support teaching in a wide range of outdoor contexts. Information about STEM ambassadors can be found on the STEM Learning website.

In addition to the STEM community, organisations such as the Royal Horticultural Society, the Woodland Trust, the Wildlife Trust and the National Trust support schools by providing education officers who provide resources and advice which helps schools make the most of their visits. Other trusts to contact include The Royal Society for the Protection of Birds, World Wildlife Fund (WWF-UK), Plantlife, Bumblebee Conservation Trust, Bat Conservation Trust, Butterfly Conservation Trust, Freshwater Habitats Trust and the British Trust for Ornithology.

And finally, don't forget parents, grandparents and other members of the school community who may be keen gardeners, allotment owners or conservationists. Make good use of the expertise and enthusiasm which is available on your doorstep.

Further reading

- A Peoples Manifesto for Wildlife: www.chrispackham.co.uk/a-peoples-manifesto-for-wildlife
- Free Bug Count App: www.opalexplorenature.org/bugs-app
- Gardening in Schools: A Vital Tool for Children's Learning: www.nottinghamcity.gov.uk/media/370608/chttphandler.pdf
- Impact of School Gardening on Learning (RHS 2010): www.nfer.ac.uk/media/2135/rhs01.pdf
- Outdoor Learning 'Boosts Children's Development': www.bbc.co.uk/news/science-environment-36795912
- Reviews of Research on Outdoor Learning: www.englishoutdoorcouncil.org/research.in.outdoor.learning.html
- Social Farms and Gardens: www.farmgarden.org.uk/your-area
- State of Nature Report 2019: www.bto.org/our-science/publications/state-nature-report/state-nature-report-2019
- State of Nature Report 2016: http://stateofnature.wildlifetrusts.org/
- STEM Learning: www.stem.org.uk/stem-ambassadors
- Transforming Outdoor Learning in Schools 2016: www.plymouth.ac.uk/uploads/production/document/path/7/7634/Transforming_Outdoor_Learning_in_Schools_SCN.pdf
- Where to See Urban Wildlife: www.wildlifetrusts.org/where_to_see_urban_wildlife
- Wildlife Gardening Forum: http://wlgf.org/

ASE Journals

- Primary Science (January–February 2015) *Transition: It's Not Just for Children* by Leigh Hoath.
- Primary Science 137 (March–April 2015) *What Difference Does a More In-Depth Programme Make to Learning?* By Athene Reiss.
- Education in Science 268 (May 2017) *Natural Connections Why Learn Outside?* By Martin Gilchrist.
- Journal of Emergent Science 16 (Winter 2019) *The Benefits of Outdoor Learning on Science Teaching* by Michele Grimshaw, Linda Curwen, Jeannette Morgan, Naomi Shallcross, Sophie Franklin and Dudley Shallcross.
- Primary Science 158 (May–June 2019) *It's Easier Than You Think! Exploring an Outdoor Pedagogy for Science Teaching* by Mark Hainsworth.
- Primary Science 159 (September–October 2019) *The Science Behind the 'Wow' Factor of Outdoor Learning* by Helen *Spring*.

Books and research articles

- Passy, R. (2014) School Gardens: Teaching and Learning Outside the Front Door. *Education* 3–13 volume, 42.
- Pinniger, B. (2015) *How to Garden and Grow: Gardening as Therapy for Children with SEND*, Accrington: LDA Publishing.
- Waite, S. (Ed) (2019) *Outdoor Learning Research: Insights into Forms and Functions*, Abingdon: Routledge.

Naturalist   Ornithologist   Botanist
Biologist   Entomologist   Zoologist
Meteorologist   Forester   Ecologist
Palaeontologist   Bryologist
Dendrologist   Plant morphologist
Lichenologist   Mycologist   Pharmacologist
Marine biologist   Conservationist
Geneticist   Taxonomist
Horticulturalist   Ichthyologist
Pharmacologist   Paleobotanist
Plant physiologist   Orchidologist
Geologist   Botanical illustrator
Malacologist   Plant pathologist
Crystallographer   Ornithologist
Biochemist   Ethnologist   Conservationist

CHAPTER 3
WORKING TOWARDS BIG IDEAS

Introduction

This book provides *models of good practice* which exemplify the teaching of science in outdoor contexts. The models of good practice are not intended for use as lesson plans, rather they provide sketches which illustrate how teachers can scaffold children's learning towards the development of big ideas in the primary years. *Subject knowledge* to support the teaching of big ideas is presented at the beginning of each chapter.

Chapters 4, 5 and 6 focus on the teaching of key scientific ideas, while Chapters 7 and 8 concentrate children's attention on ideas about science, including social and ethical issues. The chapters provide models of good practice at three age-related levels: key stage 1 (5–7 years), lower key stage 2 (7–9 years) and upper key stage 2 (9–11 years). It is envisaged that teachers will adapt the models to suit their resources, their curriculum and the needs of their children. The learning goals are consistent with the requirements of the primary school curricula in England, Wales, Scotland and Northern Ireland. They have also been influenced by the big ideas of science identified in Harlen (2010, 2015).

The chapters which focus on ideas about science are designed to broaden children's thinking about the nature of science and also provide them with opportunities to explore the impact human activity can have on the wellbeing of the natural world. The chapter on nature conservation enables children to play a part in the preservation of wildlife, by 'wilding up' the school grounds and contributing to citizen science projects.

Subject knowledge

Subject knowledge teachers require is set out in narrative form in Part 1 of each chapter. Narrative is used in a wider sense of the word, providing a contextualised account of the science from the author's point of view. Besides describing the science, the narrative serves a number of other purposes:

- It provides ideas, objects and events which children can progressively engage with at different levels.
- The story-line provides direction and continuity in children's learning across the age groups and helps teachers visualise how the ideas they teach contribute to the development of bigger ideas.
- It helps teachers to visualise the bigger picture and understand where children's learning in each stage is heading conceptually, and therefore helps them manage progression.
- Puzzling events and problem-solving scenarios can be drawn out of the narrative to arouse children's curiosity and engage them in a quest for knowledge.
- The narrative also provides a model for the nature of children's story-telling which is intrinsic to the approach to science learning fostered by the models of good practice.

Models of good practice

The models of good practice are based on a three-stage framework for managing children's science learning, which is presented in Loxley et al. (2018). However, in this book the framework has been interpreted to suit children's learning in outdoor contexts and to promote the value of *working towards understanding big ideas*.

Exploring children's ideas

Learning starts in the first stage by exploring children's ideas. Learning involves children sharing, trying out and evaluating their own ideas to solve problems and answer questions related to their experiences and enquiries in outdoor contexts. For example, when preparing a bed to sow vegetables, children may find a variety of invertebrates in the soil, including worms. Children raise their own questions to make sense of the ecology of the soil. What are the worms doing there? Are they likely to damage or benefit the crops? How many different types of worms are in the soil? What do they eat? Can they see underground? How are they suited to their habitat? There are lots of questions to answer, and enquiry activities can help children discover the answers for themselves.

Working on scientific understanding

The second stage involves working on scientific understanding. Introducing scientific ideas at this stage provides children with an alternative point of view which can help them visualise the outcomes of their enquiries in ways they are unlikely to discover for themselves. This involves providing children with access to the language they need to talk about and mentally engage with the scientific view. For example, Darwin referred to worms as 'nature's ploughs' when talking about the role they play in the garden ecosystem. As worms burrow through the soil, they digest rotting leaves and other organic matter and break it down, making it easier for plants to spread their roots and take in the nutrients they need. Other evocative language which could be used to help children visualise what worms do are 'decomposer' and 'recycler'. Worms help decompose and recycle organic material from dead plants, making the nutrition available for new plants to grow. Maybe, rather than calling them 'nature's ploughs', Darwin should have called worms 'nature's recyclers'? Children can debate the term which best describes the role worms play in the garden ecosystem. Loxley et al. (2018) refer to this stage of children's learning as the 're-describing stage' to emphasise the role figurative language plays in helping children to re-think their ideas, and consequently to persuade them to adopt the scientific view as their own.

The bigger picture

The third stage provides opportunities for children to explore the bigger picture by using and developing their scientific understanding in other contexts. For example, children can ask whether worms are nature's only recyclers. How many recyclers does nature have? A trip to the local woodland in autumn where they can explore all kinds of rotting vegetation can help children answer this question and enable them to visualise the bigger ecological picture of how nature depends on its recyclers. Working on their understanding of nature's recyclers is a step towards developing their understanding of bigger ideas about interdependence and ecosystems. Children can further develop their understanding of the ecology of the woodland by exploring the relationships between decomposers, producers and consumers.

Indicators of good practice

How children learn science is important. The quality of children's learning depends on the nature of the learning opportunities we provide for them. Wynne Harlen's report, *Working with Big Ideas of Science Education*, explores the types of activities and ways of working that help children develop their understanding of big ideas. The report suggests that indicators of good practice are likely to include children having opportunities to:

- understand the purpose of their activities;
- explore new objects or phenomena informally and 'play with ideas' as a preliminary to more structured investigation;
- make links between new and previous experience;
- work collaboratively with others, communicating their own ideas and considering others' ideas;
- present evidence to support their arguments;
- engage in discussions in defence of their ideas and their explanations;
- apply their learning in real-life contexts;
- reflect self-critically about the processes and outcomes of their enquiries.

Research shows that children learn best by sharing ideas and working collaboratively towards common goals in contexts which are familiar and meaningful. The role of the teacher is that of an active participant who guides and assists the children's learning. As the expert, the teacher takes a central role by organising learning tasks, modelling and demonstrating good practice, and helping children to think, talk and act in ways which support effective learning (Loxley et al., 2018).

Scientific enquiry

Scientific enquiry is the cornerstone of science learning through which children develop scientific skills and knowledge. Enquiries start naturally with questions or mysteries which set children off on a collaborative quest for knowledge to find an answer. Children add to the richness of the quest by speculating about possible solutions and acting to collect evidence in support of their ideas. The plot unfolds when children present their findings and engage in discussion in defence of their ideas. Through whole-class discussion a negotiated solution is reached and the enquiry brought to a satisfactory resolution. Reflecting on the outcomes of enquiries also provides opportunities for children to voice their opinions and feelings about the value of what they have learnt and what they need to do next in their quest for knowledge.

Story-telling

Story-telling is a key part of scientific enquiry because it enables children to talk about the science in their own words. Rather than just recounting facts, the re-telling of the science from their own point of view allows the lived experiences of the children to interact with scientific ideas. Hence story-telling can capture the nature of their scientific understanding and reveal its

Chapter 3 Working towards big ideas

influence on the way they think and feel. It is the link between speaking, listening, thinking and learning which makes spoken language so important. We can provide children with fascinating experiences of the natural world and excellent resources to explore it. But, unless we guide the way they use language to make sense of their experiences, their learning will be diminished and their understanding less secure.

Chapter 3 Working towards big ideas

Effective talk

Effective talk enables children to share their thinking and to collaborate so that by working in a group each child does better than they could have done alone. It is the teacher's job to model and guide the way children interact with each other, to ensure effective science learning. Classes benefit from devising a set of ground rules which help the children remember that talk is a crucial part of science learning. The following rules have been shown to promote effective talk and help children work collaboratively:

- Listen attentively.
- Include everyone in the discussion.
- Ask questions.
- Share relevant information openly.
- Challenge one another's ideas and opinions with respect.
- Ask for and give reasons for ideas.
- Seek to reach agreement before proceeding.
- Support one another during subsequent whole-class discussion.

(Loxley et al., 2018)

Talking points

Talking points is a strategy which can be used to guide group discussion. It is a resource for effective talk developed by Lyn Dawes (2012). Talking points provide starting points for discussion. For example, a talking point could be a simple statement about the behaviour of an animal, such as 'Bees only see things in black and white'. Groups discuss the idea and together try to decide whether they agree or disagree with the statement, or whether they are unsure. Each member of a group is encouraged to contribute and justify their point of view, and in this way the group works towards an agreed response. Subsequent whole-class discussion orchestrated by the teacher helps everyone to consider a range of views, share their thinking, establish areas of uncertainty for further work and generally develop their vocabulary and ideas (Loxley et al., 2018).

Publishing

Don't bury children's ideas in their notebooks. Good ideas should not be hidden away and forgotten, they should be published so other people can enjoy them.

> When writing has a purpose, the writer discovers all kinds of important stuff to do with what to write, why write, how write and much more. So, to my mind, we should reconfigure, reframe and reinvent 'writing in schools'. We should think of schools as publishing-performing houses for the exposure and circulation of writing – writing by anyone who works in a school community – pupils, teachers, non-teaching staff – and beyond: parents, grandparents, carers, assistants and so on.

(Michael Rosen, accessed 08/2019 online)

Science publishing in primary schools can be part of a wide genre of writing, such as poetry, drama, short stories, music reviews, news articles, book reviews, film reviews, sport reviews and so on. Outdoor learning provides children with lots of interesting science to write about. They can blog about garden science, visits to wildlife areas, wildlife conservation or citizen science projects. They can tell stories about fascinating wildlife which they discovered. Publishing science for an audience requires children to use their own 'voices' to describe the scientific ideas and enables them to experience the satisfaction that authors get from sharing their ideas with others.

Where to publish are decisions schools have to make in accordance with their e-safety policy. There is a wide choice of blogging platforms, including Quadblogging which links schools in different parts of the world together in fours, so that children have a guaranteed audience for their blogs. Collaborating with other schools can be very exciting and can open children's minds to new ideas and new ways of seeing the world. How to prepare blogs for publication is another matter which needs consideration. To a certain extent, the content of the blogs will need to be edited. How this is done is, again, a matter for individual schools. However, the editing process can provide opportunities for children to re-think their ideas in ways which help them deepen their understanding of the science.

Blogs are not the only way children can publish their scientific ideas. Use newsletters, school magazines, science days, school-based science conferences, designated pages on the school website and so on. Schools should take every opportunity to publish and celebrate the children's science. Scientists strive for the satisfaction of getting their work published. As a young man, Darwin wrote how delighted he was after finding that his discovery of a new type of beetle had been published. We can help foster the same enthusiasm for science by helping children publish their discoveries.

Formative assessment

Formative assessment is an integral part of good practice. It is a continuous process in which information about children's ideas and capabilities is used to help move their learning forward towards the development of bigger ideas.

Opportunities for formative assessment arise whenever children engage in discussion about scientific ideas. Well-judged questions enable teachers to probe children's thinking and assess their understanding of the scientific ideas. *Talking points* can be useful for assessment, as the process of explaining their thinking lays bare the limitations of the children's ideas. Misconceptions can be identified and addressed as part of group or whole-class discussions. Talking points also provide opportunities for peer and self-assessment. Working in small groups allows children to compare and evaluate ideas and enables them to identify weaknesses in their own understanding.

Other opportunities for formative assessment are provided when children engage in solving puzzles, scientific enquiry, modelling through drama, story-telling, publishing and describing their ideas through drawings. Listening to children's talk, challenging their ideas and probing the reasons for their thinking enable teachers to identify their learning needs and assess their understanding of the key scientific ideas.

Health and safety

The very nature of out-of-school learning is collaborative, and its success depends on the children, teachers and support staff working together. The outdoors presents different risks than those presented in the classroom, and children must be supervised even for short activities within the school grounds. All schools have a policy for the safe conduct of outdoor learning, and many schools have a designated member of staff with responsibility for ensuring that all visits comply with this policy. It is essential that a risk assessment is carried out and a record kept which can be used to inform subsequent visits. However, each visit should have its own up-to-date risk assessment.

A prior visit to a new outdoor site enables teachers to assess the hazards and also to plan learning activities. Some wildlife sites have their own education programmes, in which case teachers should consult the staff when planning their visit. It remains the *teacher's duty* to assess any management, hygiene and hazard risks. Teachers need to know that the activities which they plan for their children are inherently safe. Children need to be instructed how to behave when working in outdoor contexts and to be made aware of any risks involved.

The Association for Science Education (ASE) (2011) publication *Be Safe!* provides extensive guidance on health and safety matters. When planning activities outlined in this book refer to the relevant ASE *Safety Codes* for guidance. The ASE have published safety codes for:

- Studies out of the classroom (p 13).
- Gardening (p 14).
- Food hygiene (p 15).
- Using plants (p 18).
- Keeping animals (p 21).
- Handling animal materials (p 22).

As well as safeguarding the wellbeing of the children, activities should also be designed to take care of the plants and animals being studied.

Further reading

- Association for Science Education. (2011) *Be Safe! Health and Safety in School Science and Technology for Teachers of 3 to 12 year olds* (4th ed.), Hatfield: Association for Science Education.
- Dawes, L. (2012) *Talking Points: Discussion Activities in the Primary Classroom*, London: Routledge.
- Harlen, W. (Ed) (2015) *Working with Big Ideas of Science Education*, published online by IAP.
- Harlen, W. (Ed) (2010) *Principles and Big Ideas of Science Education*, published online by IAP.
- Loxley, P. et al. (2018) *Teaching Primary Science: Promoting Enjoyment and Developing Understanding*, London: Routledge.

Websites

- Association for Science Education: www.ase.org.uk
- Big Ideas of Science Education: www.ase.org.uk/bigideas
- Michael Rosen on blogging: https://michaelrosenblog.blogspot.com/2012/07/blogging-for-schools-writing-for.html
- Primary Science Teachers Trust website: https://pstt.org.uk/resources/curriculum-materials/assessment
- Quadblogging: http://quadblogging.net/

Chapter 3 Working towards big ideas

Quest for knowledge   Structured Investigations
Probing children's thinking   Talking points   Narrative
Making sense of experiences   Scientific understanding
Working collaboratively   Being an active participant
Defending ideas   Modelling   Presenting evidence
Reflecting on outcomes   Supporting arguments
Sharing ideas   Negotiating a solution   Science Day
Continuity of learning   Presenting an alternative view
Listening to children's talk   Science conferences
Contextualising accounts of science   Re-describing
Solving problems   Arousing curiosity   Speculating
Applying learning   Working with other schools
Fostering enthusiasm   Collecting evidence
Exploring informally   Broadening thinking
Managing progression   Accessing scientific language
Talking points   Using ideas in new contexts
Re-thinking   Publishing science for an audience
Enquiring   Good practice   Visualising the bigger picture
Towards the understanding of big ideas

Horse chestnut joins list of trees in danger of extinction (28/9/19)

Vroom to shroom: underground car park used to grow mushrooms (1/10/19)

Labradoodle, Designer Dog (26/9/19)

Beetles species named after Greta (26/10/19)

DNA of 66,000 UK species to be unlocked (2/11/18)

Amber specimen shows spiders had tails (6/2/18)

Attenborough gets angry (19/10/19)

Huge mammalian ancestors walked with dinosaurs (23/11/18)

Artificial leaf created to produce clean fuel (22/10/19)

Is this England's tree of the year? You decide (9/9/19)

Bird feeders send goldfinch and wood pigeon populations soaring (22/5/19)

Insects have 'no place to hide from climate change' (2/4/19)

British bluebells saved from extinction (8/5/19)

Plastic particles 'can make their way to top of food chain' (1/2/19)

Three billion birds have disappeared since 1970 (in North America) (20/9/19)

'Hedgehog champions' needed to halt sharp decline in population (7/2/19)

Toad survey will assess population (29/9/18)

One million seeds in storage vault (27/2/18)

Spending time in nature 'good for children's schoolwork' (7/11/19)

50 million trees to create new 'forest corridor' (8/1/18)

Stop mowing your lawn and let flowers bloom, public urged (24/5/19)

Robotics sows the seeds of change down on the farm (4/12/18)

Scientists 'must engage public to make progress' (26/11/18)

(All headlines published in the i newspaper)

CHAPTER 4
INTERDEPENDENCE

Big idea: *Living things within an ecosystem often depend on, or compete with, other living things for food and other resources which they need to survive.*

Part 1: Subject knowledge

This part presents subject knowledge that teachers require to support children's learning towards the big idea. The ideas presented go beyond the requirements of the National Curriculum to provide levels of subject knowledge which enable teachers to meet the needs of children with different interests and abilities.

The topics include:
- Learning through experience
- Thinking and talking with scientific ideas
- Germination and photosynthesis
- Why we need to 'feed' plants
- Interdependence
- Ecosystems
- Competition for resources
- Biodiversity

Part 2: Working towards the big idea

Each topic aims to move children's understanding further towards the big idea. The journey starts when children explore the conditions plants need to grow, and experience how animals in the garden feed on them. Children then focus their attention on plants as producers of food, and explore how animals in the garden depend, directly or indirectly, on the food they produce to survive. They learn how to describe feeding relationships using food chains

Chapter 4 **Interdependence**

and webs. Children build on their understanding of feeding relationships, to learn how living things within an ecosystem depend on, and compete with, other living things for food and other resources.

The topics are:

- Food provided by plants (5–7 years)
- The producers (7–9 years)
- Ecosystems (9–11 years)

Part 1: Subject knowledge

Learning through experience

By giving children opportunities to grow their own vegetables in the school garden, they can learn through experience the conditions plants need to grow strong and healthy. Generally, plants require water, light and a suitable temperature to grow, and vegetables are no exception. In addition, vegetables need well-composted soil to produce healthy crops. Children can develop an understanding of the structure of plants by exploring the different parts which they eat. With a little guidance, knowledge gained from growing vegetables can be used by children to make sense of what is meant by a balanced diet. In the garden, children start to explore the ecology of the garden by investigating the pests that feed on their vegetables.

Thinking and talking with scientific ideas

When growing their own vegetables in the school garden, there are lots of fascinating things children can discover. However, what children discover for themselves only provides them with fleeting insights into the ecology of the garden. To appreciate the bigger picture children need to learn to think with scientific ideas. For example, by learning to think of plants as the *producers* and other living things as the *consumers*, children can begin to talk about how living things depend on each other to survive. As their understanding of ecosystems develops, children are more able to appreciate the impact human activity can have on the wellbeing of wildlife in the UK and in other parts of the world.

Germination and photosynthesis

Seeds contain a store of starch to fuel the growth of the embryo plant contained inside. When water enters the seed, the process of breaking down starch into sugar begins. Sugar molecules release the energy they contain, and this is put to use to build the new root and stem. This early stage of root and stem development is known as germination.

Once the first leaves emerge above the soil the plant can now produce its own sugars by a process called photosynthesis. The raw materials for photosynthesis are carbon dioxide and water. Carbon dioxide enters the leaves through pores called stomata on the underside of the leaf, and water is absorbed by the roots and travels through xylem tubes to get to the leaves. When light is absorbed by the leaves, carbon dioxide and water are converted to glucose. The by-product of photosynthesis is oxygen, which passes out through the pores on the underside of the leaf into the air. This oxygen supports life on earth.

Plants cannot store large amounts of glucose, and what is not used immediately is changed into other chemicals. Some is converted into other sugars, which are transported from the leaves to all the other parts of the plant through a set of pipe-like structures called the phloem. Some is converted into starch, a complex energy-rich carbohydrate, which can be stored in different parts of the plant. Some is converted into cellulose and used to make the cell walls of the plants. Glucose is also a building block for making proteins and fats. This means that most of the 'stuff' that a plant is made of comes from carbon dioxide in the air and water from the soil.

Why we need to 'feed' plants

If plants make their own food, why does a Venus flytrap eat insects? And why are there shelves full of 'plant foods' at the garden centre? The answer to both questions is the same. Flies and 'plant foods' both provide nutrients or minerals. Even though plants make their own food through photosynthesis, they need these nutrients in order to maintain their health. The Venus flytrap is found growing in poor soil conditions which do not provide enough nutrients. It extracts and absorbs the minerals from the fly's body. Plant foods provide minerals such as potassium, magnesium, phosphorus and nitrogen which may be missing from the soil. Like humans and other animals, plants require a range of minerals to stay healthy. In fact, we get many of the minerals and vitamins that we need to stay healthy from eating plants. When children 'feed' their growing vegetables, they can be assured that the minerals they put into the soil will in turn help keep themselves fit and healthy.

Interdependence

Pollinators are crucial to the wellbeing of any garden, and their relationships with their preferred plants exemplifies the way living things depend on each for their survival. Pollinators depend on plants for food, while the plants need the help of the pollinators to reproduce. It is not only pollinating insects and flowering plants which depend on each other; the idea of interdependence can be witnessed through the interconnected behaviours of all the living things in the garden and other green spaces.

Interdependence is a big idea because it helps us create in our minds a picture of how living things throughout the world depend on each other for their survival. Without plants to provide food and oxygen, animals including ourselves could not survive. Consequently, our wellbeing is intrinsically dependent on the wellbeing of other living things on the planet. By damaging the planet, we inevitably damage our own wellbeing. Interdependence is a big idea children can explore in the garden and then use to influence their thinking about issues such as intensive farming and the destruction of native woodlands. Refer to Chapter 8 for more information about wildlife conservation.

Ecosystems

Interdependent organisms living together in particular environmental conditions form an ecosystem. A stable ecosystem generally contains primary producers (plants) capable of harvesting energy from the sun. When animals eat the plants, the energy is passed through the food chain by primary consumers (herbivores) and secondary consumers (carnivores). Primary consumers, such as snails, feed directly on the plant, while secondary consumers get their share of the energy by consuming the snails. Decomposers (bacteria and fungi) work at the bottom of the food chain, feeding on waste products and dead plant and animal tissue. The decomposers recycle organic materials back into the soil so new plants can grow. Animals such as worms, slugs and snails break down dead leaves and other organic material, helping to make the job of the decomposers a bit easier. The relationship amongst plants and animals can be represented as food chains and food webs which show how energy is passed along from the primary producer to the different types of consumers.

In an ecosystem, some animals will be dependent on plants to provide for other needs, as well as for food. For example, a nettle patch in a garden not only provides food for certain caterpillars and other invertebrates but also provides shelter and protection. The stinging hairs of the nettle provide a defence against animals which would otherwise destroy their habitat, and they also provide protection against all but the most agile predators. Many nettle patches provide homes for aphids which swarm around the fresh spring growth and consequently provide food for ladybirds. Aphids are also eaten by blue tits and other birds agile enough to navigate the stems. In late summer nettles produce large quantities of seeds, which are a food source for a variety of birds.

Competition for resources

In any ecosystem there is competition for the available resources. To survive, plants compete for sunlight, water, nutrients and space to grow. Wildflowers compete successfully for these resources in a woodland by growing and flowering before the deciduous trees produce their leaves. Flowering plants also compete to attract the

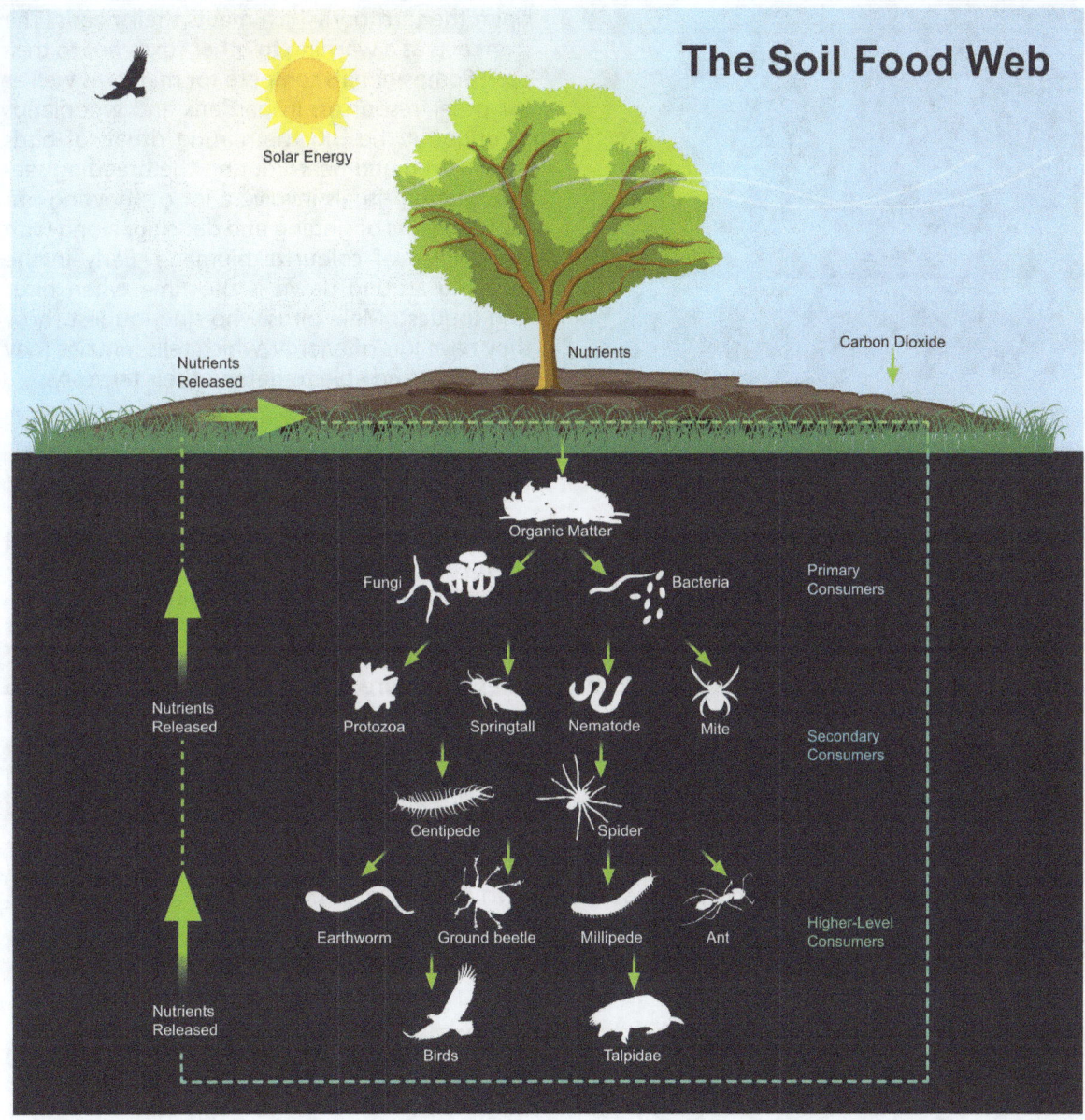

pollinators they need to help them reproduce. Their flowers are often brightly coloured to attract the attention of insects and structured to enable the insects to access their nectar and pollen. Some plants produce flowers which attract certain types of pollinators. For example, foxgloves have large tubular flowers with clearly marked spots and a landing strip which is perfectly suited to bumblebees.

Animals compete for the resources they require in different ways. Many birds and mammals are territorial. Birds, such as robins, choose a territory because it can meet their needs for food, water, shelter and nesting sites. Once a male robin has chosen its territory, it will defend it aggressively against other males. Some mammals, such as foxes, are also territorial. Foxes use scent to mark and

claim the territory which meets their needs. The scent acts as a warning to other foxes not to trespass. Some animals compete for mates, as well as for other resources. In gardens and woodlands throughout the UK, the mating rituals of birds can be seen and heard during the breeding season. Mating rituals involve a lot of showing off, including lots of singing and dancing, along with the display of colourful plumage. Early in the morning around dawn is the time when birds sing loudest. Male birds who sing loudest show they have lots of energy, which tells females they are strong and able to defend their territory.

Biodiversity

An ecosystem which is species-rich is more resilient and adaptable to environmental changes than one in which the range of species is limited. In a system where species are limited, the loss or temporary reduction of any one species could disrupt the food chain with serious effects on other species. In habitats rich in biodiversity, the loss of one species is less likely to have such a major effect on the stability of the system. If one species fails in an ecosystem supported by a wide variety of living things, then it is likely there will be other species which are able to keep energy flowing to maintain the system. For example, if a pollinating species goes extinct, a wildflower meadow with 20 other species is likely to adapt better than a meadow with only one.

A biologically diverse environment can be stunning and utterly fascinating. Spending time in nature provides experiences and opportunities which can inspire us aesthetically, as well as improve our physical and mental health. All it takes is one step into a natural woodland or a walk through a landscape of wildflowers to make us realise how lucky we are to be alive, and how much we owe to the great diversity of species with which we share the world. Refer to Chapter 8 for information and activities related to ecosystem services and wildlife conservation.

Part 2: Working towards the big idea

Models of good practice

Topic: Food provided by plants

Age group: 5–7 years

Learning goals

Children take a step towards the big idea when they learn to grow plants as sources of food. The topic starts by exploring the different parts of plants which children eat and goes on to

Chapter 4 **Interdependence**

link the ideas to the health benefits of eating vegetables. By growing their own vegetables children learn how plants require water, light and a suitable temperature to grow. In the later part of the topic, children start to develop their understanding of the ecology of the garden by exploring the parts of plants that animals prefer to eat and by describing simple food chains.

Working scientifically

In this topic children will:

- ask simple questions;
- observe closely using simple equipment;
- perform simple tests;
- identify different edible plants;
- use their own ideas and scientific ideas to answer questions;
- gather and record data to help answer questions.

Health and safety

Check whether the seeds you intend to sow have been treated with pesticides. Teach children never to eat the seeds. Safeguard against children with allergies eating sunflower seeds grown in the garden. Plan all gardening activities to include appropriately sized tools and equipment, as well as considerations of safety and hygiene. Wash food crops before eating them. Risk assess any outside visits. Refer to the relevant safety codes in the ASE publication *Be Safe!* (2011) when planning to teach the activities in this topic.

Exploring children's ideas

Introduce the topic in the autumn term by talking about plants as sources of food. How well do children know what they eat? Ask them to talk about their favourite vegetables. Can they describe a vegetable? What is it? Which vegetables do they like to eat? Which don't they like? Show children a range of common vegetables and ask them to name them. Do they know where they come from?

Talking points: true, false or not sure?

- Vegetables come from supermarkets.
- Vegetables are grown on farms.
- Apples grow on trees.
- Carrots grow on trees.
- Chips are grown on trees.

- Tomatoes are parts of a plant.
- All vegetables are parts of plants.

Working in groups, children discuss the talking points. Listen to the reasons for their ideas and assess what they know about edible plants. Use video and pictures to establish that vegetables come from plants and are grown in gardens, on allotments and on farms. Establish that a vegetable is the part of a plant that we eat.

What part of the plant do we eat?

If you grow vegetables in your school garden, take the children to have a look at what is being grown. See if they can name the plants and are aware which part we eat. Lift selected plants so children can talk about the parts they eat. Use terms such as leaf vegetables, stem vegetables, root vegetables and fruits. Take photographs of different edible parts of the plant.

Organise a trip to a local community garden, allotment or another place in your neighbourhood where vegetables are grown. Contact your local council or visit the Social Farms and Gardens' website to find a community garden near you. Plan the visit so children can explore the different types of edible plants and find out how they are grown. Ask permission to lift selected plants so the children can see the edible parts. Take photographs of the different vegetables. Arrange for the children to do simple tasks such as watering, weeding and perhaps some planting. If possible, gain permission to bring some vegetables back, which can be prepared and eaten in the classroom.

Things to talk about

Back in the classroom, listen to children's stories about what they learnt from their visit. Encourage them to talk about the different plants and which parts are edible. Which parts do they like to eat? Which plants do they eat at home? Which have they never eaten? Which would they like to try?

Create a large wall display of a plant showing different edible parts. Start by drawing a very large plant with roots, a stem and leaves. Using the photographs, talk about the different vegetables in the school garden and community gardens. On what part of the plant were the vegetables found? Children make cardboard models of the different types of vegetables and attach them to

Chapter 4 **Interdependence**

the appropriate parts of the plant display. On a table at the base of the display arrange a selection of the real vegetables.

Minestrone soup and fruit salad

Talk about how vegetables make delicious soup which is good for the children's health. Link this to the work you do on healthy eating, and remind children about the need to eat fruit and vegetables every day. Purchase a range of fruits and root vegetables to make minestrone soup and fruit salad. Can children identify those that grow above the ground and those which grow below? Ask children to sort the food into two groups: those which they will use to make their soup and those they will use to make their fruit salad. Discuss reasons for children's choices. Children help make a healthy meal by peeling and cutting up the vegetables under the supervision of an adult.

Hot seating and snap

Give each child, or small group, a label and help them write the name of a vegetable on it. Without revealing the name of the vegetable, children describe their vegetable and talk about which part of a plant it represents. The rest of the class try to name the vegetable. Another game is to divide the class into groups. Each group has labels with the names of vegetables on them. This is a game of snap, where one group describes a vegetable and the other groups have to match it to the name of a vegetable on one of their labels. In both games children should be encouraged to justify their responses. Use the activity to assess children's progress towards the learning goals.

Which are the best-tasting salad leaves?

Spring is a good time to plant easy-to-grow vegetables. Ask children for their advice about growing plants. Find out what they know and what experience they have. Listen to their ideas and probe their understanding.

Bring in a range of salad leaves which are easily available such as lettuce, basil, baby spinach, rocket, coriander, chervil and parsley. Try to include leaves of different colours. The purpose of the enquiry is to discover which they prefer to eat and why. Working in groups, children collaborate to decide the best way to test the leaves. Encourage children to think about the influence scent, colour, texture and shape of the leaves may have on their choice. Groups decide on their own tests. Encourage children to describe their experiences and give reasons for their ideas. Which salad leaves would they like to grow?

31

Chapter 4 Interdependence

How do we grow salad leaves in the garden?

With support, children grow microgreens in raised beds or containers in the garden, or if necessary in pots on windowsills in the classroom. Microgreens are plants that can be harvested for their leaves in just a week or so and can be used to add flavour and nutrients to a salad dish or pizza topping. Common varieties of microgreens include rocket, basil, beetroot, broccoli, cabbage, celery, chard, chervil, coriander, kale, mustard, kohlrabi, lettuce, parsley, peas and radish. When growing microgreens in garden beds make sure the soil is finely raked. In containers use fine-textured potting soil and follow the planting instructions on the packaging.

There are a number of questions children can answer by enquiry, when growing microgreens.

- Do microgreens need water to grow?
- Do microgreens need light to grow?
- Do microgreens grow best in sunny or shady conditions?
- Which type of microgreens grow fastest?
- Which type of microgreens grow the biggest leaves?
- Which type of microgreen grow the longest roots?

Help children plan their investigations. Children record the growth of the plants from sowing until they are harvested. Take photographs and create a timeline showing different stages in the growth of the plants from germination to harvest. Based on the outcomes of their experiments, children devise a set of simple instructions for growing microgreens. Encourage groups to justify their instructions and use their ideas to assess their progress towards the learning goals.

Information sources

- Design a children's allotment: www.nsalg.org.uk/growing-advice/design-a-childrens-allotment/
- Social farms and gardens: www.farmgarden.org.uk/

Working on scientific understanding

In this part, children have opportunities to talk about growing edible plants from a scientific point of view and, by investigating simple feeding relationships, start to develop a picture of the ecology of the garden.

Start by talking about children's experiences of growing microgreens. Help them describe the way the microgreens grew from tiny seeds. Talk about growing roots, stems and leaves. Listen to children's responses and encourage them to talk about how they helped the microgreen seeds to grow. Broaden the discussion to talk about seeds in general, and how they are waiting for the right conditions to grow. Use video clips and other images to illustrate how plants grow. The BBC clip 'What does a plant need to grow?' is useful because it features growing a sunflower, which can be used to initiate a scientific enquiry.

Growing sunflowers

Sunflowers are easy to grow and produce edible seeds. Working in groups, children talk about how they can grow sunflowers in the school garden. Encourage them to discuss the best conditions for growing the plants. Listen to their ideas and assess their understanding. Sunflowers grow best in full sun, but children can experiment by also trying to grow some plants in partial shade. This will enable them to recognise the important part sunlight plays in plant growth. Keep soil moist in the growing season.

With adult support, groups prepare containers and beds in areas around the school. Slugs and snails like to eat young sunflower shoots, so encourage children to think of ways they can protect their plants while they grow. Each week children record the progress of their plants by measuring how much they have grown, the number of leaves and, later on, the size of the flower head. Children make sketches and take photographs of their development. Groups record the weekly progress of their sunflowers on a large chart in the classroom. Encourage children to talk about the effect of the sun on their sunflowers. After the flower head turns brown the seeds can be harvested, and children can make their own seed packets to take some home. Based on the outcomes of their enquiry, instructions on how to best grow the seeds at home can be included in the packet.

Most parts of a sunflower can be eaten, but it is the hulled seeds which are most popular. Check the school health and safety policy before allowing children to eat sunflower seeds. Do not allow children with nut allergies to handle them.

Which part of the plant do animals eat?

Children plant unprotected sunflower seedlings in the garden to find out which animals like to feed on them. Children will need to keep a careful eye on the seedlings to see which pests are feeding on the young shoots. Look out for the giveaway signs of slippery snail and slug tracks to identify the culprits. Check the leaves for caterpillars and small insects. Sunflowers attract different kinds of pollinators including bees and hoverflies. In the summer, children can observe the bees

collecting nectar and pollen, and when the seeds are ripe tits and finches may be attracted to the garden to feast on them.

Throughout the growing season children record the animals which feed on different parts of the sunflowers and other plants in the school garden. Create a giant display of the sunflower which illustrates the parts eaten by different animals. Children produce simple food chains such as *sunflower – snail – hedgehog*, or *sunflower – caterpillar – bird*. Introduce children to the terms carnivores, herbivores and omnivores.

Bird café

Children plan investigations to find out which types of seeds birds like best. Do all birds like the same types of seeds? Is the size of the seeds important? Which kind of birds like sunflower seeds? Seeds can be bought commercially so that they are available to the birds all year round. Use a number of feeders situated close together, each with a different type of seed. Don't forget to put out some water. Set up a wildlife video camera to record the birds which visit the feeders. Children present their findings at a school assembly. Safeguard children with nut allergies.

Exploring the bigger picture

Children further develop their understanding of food chains by exploring the range of predators in the garden and a local park. Children learn that animals survive by eating plants or eating other animals which have eaten plants.

We're all going on a predator hunt

A wide range of predators can be found in the school grounds or a local park. Before going out on a predator hunt, children need to learn about the types of predators they will be hunting for. Help them use information sources to identify the predators they are likely to find in the school garden or nearby park. These will mainly be invertebrates as such ladybirds, ants, spiders, earwigs, centipedes, ground beetles and rove beetles, as well as different types of birds. Children may also

find frogs and toads, especially if you have a pond. Hedgehogs, mice and bats are nocturnal animals, so children are unlikely to see these active during the day.

Working in supervised groups, children search the school grounds or nearby park looking for predators. Take magnifiers and specimen jars so children can collect and closely observe the invertebrates. Remind them to handle the creatures carefully and return them unharmed to where they were found. Places to look include the compost heap, beneath leaf litter, under logs or stones, in cracks in walls, and on the stems and leaves of plants. Use sweep nets to explore long grass, and use a white sheet to collect invertebrates which fall out of trees after shaking lower branches. Take photographs of the creatures and also where they were found. Use information sources to talk about what the creatures eat. Back in the classroom create simple food chains which include part of a plant, the prey and the predator. Here are some examples:

- flowers – butterflies – birds
- leaves – slugs – frogs
- leaves – snails – hedgehogs
- flowers – moths – bats
- flowers – bees – spiders
- leaves – aphids – ladybirds

Use children's photographs and images from the web to illustrate the food chains.

Children's stories: a guide to garden predators

With support, children produce an illustrated magazine entitled *A guide to garden predators*. Working in small groups, children contribute a page to the magazine which focusses on a particular predator. The predator can be one they discovered on the hunt or a predator they have discovered using information sources. Each page should include information about the predator and its habitat, and at least one food chain. In the role of the editor, the teacher needs to guide children's ideas to ensure the magazine is as wide ranging as possible. Photographs taken on the hunt can be used to illustrate the magazine, along with children's drawings. Discuss children's ideas as they produce the magazine and assess their progress towards the learning goals.

Making the school garden frog, toad and bat friendly

Compost heaps and ponds are good resources for frogs, toads and bats. Bats swoop low over ponds to feed on insects such as adult caddis flies and mayflies. Bats also feed on moths. Grow white or pale-coloured flowers which attract moths at night. Place bat boxes in sheltered places on tree trunks and walls, away from the hustle and bustle of the playground. Log piles, hedges and large stones provide ideal places for frogs and toads to shelter and hibernate in the winter. For more information refer to the RHS, Froglife and Bat Conservation Trust websites. More information for making the garden more wildlife friendly can be found in Chapter 8.

Information sources

- Bat Conservation Trust: www.bats.org.uk/
- Froglife: www.froglife.org/who-we-are/
- Making a pond: www.froglife.org/wp-content/uploads/2013/06/Froglife_JustAddWater_2011.pdf
- RHS Amphibians: www.rhs.org.uk/advice/profile?pid=493
- RHS Bats: www.rhs.org.uk/advice/profile?pid=759
- RHS Sunflowers: www.rhs.org.uk/education-learning/gardening-children-schools/family-activities/grow-it/grow/sunflower
- RSPB: www.rspb.org.uk/birds-and-wildlife/advice/how-you-can-help-birds/feeding-birds/safe-food-for-birds/
- Take action for wildlife: www.wildlifetrusts.org/actions
- What does a plant need to grow? www.bbc.com/bitesize/articles/zxxsyrd

Topic: The producers

Age group: 7–9 years

Learning goals

Children make progress towards the big idea by learning how plants produce their own food. The topic starts by exploring the best conditions for growing edible plants. Children learn how soil contains nutrients which the plants need for healthy growth, and how water and sunlight play a fundamental part in a plant's development. Children work on their understanding of the functions of the different parts of a plant and learn how the parts contribute to the production of food. Later on, the topic provides opportunities for children to explore the bigger picture by encouraging them to visualise the garden as a managed ecosystem which can provide for a large diversity of living things. Children learn that animals are ultimately dependent on food produced by plants for their survival and that feeding relationships can be represented as food chains and food webs.

Working scientifically

In this topic children will:

- set up practical enquiries to answer questions;
- make systematic and careful observations;

Chapter 4 **Interdependence**

- record and report findings appropriately;
- use results to draw conclusions and make predictions;
- use scientific evidence and ideas for problem solving;
- apply scientific ideas to real-life situations.

Health and safety

Check whether the seeds you intend to sow have been treated with pesticides. Teach children never to eat the seeds. Plan all gardening activities to include appropriately sized tools and equipment, as well as considerations of safety and hygiene. Wash food crops before eating them. Risk assess any outside visits. Refer to the relevant safety codes in the ASE publication *Be Safe!* (2011) when planning to teach the activities in this topic.

Exploring children's ideas

Autumn is a good time for children to prepare their vegetable beds and choose which vegetables they would like to grow in spring. Planning ahead is important so that they can plant their vegetables at the right time and provide the right conditions for them to grow. Listen to what children know about growing plants and talk about the conditions vegetables need to grow.

Soil testing

Take children out into the school garden to identify areas which can be used to grow vegetables. Talk about how the area should not be too exposed to the wind, but should be open to the sun. A south-facing garden is ideal. Talk about the soil. Why are plants grown in soil? Discuss children's responses. Point out that the soil must be fertile, meaning that it should contain all the ingredients plants need to grow strong and healthy. Introduce children to the idea that soil is a mixture of ingredients, just like a cake. To discover the ingredients children carry out the following tests:

1. Is the soil heavy clay, or light and sandy?

Groups collect samples from around the school garden to test the nature of the soil. A simple way to assess whether the soil is heavy clay or sandy is to knead a golf-ball-sized amount with a small amount of water. If the damp soil is pliable and can be made into a ball or a flat sausage shape, then it is a clay soil. On the other hand, if it cannot be kneaded it is likely to be sandy soil. Another way of testing soil is find out how well it drains. Children devise experiments to discover the best-draining soil. Clay soils tend to become waterlogged, while sandy soils are often free draining.

2. Is the soil acid or alkaline?

Simple pH testing kits can be purchased from gardening shops. Children follow the instructions that come with the kit. Use the kits or other devices to compare the pH of the soil to the juice of lemons, limes, oranges, beetroots, tomatoes and other edible plants. Vegetables do best in soils of around pH 6.5, which is slightly acidic.

3. What else is in the soil?

Using samples of soil from the garden, children plan how to separate out the ingredients. They start by picking and sorting the bigger ingredients into organic and non-organic materials. Then they can separate the ingredients using progressively finer sieves. Finally, they mix the remaining ingredient with water in a clear plastic bottle, shake it up and let it settle. The light organic material can be found at the top, with the heavier rock-based materials sinking to the bottom.

Groups present and compare the results of the three tests with the rest of the class. What do they think soil is made from? Children debate which areas provide the best conditions to grow vegetables. If the soil is very poor, give children the option of growing their vegetables in containers using soil-based potting compost. Children can separate the ingredients in the potting compost and compare it to the soil around the school.

Growing vegetables

Children use the outcomes of their enquiries to choose areas of the garden where they can grow their vegetables. If necessary, to improve drainage they add compost to the soil and dig in slow-release organic fertiliser to add nutrients which improve the fertility of the soil. Talk about how compost adds organic materials to the soil and how the minerals contained in the fertiliser support the health and growth of the plants.

Choosing vegetables to grow in the school garden can be problematic, as seeds sown in spring may not be ready for harvest until late summer or autumn. Buying plugs (seedlings) can help solve this problem. Using plugs instead of seeds can save a number of weeks of growing time, so vegetables can be harvested before the summer holidays. Crops such as beetroot, carrots, cucumber, French beans, lettuce, courgettes, peas, first early potatoes, radish, spinach and turnip are what the RHS call speedy crops and can be grown in less than three months.

When choosing which vegetables to grow, children should research the possible sowing and harvesting times. Encourage children to choose vegetables that they harvest at different times in the school year. Each group should produce its own crop planner, with a timeline for planting and har-

vesting their vegetables. Look for advice on the RHS website to help children plan their vegetable garden. Design labels to include the name of the crop, when it was planted and the expected harvest time.

Keeping a garden journal

Keep a garden journal to make weekly records of children's activity in the garden. Save seed packets, plant tags and photographs of different crops. Make notes about the progress of the crops, including successes and failures. Record plans and planting schedules, as well as a sketch of the garden layout season by season. Record rainfall and temperature. Make notes about the use of compost and fertilisers and the problems with garden pests. Include photographs of the children working in the garden, as well as wildlife such as birds and invertebrates. Include tips, images and ideas from gardening magazines. Use the journal to help children reflect on both the development of their gardening skills and their science learning.

Plant science

Children design their own tests to discover the best conditions for growing vegetables. Here are some enquiries they could consider:

- How does the amount of water affect the growth of the plants?
- How does the frequency of watering the plants affect their growth?
- How does the amount of compost added to the soil affect the growth of the plants?
- How does adding organic fertiliser to the soil affect plant growth?
- Does the distance between the plants affect how well they grow?
- How does growing vegetables in shady rather than sunny areas affect their growth?

Encourage children to think of themselves as plant scientists and the garden as a place for experimentation and discovery. Not all plants like the same growing conditions, and only by working scientifically will they be able to discover the best ways to grow their chosen vegetables. Use organic (natural) fertilisers such as blood and bone meal, chicken manure pellets and seaweed fertiliser, which are environmentally friendly.

Compost or fertiliser?

Adding lots of compost improves the health of the soil and helps grow stronger, healthier vegetables. However, too much fertiliser can damage the health of the soil and create sappy, leafy growth, which is vulnerable to attack by pests. To test whether vegetables are better grown in compost-rich soil or fertiliser-rich soil, children can set up comparative tests using containers.

Gardening magazine

Children publish their own gardening magazine which reports on all the work they do in the garden and the crops they have produced. Part of the magazine can be devoted to garden science, in which they report the results of their enquiries and try to explain events in the garden from a scientific point of view. Discuss the ideas they publish in the magazine and assess their progress towards the learning goals.

Harvest festival

Organise a show for Harvest Festival in which children display their produce from the garden, along with artefacts, paintings, photographs and cakes, which they have produced as part of the Design Technology and Art curriculum. It you want to be more ambitious, turn the show into a community affair with opportunities for parents to contribute. Categories could include Vegetables and Fruit, Flowers, Floral Arrangements, Cookery, Handicrafts, Artwork and Photographs.

Information sources

- Design a children's allotment: www.nsalg.org.uk/growing-advice/design-a-childrens-allotment/
- RHS campaign for school gardening: https://schoolgardening.rhs.org.uk/home
- Veg crop planner: www.rhs.org.uk/advice/pdfs/vegplanner.pdf
- Vegetable crop planner: https://schoolgardening.rhs.org.uk/resources/info-sheet/vegetable-crop-planner

Working on scientific understanding

In this part children work on their understanding of how plants produce their own food. The approach is to focus children's attention on the functions of the different parts of the plant, and help them visualise how a plant uses its roots and leaves to collect the 'ingredients' it needs to make its own food. Start by discussing what children know about the functions of the parts of a plant.

Talking points: true, false or not sure?

- Plants need water, light, air and nutrients to grow.
- Plants take in water through their leaves.
- Plants use their roots to take in water and nutrients from the soil.
- Roots prevent a plant falling over.
- Plants collect light from the soil through their roots.
- Plants collect sunlight with their leaves.
- Air gets into plants through their flowers.
- Air can pass through tiny holes in the leaves.
- Plants use water, light, air and nutrients from the soil to produce food.

Groups work collaboratively to address the talking points and share their ideas with the rest of the class. Focus discussion on the reasons for their responses. Address misconceptions and talk about how leaves and roots play an important part in collecting the 'ingredients' needed to make the food plants require to grow and keep healthy.

How do plants produce food?

The purpose of this enquiry is for children to discover how water and other nutrients from the soil travel into and around a plant. Groups start by exploring how water travels up the stem of a plant into its leaves and flowers. Use white carnations or chrysanthemums stood in a container of coloured water. Use food dye. Help children cut the end of the stem with a sharp knife so it is not crushed. Talk about how the water carries the food dye around the plant, and compare it to how water carries nutrients from the soil around a plant. Groups then dissect their plants and using magnifiers explore the structure of the stems leading to the leaves and flowers to find out how the water travelled through the plant.

Children repeat the previous experiment using cabbage leaves. Place the stem of a cabbage leaf in coloured water and wait to see what happens. Remember to help them cut the end of the stem with a sharp knife. Observe and record what happens at regular intervals during the day. Take photographs. Children dissect the leaves and use magnifiers to inspect the paths taken by the dye in the veins.

Leaves are 'food-making machines'

Groups collect different types of leaves from the school grounds or nearby park to observe in detail back in the classroom. They look at the shape of the leaf, what its edges are like, whether it has one or more main veins, the pattern made by the side veins and whatever else the children find interesting. Use magnifiers and microscopes to look closely at the underneath of the leaves to identify the little holes (stomata) through which air (carbon dioxide/oxygen/water vapour) goes in and out of the plant. Talk about leaves as food-making machines (organs) which first collect the ingredients (air, water and nutrients) and then combine them to make food. Draw their attention to the role light plays in producing food. Leaves absorb light and use its energy to 'cook up' the ingredients into a sugary food, which is stored in different parts of the plant. Talk about how plants use some of the food to grow, and how they store the rest in their leaves, fruits, stems and roots, which provide food (vegetables) for us and other animals to eat. Illustrate the point by identifying different vegetables, such as leaf vegetables (lettuces), fruit vegetables (tomatoes), stem vegetables (potatoes) and root vegetables (carrots).

Chapter 4 Interdependence

Scientific drawings

Children sketch the anatomy of a plant showing the pathways through which water and nutrients travel and the holes through which air gets into the leaves. Discuss children's pictures and assess their progress towards the learning goals. Use animations from video clips on the web to help children visualise how a plant takes in water and nutrients through its roots, and how it takes in air and absorbs light through its leaves.

Artwork

Children create their own artwork based on the shapes of different kinds of leaves. They can use a combination of printing, painting, pressing and rubbing techniques to create their own unique collages inspired by nature. Introduce children to the work of William Morris, who used a lot of leaf and fruit motifs.

Things to talk about

Which nutrients do children get from eating parts of plants? Compare nutrients in the soil to the vitamins and minerals children get from their food. Plants need essential minerals such as calcium, iron, potassium, magnesium, phosphorus and nitrogen to keep healthy. They get these nutrients from the soil. Where do children get their minerals from? What nutrients do they get from eating vegetables? Groups use information sources to find out about the essential nutrients which they get from eating vegetables, such as carbohydrates, proteins, fats, vitamins and minerals. Link the ideas to the work you do on healthy eating. You may have vegan or vegetarian children in your class. Talk to them about what they eat. Children plan a vegan meal which provides the nutrients they need for a healthy diet.

How well do plants grow without nutrients?

Children plan their own investigations to compare how well plants grow in different soil conditions in the garden. For example, children compare how well radishes grow in agricultural sand without any nutrients, in sand mixed with compost, in sand mixed with organic fertiliser and in sand mixed with compost and fertiliser. Focus children's attention on fair testing, and talk about the control of variables. Which conditions need to be the same for all the plants? Encourage children to predict the outcomes of their experiments. Children should justify their predictions.

Record and plot the growth rate of the plants. After about four weeks when the radishes are formed, compare the size and taste of the radishes. Compare outcomes with children's predictions.

Discuss the benefits of growing vegetables in nutrient-rich (fertile) soil. Use this activity to assess children's progress towards the learning goals. See the Science and Plants for School (SAPS) Gardening for Primary Schools website for more investigations. Invite parents or guardians who grow vegetables to share their experiences with the children.

Information sources

- SAPS: www.saps.org.uk/primary/beyond-the-classroom/233-gardening-for-primary-schools-suggestions-for-investigations
- Social farms and gardens: www.farmgarden.org.uk/
- What do a plant's roots and stem do? www.bbc.com/bitesize/articles/zcxh4qt
- What does a plant need to live? www.bbc.com/bitesize/articles/zcmtk2p

The bigger picture

Having explored how plants produce their own food, children start to develop a bigger picture of the ecology of the garden by exploring the diversity of animals which feed on them. Activities in this part help children to visualise how food produced by plants (producers) is consumed directly or indirectly by different types of animals (consumers).

Talk about how we are dependent on food produced by plants. Could we survive without plants? What would we eat? Working in groups, children debate the idea of a world without plants. Groups share and justify their ideas and develop an argument for whether we could or could not survive without plants.

Talking points: true, false or not sure?

- There are lots of things to eat other than plants.
- If all the plants die we could still eat meat.
- If there were no plants, we could drink more milk.
- I don't eat plants anyway; we get our food from the supermarket.
- I prefer burgers and chips rather than eating vegetables.
- Without plants there would be no meat to eat.
- If there were no plants we could still eat fish.

Groups discuss the talking points and provide reasons for their responses. Groups come together to share their ideas. Challenge misconceptions. Focus their attention on the idea that animals cannot produce their own food. Animals are consumers which rely directly or indirectly on the food plants produce to survive. Illustrate with some simple food chains connected to the talking points, such as:

- Grass – cows (milk) – humans
- Grass – cows (burgers) – humans
- Tiny sea plants – prawns – cod – humans

Hot seating

Write the names of common meals on cards such as baked beans on toast, eggs and bacon, sausage and chips, spaghetti and meat balls, fish fingers and so on. Without naming the meal, children in the hot seat describe what the food looks like and why it would not exist without plants. The rest of the class try to identify the meal. Once they get the idea, children can make up their own meals. Use the activity to assess children's progress towards the learning goals.

Garden ecology

Ask children, which are the biggest pests in the garden? Which creatures cause most damage to your vegetables? Children use information sources to learn about the different types of pests. Groups find out what the animals look like and where in the garden they are likely to find them. According to the RHS, caterpillars, slugs, snails, beetles, aphids and ants are among the most common garden pests.

Which pests live in the school garden?

Working in groups, children plan an investigation to identify and map the location of common pests that live in the school grounds (or a local park). The investigation should include all the different types of plants, not just vegetables. Take photographs of host plants and the damage the pests have caused. Children use magnifiers to observe and help identify the pests. Back in the classroom groups report their findings and pool their results to create a giant map of the school grounds with the locations of the different types of pests, and information about which plants they eat. Children use appropriate sources to collect information about predators which feed on the pests.

Pests can be our friends

Discuss how pests are part of the garden ecosystem. Some garden animals are classified as pests because they damage the growth of certain plants, including vegetables. However, pests are an important part of the ecology of the garden. By removing primary consumers such slugs and snails from the garden, we are also removing a source of food for a large variety of predators including birds, hedgehogs, ground beetles, toads, frogs, slow worms and shrews. Hence, by removing pests we are also likely to limit the range of the animals that visit the garden. If we want to maintain a wildlife-friendly garden, we must not think of plant-eating animals as pests, but instead see them as an important part of the garden's ecosystem.

Food chains and food webs

Help children work on their understanding of food chains by explaining how all animals rely on the food produced by plants to survive. This is because, unlike plants, animals cannot produce their own food. In an ecosystem some animals get their food directly from plants by eating them, while others get their food indirectly from plants by eating animals that have already consumed plants. This means nutrients in the food produced by the plants are transferred from producer to primary consumer to secondary consumer and so on up the food chain. For example, in the garden a slug may feed on a lettuce seedling, then the slug itself may be eaten by a frog, which consequently is eaten by a bird such as a crow. This means that energy and nutrients stored in the lettuce and other plants eaten by the slug have been passed up the food chain, eventually being used by the crow to keep healthy.

Tell children the story of how pests such as slugs and snails are vital to the ecology of the garden. Illustrate the point by producing a food chain, for example:

lettuce	slug	frog	crow
producer	primary consumer	secondary consumer	tertiary consumer

Children add more consumers and turn the chain into a web, more accurately reflecting the feeding relationships in the garden. Groups produce their own food chains and webs which include garden pests. Children explain how wildlife would suffer if all the pests were removed from the garden.

Controlling pests in the garden

Pesticides not only kill off the pests but also are likely to harm their predators. They can also have damaging effects on the health of children who eat vegetables with traces of pesticide on them. The ASE advise that pesticides should *not* be used in a school garden.

Natural pest control provides opportunities for children to discover wildlife-friendly ways of protecting their crops against common garden pests. Here are some ideas for children to investigate:

1. Encourage more natural predators into the garden.

Allow natural predators to control the pests by making the garden attractive to a wide variety of wildlife. Increasing the number of predators in the garden will help reduce the number of pests.

Chapter 4 **Interdependence**

Working in groups, children plan ways of attracting more predators to the school gardens and grounds. Each group can focus on a specific type of predator and use information sources to find out about its preferred habitat. To attract it to the garden children need to provide for the predators' basic needs. Just including a source of water in the garden will attract wildlife. Create small ponds around the garden using containers buried in the ground. Ponds quickly become habitats for many types of animals, especially frogs and toads. When creating a pond make sure animals can easily get in and out of it. Long grass, weeds, dead wood and log piles provide hiding places for small mammals, and don't forget to provide nesting boxes for birds, bats and hedgehogs. Refer to Chapter 8 for more ideas to attract wildlife.

Having done their research, groups can take action to attract predators into the school grounds/garden. Throughout the school year children monitor the use of the garden by birds and look out for signs of other predators. Set up wildlife cameras in the vegetable garden to monitor the activities of snails and slugs, and the predators that feed on them. Look out for empty snail shells as evidence of predators at work.

2. Create physical boundaries around your plants.

To prevent slugs and snails from devouring young plants, children could think of creating boundaries around the plants which prevent the creatures reaching the plants. Slugs and snails do not have legs, so it is likely they may have difficulty travelling over loose, uneven surfaces. Some gardeners use broken egg shells or sharp gravel to protect their plants. Working in groups, children can come up with their own ideas and test them out in the vegetable garden. Children need to work scientifically to discover whether their boundaries are successful. This involves comparing protected and unprotected plants within the same beds.

3. Companion crops.

Companion plants are grown alongside other plants which gardeners want to protect from pests. The purpose of the companion plant is to attract pests away from the plants gardeners value, or to attract predators which feed on the pests which are likely to attack their more valued plants. When gardeners talk about companion planting they are often thinking about marigolds. Marigolds are planted alongside plants which are susceptible to attack by aphids. Marigolds attract pest-munching insects such as ladybirds which can devour great numbers of aphids. They also attract hoverflies whose larvae feed on aphids. Children test whether marigolds are effective by growing them alongside vegetables which are susceptible to aphids. Children collect data on the numbers of hoverflies and ladybirds the marigolds attract, and whether they have an effect on aphid populations. Be warned! Marigolds can attract slugs so trying to solve one problem may create another. If things get bad then pick off pests by hand and put them in another part of the school grounds where they can do less harm.

Visit to a community garden

Organise a visit to a community vegetable garden or allotment to find out how they protect their crops from garden pests. In advance arrange activities which children can do to help volunteers in the garden. Also, prepare questions for children to ask and look out for new things to grow in the school garden. Visit the Social Farms and Gardens' website, or contact the local council to locate your nearest community garden.

Information sources

- Companion plants: www.bbc.co.uk/gardening/basics/techniques/organic_companionplanting1.shtml
- Companion planting: www.thompson-morgan.com/companion-planting-guide
- Social farms and gardens: www.farmgarden.org.uk/

Topic: Ecosystems

Age group: 9–11 years

Learning goals

Children make progress towards the big idea when they work on their understanding of how living things within an ecosystem depend on, and compete with, other living things for food and other resources. In this topic, children turn their attention to the important role decomposers play in the ecology of the garden, and how a stable ecosystem consists of producers (plants), consumers (animals) and decomposers (bacteria and fungi). Children focus their attention on the bigger picture by examining feeding relationships in a woodland habitat, which helps them appreciate why biodiversity is essential for a healthy and stable ecosystem. Opportunities are provided for children to learn how wildlife competes to survive and to engage with the struggle for survival of our native ladybirds.

Working scientifically

In this topic children will:

- plan scientific enquiries to answer questions, including the control of variables where necessary;
- make detailed scientific observations and take measurements over an extended time period;

Chapter 4 **Interdependence**

- record data and results using scientific diagrams and appropriate graphs;
- report and present findings from enquiries in oral and written form;
- use evidence to support or refute arguments.

Health and safety

Check whether the seeds you intend to sow have been treated with pesticides. Teach children never to eat the seeds. Plan all gardening activities to include appropriately sized tools and equipment, as well as considerations of safety and hygiene. Wash food crops before eating them. Risk assess any outside visits. Do not touch, collect or consume wild mushrooms or other fungi. Refer to the relevant safety codes in the ASE publication *Be Safe!* (2011) when planning to teach the activities in this topic.

Exploring children's ideas

According to the Wildlife Gardening Forum, an ordinary garden supports more than 8,000 species of insects alone. This is not to mention all the other invertebrates including worms, woodlice, centipedes, millipedes, slugs and snails; and then of course there are vertebrates such as birds, frogs, toads, mice, hedgehogs, bats . . . the list goes on! Talk about the garden or school grounds as an ecosystem, in which plants, animals and other living things depend on each other to survive.

Activities in this part focus on the important role decomposers play in the ecology of the garden, and how a stable ecosystem consists of producers (plants), consumers (animals) and decomposers (bacteria and fungi). Encourage children to speculate about the meaning of the term decomposers. Can they imagine the job they do in the garden?

Detritivores and decomposers

Autumn is traditionally a good time to tidy up the garden and to prepare the soil in anticipation of the plants you want grow in spring. It is also a good time for children to explore the ecology of the garden, especially the role the detritivores and decomposers play in recycling organic material back into the soil. Before tidying up the garden, ask children to imagine what would happen to the leaf litter if it were left on the ground? They can start with the talking points.

Talking points: true, false or not sure?

- The leaf litter would continue to pile up year on year.
- The leaf litter would be blown away by the wind.
- The leaf litter would be washed away by the rain.
- The leaf litter would be collected by birds to make their nests.
- Animals would eat the leaf litter.
- The leaf litter would slowly rot away.

Working in groups, children discuss the talking points and try to arrive at an agreed response to what would happen to the leaf litter. Bring the class together, so that groups can share and justify their ideas.

Things to talk about

Talk about invertebrates such as woodlice which feed on rotting vegetation (detritus). Woodlice are called detritivores because they feed on the detritus of decomposing plants. Slugs, snails, worms and other types of invertebrates are also detritivores, which help 'clean up' nature's dead material. Children use information sources to learn about the different types of detritivores they expect to find in the school grounds. Use images from the web to create a display.

Survey of detritivores in the school grounds

Working in groups, children survey all areas of the school grounds to map the different types of detritivores. They can survey different types of leaf litter, search in vegetable and flower beds, look under twigs and logs, carefully rummage through grass cuttings and under hedges. If your school grounds are not suitable, children can carry out the survey in a local park. Back in the classroom, groups share their results and produce a map of the school ground or park, showing the habitats in which they found detritivores. Use the results to discover whether different types of detritivores have food preferences, or whether they all eat the same types of plant material. Children publish the outcomes of the enquiry in the school science magazine.

Exploring the ecology of a compost heap

Compost is often described as food for the soil, and gardeners refer to it as black gold because it is crucial to the success of any garden. The health of the soil in the school garden depends on the compost children add to it. Compost conditions the soil, making it loose and absorbent, and it increases the amount of water the soil can hold. Compost also releases nutrients slowly into the soil, providing plants with a steady, balanced diet to keep them growing strong.

To explore how compost is made children can set up a leaf compost heap in autumn. Construct the bin using four sturdy canes and some wire netting. Details can be found on the RHS website.

Collect lots of fallen deciduous leaves to fill the bin. Make sure they are disease free. With permission from the local council, collect leaves from a nearby park if you cannot find enough in the school grounds. Keep the leaves damp throughout autumn and winter. Take photographs of the leaves and record their conditions.

As spring arrives, children should check on the progress of the leaves. Do they appear to be decomposing? How have they changed since autumn? Which invertebrates can they find in the compost heap? What are they doing there? Children use information sources to identify the invertebrates and classify them into groups such as insects, arachnids, crustaceans, myriapods, molluscs and worms according to physical characteristics. They can further classify them by identifying the primary and secondary consumers and create food chains and simple webs. Finally, groups sample the populations by taking equal amounts of leaf litter from the bottom, middle and top of the bin and record the numbers of different types of invertebrates. How many types of detritivores inhabit the compost? Which types are most popular?

Children continue to record data on the decomposition of the leaf litter at regular intervals throughout spring and summer to answer questions such as:

- At what time of the year do the leaves decompose quickest?
- Which invertebrates (detritivores) are feeding on the leaf litter?
- How do the populations of invertebrates change from early spring to late summer?
- Which types of invertebrates have the highest populations?
- Are there more detritivores or predators in the leaf litter?

Where appropriate, children record the data collected using bar and line graphs.

If you have an established compost heap which contains a mixture of different type of rotting vegetation, children can compare the types of invertebrates in there with the ones in the leaf compost. Talk about children's food chains and webs, and discuss how the detritivores are responsible for breaking down the rotting leaves, along with a lot of helpful fungi and bacteria which they may not be able to see. Use their webs to assess their progress towards the learning goals.

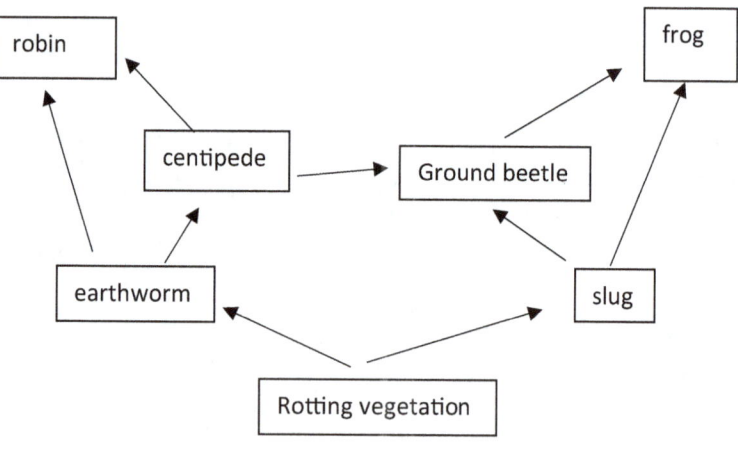

Preparing the soil for growing vegetables in spring

Early autumn is a good time to add compost to your vegetable beds in preparation for sowing crops in spring. Before the children start digging, find out what they know about the purpose of composting the soil.

Talking points: true, false or not sure?

- Compost keeps the soil warm.
- Compost kills the weeds.
- Compost kills the worms.
- Compost provides food for the worms.
- Compost provides food for the plants.
- Compost adds nutrients to the soil.
- Compost helps keep plants healthy.

Working in groups, children discuss the talking points. Groups come together in whole-class discussion to share the reasons for their responses. Address misconceptions.

Testing commercial compost

Children will need to choose compost that suits their soil and the vegetables they intend to grow. A vegetable garden will do best on soils of around pH 6.5. Kits to test the pH of your soil are available from garden centres. If your soil is acidic and low in organic matter, mushroom compost is a useful choice. Children research the different types of compost and their uses on the web.

Working in groups, children test different types of commercially produced compost for their pH and organic content. To explore the organic content, children mix samples of compost with water, shake up the jar and see how much organic material floats to the top. They can compare the texture and pH of the commercial compost with compost produced in the school bin. It may be a good idea to use a mixture of commercial and home-produced compost in the vegetable garden.

How does composting affect the ecology of the soil?

While the soil is still warm, children dig over their beds and remove any weeds. Look for invertebrates in the soil and see if children can find any detritivores. Lots of worms suggest a fertile soil. Randomly sample the numbers of worms and other detritivores in measured volumes of soil to record the populations. Create simple food chains or webs to depict the ecology of the soil habitat.

Children dig lots of suitable compost into the soil, and then mulch their plots to reduce the growth of weeds. Before planting vegetables in spring, children randomly sample the soil to discover the effect the compost has had on the populations of detritivores and their predators. Children review and update their food webs. In summer children can repeat the sampling experiments to see whether the numbers of invertebrates have changed. Children publish their findings on the school blogging platform.

Growing sugar snap peas

Hardy vegetables can be planted as early as March. The SAPS website suggests that sugar snap peas are an ideal crop for primary schools. If planted early in the year they will flower within

12 weeks and produce peas by the end of July. The peas are safe and delicious to eat, either raw or cooked.

Children plan enquiries to test the effects compost has on the growth of their vegetables. The main crop of peas can be planted in the composted beds, while a small number of seeds can be planted in a control bed which has not been composted. Other than the difference between the two soils, all other growing conditions must remain the same. Vegetables need regular watering in dry weather. When they start to grow the peas will need supporting with twigs or canes combined into a tent shape. Refer to the RHS website for more information. If you want to save time, grow the peas from plugs.

An interesting experiment would be to grow the peas without compost, in containers filled with agricultural sand and fertiliser. Children could compare organic and manufactured fertilisers, both of which contain the essential nutrients plants need to grow. Keep other conditions the same as the plants in the beds. Children regularly monitor the growth of the peas, and compare the health of the plants growing in different conditions. Use information sources to compare the advantages and disadvantages of both types of fertilisers. Which best support the garden ecosystem?

Provide opportunities for children to present the outcomes of their enquiries at a school assembly, where the peas can be enjoyed by all.

Working on scientific understanding

Children work on their understanding of how dead vegetation (detritus) is recycled back into the soil by the action of detritivores and decomposers. Although the detritivores break up and shred the dead vegetation, it is bacteria and fungi that do the decomposing. Decomposers play a crucial role in maintaining ecosystems by recycling nutrients from waste products and dead organisms back into the soil, making them available to growing plants. Therefore, in a stable ecosystem there are producers of food (plants), consumers (animals including detritivores) and decomposers (bacteria and fungi).

Things to talk about

Show children the BBC Bitesize time-lapse video of decaying fruit. Discuss how mould (fungus) and bacteria break down (decompose) the organic material, and how similar types of fungi and bacteria can be found in soil. Talk about how mushrooms are probably nature's most visible decomposers. Along with other types of fungi, mushrooms help decompose rotting vegetation. The part we call a mushroom is the fruiting part of the fungus, the equivalent to an apple on a tree. The main part of the fungus lives out of sight, either beneath the soil or inside wood or any organic material it feeds on. If a mushroom pops up on your lawn, you can be sure that hidden underground is a mass of very thin, thread like structures called hyphae, which are responsible for digesting organic material in the soil. Children use information sources to find out about different types of bacteria and fungi and how they help recycle nutrients from dead vegetation back into the soil.

Exploring mushrooms

Children hunt for mushrooms as part of an autumn walk to a local park or woodland. Take photographs and use information sources to identify the different types of mushrooms. Do not touch or collect them. Record all the places mushrooms like to grow; for example, at the base of trees, on trees, on rotting logs and in the ground. What are the most unusual places children find mushrooms growing? Point out that the mushroom is only part of a larger organism (fungus) that lives beneath the soil or inside the rotting wood. Wearing protective gloves, children can carefully use

suitable equipment to explore the ground beneath a mushroom to discover its hyphae. Encourage children to record the detritivores (worms, woodlice etc.) which share the mushroom's habitat. Also, record invertebrates which can be found feeding on the mushrooms.

Ask children whether they think a mushroom is a type of plant. What do they have in common with plants? Compare neighbouring plants with the mushrooms.

Talking points: true, false or not sure?

- Mushrooms are not plants because they have no leaves.
- Mushrooms have fruits so they must be plants.
- Plants do not grow on rotting wood.
- Mushrooms must be plants because they grow in the same places.
- Mushrooms are not plants because they do not produce their own food.
- Mushrooms are not producers; they are consumers because they feed on plants.

Use children's responses to the talking points to focus children's attention on the differences between plants and mushrooms. Plants need sunlight to produce food in their leaves. Mushrooms rely on digesting dead vegetation to get their food. From this perspective mushrooms are consumers not producers, and therefore are not plants. Encourage children to use their findings to speculate about the types of animals which feed on mushrooms and to construct and justify simple food chains such as dead plants – mushrooms – slugs – birds. Use children's responses to the talking points to assess their progress towards the learning goals.

While on their mushroom hunt children look out for mould growing on rotting wood or dead leaves. Take photographs and listen to what children know about mould. Remind them that mould are fungi and are decomposers like mushrooms. They are important parts of the ecosystem of the woodland. Remind children not to touch the mould.

In what conditions does mould grow best?

Back at school, children look for mould growing in the compost heap and other parts of the garden. This can set children on a quest for knowledge about the conditions in which mould grows best. Use foods such as bread, different types of fruit and other vegetables, cheese, bread or cake. Do not use meat or fish. Cut the food up into smallish pieces about the size of a grape. After dipping the food in water, place the pieces next to each other inside a largish see-through plastic jar which is resting on its side. Do not stack the food. Close the container with a secure lid, and never open it. Groups can leave containers in different light and temperature conditions. They can also set up control experiments in which they place the same foods without dipping them in water. Children observe and use cameras to record the growth of mould in their containers each day until the mould is well established. Which are the foods with the most mould? Use the photographs to create a display which illustrates the conditions in which mould grows best. Children use information sources to explore other types of fungi which help recycle organic material.

Things to talk about

Talk about how fungi are aided in their work by some of nature's smallest organisms, bacteria. Both bacteria and fungi can be found hard at work in the garden busily breaking down and recycling rotting fruit and other organic material. Make it clear that bacteria are too small to see without a powerful microscope. Use the BBC clip *Understanding the size of bacteria* to help children imagine how small they are. Bacteria are so small that 250,000 could fit on a spot the size of a full stop, and a billion could be found living in a single gram of soil. Children explore photographs of different types of garden-friendly decomposer bacteria on the web. Type in 'decomposer bacteria' or 'probiotic bacteria' into the search engine. Groups report what they find to the rest of the class.

Beatrix Potter the scientist

Beatrix Potter is well known as an author of children's books, but she is less well known for her scientific work. Beatrix was an inquisitive child who was fascinated by the wildlife she discovered in the woods close to her home. Her uncle was a chemist who encouraged her interest and allowed her to use his microscope to study the local plants, fungi, insects and other invertebrates. She drew each of them in great detail.

Fungi fascinated Beatrix the most. By the time she turned 21, she was already an accomplished mycologist. Her drawings of lichens illustrated how they consisted of two different organisms that lived together, an alga and a fungus. She was the first person in the UK to recognise this fact. Beatrix went on to develop a theory about the symbiotic relationship between the alga and fungus and also produced a scientific study on mushroom reproduction. Because she was a woman, there were few opportunities to present and publish her research. At that time scientific societies were male-only institutions. It is said that Beatrix turned to writing children's literature because she found it impossible to pursue a scientific career.

Working in groups, children use information sources to research the life and work of Beatrix Potter. Explore children's attitudes to women in science. Is there any reason why women should not take up scientific careers? Children research women's achievements in science from the time of Beatrix Potter until the present day. Can they find any women scientists who were not given the recognition they deserved?

Following in Beatrix Potter's footsteps

Children use information sources to discover the different types of lichens which grow in the UK and to explore the symbiotic relationship between alga and fungus. Arrange for children to survey the lichens that grow in the school grounds, the local park and other suitable places in your area. Cemeteries and churchyards can be good places to study lichens. Take photographs and report the outcomes of the survey on the school blogging platform.

Children use information sources to discover the nature of Beatrix Potter's research about mushroom reproduction and explore for themselves how mushrooms reproduce. Find out how to grow edible mushrooms in the school garden.

Chapter 4 Interdependence

Story-telling: life in a compost heap as told by a snail!

Story-telling can help children work on their scientific understanding of natural phenomena by helping them visualise the relationships between the main protagonists. In this case the story is about ecosystems, and the main protagonists are detritivores and decomposers, as well as other characters such as predator invertebrates, birds and small mammals. Children use information sources to identify and discover interesting facts about the protagonists, but the story must not be based simply on a series of facts. Like all stories, it should be structured around a story-line, and told in the author's own words. Children work in groups to share and edit their stories. They could illustrate their stories and publish their own picture story books. Use children's stories to assess their progress towards the learning goals.

Ecosystem modelling

Divide the class into two groups, and provide each group with a set of cards on which they can write the names of the invertebrates and other animals which they think are part of the ecosystem of a compost heap. Each child should have a card with the name of an animal on it, and each group should have a card labelled 'decaying vegetation'. Also provide each group with a ball of string. Take groups out into the playground and ask each group to use the string to create a giant food web, which links the animals together. One child in each group should represent the decaying vegetation and may need to tie together the ends of a number of strings. In the end, each child in the group should be part of the food web. The group with the most valid links is the winner. Discuss the links with each group and address misconceptions.

Information sources

- Beatrix Potter: www.famousscientists.org/beatrix-potter/
- Decaying fruit: www.bbc.com/bitesize/clips/zwx76sg
- How do ecosystems work? www.bbc.com/bitesize/articles/z2pqfcw
- The British Lichen Society: www.britishlichensociety.org.uk/
- Understanding the size of bacteria: www.bbc.com/bitesize/clips/zkptsbk

The bigger picture

In spring, children turn their attention to the woodland and how wildlife compete for the resources they need to survive. Visit websites run by the Woodland Trust, Wildlife Trust, National Trust and other conservation groups to find suitable wildlife areas near your school.

  Start by asking children whether they like going outside on wet, winter days. Would they rather stay warm and dry at home, or get soaking wet in the rain? Talk about how their homes provide them with shelter from the weather and keep them safe at night. Ask them, what do animals do when the weather is bad? Where do they shelter? Provide children with pictures of woodland animals such as birds, foxes, hedgehogs, mice, beetles, bees and butterflies. Working in groups, children discuss what they think these creatures eat and where they live in the woodland. How do they shelter from bad weather and predators? Groups present their ideas to the rest of the class. Use video clips and images to develop children's ideas.

Visit to local woodland

Before the visit, talk about how the woodland provides for the needs of the wildlife. To flourish the animals need water, food, shelter and a safe place to raise their young. The purpose of the visit is to find out where different types of animals find the resources they need.

Prepare for the visit by talking about the most likely places children will find different types of animals. At first glance life in a woodland seems to be all about plants, especially trees, bushes and grass. It is only when children sit quietly they start to hear the birds, and then when they look carefully underneath things they start to discover the range of animals that live there. Make a list of the places where children think animals may be found. Start with the woodland floor and work upwards. A woodland is an ideal place for children to explore because the vast majority of animals can be found either on or close to ground level. Places for children to look include holes in the ground, at the base of trees, under rocks, under logs, inside fallen tree trunks, in the undergrowth and detritus, in the long grass, in shrubs and bushes, on the underside of leaves and in cracks in the bark of trees. In fact, creatures can be found anywhere there is space for them to shelter. Look out for nesting birds and try not to disturb them.

Where possible, children should use magnifiers to observe invertebrates in the places where they find them. Use pooters if necessary to safely examine tiny insects and sweep nets to explore long grass. Information cards or apps on your mobiles can be used to identify the minibeasts. Talk about whether the animals are herbivores, carnivores or omnivores. Sketch out simple food webs. Discuss how omnivores can be both primary and secondary consumers. Speculate about where the different animals find the resources which they need to survive. Which animals eat leaves? Which animals feed on the flowers? What do the birds eat? Children take photographs and make notes and drawings to record the different types of animals and their habitats, which they can use to create a display of woodland life back in the classroom. Talk about the detritivores and decomposers, and take photographs of rotting vegetation as evidence of their work.

Chapter 4 Interdependence

Story-telling

Back in the classroom children use the photographs of the woodland habitats to tell stories of what they discovered. Focus talk on the idea that plants in the woodland not only provide food for the animals but they also provide shelter and places to hide. Create a large woodland display using the photographs with children's annotations. Add to the display pictures of mammals, birds and amphibians which live in woodland, but which children may not have managed to see. Help children to create food webs using plants and animals from the woodland display. When telling their stories encourage children to use words such as habitat, decomposer, detritivore, primary consumer, secondary consumer, tertiary consumer and food source to describe the ecosystems. They can also use terms such as herbivores, carnivores, omnivores and predators when appropriate. Use the activities to assess children's progress towards the learning goals.

Things to talk about

Talk about competition as a struggle for survival among living things in a given environment, such as woodland. Use ideas from Part 1 to discuss how living things in the woodland compete for resources. Focus children's attention on how plants compete for sunlight, space and pollinators, and how animals compete for mates, food and other resources. Describe how animals are territorial, using robins and foxes as examples.

Role play: mating rituals

Mating rituals involve a lot of showing off, including lots of singing and dancing. Early in the morning around dawn is the time when birds can be heard singing loudest. The louder a male bird is able to sing the more likely he is to attract the attention of a female, who is looking for a strong, energetic mate who is able to defend their territory. Children listen to recordings of different birdcalls on the RSPB website. Having listened to a variety of common birds, groups compete to see how many birds they can recognise from their 'voices'. Children role play a bird of their choosing and act out mating rituals designed to attract a partner.

Plant defences

Ask children whether they have been stung by a stinging nettle or been pricked by the thorns on a rose bush. Encourage children to speculate about the purpose of these adaptations. Groups use information sources to discover the variety of ways plants protect themselves against being eaten by animals.

Though we may not like stinging nettles they are an important food source for the caterpillars of some of our favourite butterflies. Stinging nettles support more than 40 kinds of insects, which are provided protection from predators by the plant's sting. In spring, aphids and other insects swarm around fresh growth providing food for ladybirds. The ladybirds in turn provide food for a variety of birds and small mammals. Children use information sources to explore the ecology of the nettle patch and create a food web to represent the feeding relationships. Use the activity to assess children's progress towards the learnings goals.

Story-telling: how wildlife compete to survive

Working in groups, children use information sources to research the ways different types of animals and plants compete for the resources they need. Based on their research, groups write a blog entitled 'How wildlife compete to survive'. Children focus on garden and woodland habitats or broaden the theme of the blog to include other types of habitats in the UK and worldwide. Help children edit the blogs and display them in the classroom or post them on the school's blogging platform. Use the blogs to assess children's progress towards the learning goals.

Native ladybirds under threat

In 2004 a new kind of ladybird arrived in Britain with a voracious appetite and is threatening the existence of some of our native ladybirds. The Harlequin is the most invasive ladybird on earth. It is native to Asia, but over the years it has colonised different parts of the world, including the USA, South America, parts of Africa and most of Europe, and now is eating its way across the UK.

Unlike most other ladybirds, the Harlequin is not a fussy eater. Once it has devoured the aphids in the crops, it then gobbles up other ladybird eggs and larvae, and even the eggs and caterpillars of moths and butterflies. The Harlequin easily out-competes native ladybirds for food, and that is why scientists believe some of our natives are becoming scarce. Children use information sources to profile different types of native ladybirds, and compare them with the Harlequin. Encourage children to speculate about ways native species can be saved. Can natives save themselves? Can they learn to compete with the Harlequin, or is it up to us to save them?

Ladybird survey

The purpose of the *UK Ladybird Survey* is to record all species of ladybird found within the UK, and to monitor the effects the Harlequin is having on ladybird populations in different areas. The survey provides a great opportunity for children to learn more about the ecology of green areas near the school, and also to contribute to important scientific research.

Ladybirds can be found in a wide range of habitats, including gardens, parks, allotments and other green areas. In most cases, their bright colours make them easy to find and they can be often be spotted on the underside of leaves or munching aphids on plant stems. They can also be found in leaf litter or in crevices on the bark of trees. More rigorous searching techniques involve shaking bushes and branches of trees to dislodge the insects, and then catching them in a white sheet, and also using sweep nets to 'sweep up' insects hiding in long grass and other low-growing vegetation.

The easiest way to submit children's findings is by using the online recording form on the Ladybird Survey website. The website is a great source of information about ladybirds and has a range of interesting blogs and activities. Children publish their own ideas about ladybirds in the school science magazine or on the school blogging platform. They could even create their own illustrated ladybird book.

Creating wildlife habitats in the garden

Based on the outcomes of their woodland enquiry, children use natural resources to provide habitats for different types of animals in the garden. Refer to Chapter 8 for ideas. Children monitor the habitats through the spring term, and hopefully into the autumn of the following school year to record the animals which choose to live there.

Artwork: landscapes of the woodland ecosystem

Children paint large pictures of the ecosystem of the woodland depicting the different types of producers, consumers and decomposers. The paintings should depict the different ways plants, animals and other living things depend on each other. Children use information sources to help them visualise the bigger picture. Based on their paintings, groups get together to create food webs which they present to the rest of the class. Working collaboratively, the class combines information from the individual food webs to produce a giant web which represents the ecology of the woodland. Which organisms have the most links? What would happen to the ecology of the woodland if these organisms were removed from the woodland? Talk about how all the animals in the woodland ultimately depend on plants for their survival. Photographs of the paintings can be used by the children to publish an illustrated booklet entitled *The Woodland Ecosystem*. Use this activity to assess children's progress towards the learning goals.

Gardening in a changing climate

In 2017, the RHS launched the report *Gardening in a Changing Climate*. It highlights the increasing importance of gardens in the future, with regard to delivering the ecological services formerly provided by the natural environment. The report also provides recommendations on how gardeners can adapt to climate change through plant choice and garden design.

Children use information sources to discover how the climate is predicted to change in the coming years, and plan a garden for the 22nd century. As well as choosing appropriate plants to grow, they will also need to plan the garden to limit global warming and to cope with extreme weather events, such as flooding and drought. They also need to plan the garden's ecosystem based on their choice of plants and by predicting the kinds of primary and secondary consumers that will exist at the time. Use the activity to assess children's progress towards the learning goals.

Information sources

- Bird territory: www.thespruce.com/how-birds-claim-territory-386444
- Decaying fruit: www.bbc.com/bitesize/clips/zwx76sg
- Find a bird and birdcalls: www.rspb.org.uk/birds-and-wildlife/wildlife-guides/bird-a-z/
- Garden animals: https://bbsrc.ukri.org/documents/real-bugs-cards-pdf/
- Gardening in a changing world: www.rhs.org.uk/science/gardening-in-a-changing-world/climate-change
- Growing veg: www.rhs.org.uk/advice/grow-your-own/vegetables/radishes
- Harlequin ladybird: www.coleoptera.org.uk/coccinellidae/harlequin-ladybird-has-landed
- Invertebrates: www.bbc.com/bitesize/clips/zmj8q6f
- Techniques for monitoring ladybirds: www.coleoptera.org.uk/coccinellidae/techniques-monitoring-ladybirds
- UK Ladybird Survey: www.coleoptera.org.uk/coccinellidae/home
- Woodland animals: www.woodlandtrust.org.uk/visiting-woods/trees-woods-and-wildlife/animals/

Further reading

Websites

- Gardening in Changing Climate Report: www.rhs.org.uk/science/pdf/RHS-Gardening-in-a-Changing-Climate-Report.pdf
- Harlequin Ladybird: www.ceh.ac.uk/news-and-media/blogs/decade-recording-harlequin-ladybirds-uk
- Harlequin Ladybird: www.buglife.org.uk/bugs-and-habitats/harlequin-ladybird
- Wildlife Gardening Forum: http://wlgf.org/

Books

- Bone, E. and Wheatley, A. (2015) *Gardening for Beginners*, London: Usborne.
- Ikin, E. (2016) *Garden Friends: Plants, Animals and Wildlife That Are Good for Your Garden*, London: National Trust.
- Loxley, P., Dawes, L., Nicholls, L. and Dores, B. (2018) *Teaching Primary Science: Promoting Enjoyment and Developing Understanding*, Abingdon: Routledge.
- Loxley, P. (2018) *Practical Ideas for Teaching Primary Science: Inspiring Learning and Enjoyment*, Abingdon: Routledge.

Chapter 4 Interdependence

- RHS. (2008) *Grow It Eat It*, London: Dorling Kindersley.
- Watts, A. (2011) *Every Nursery Needs a Garden*, Abingdon: Routledge.ASE JournalsPrimary Science 132 (March–April 2014) *Insects: Little Things That Run the World* by Luke Tilley.
- Primary Science 143 (May–June 2016) *Horticulture in Schools* by Robert Milne.
- Primary Science 142 (March–April 2016) *Gardening Provides Valuable Time to Talk* by Margaret Boyd.
- Primary Science 146 (January–February 2017) *Urban and Branch Reform: Teaching City Kids About Urban Trees* by Mark Walker.

Puffball   Common Eyelash   Honey Fungus
Glistening Inkcap   Fly Agaric   Amethyst Deceiver
Hen of the Woods   Witches' Butter   Stinkhorn
Blushing Wood Mushroom   Yellow Stainer
Scarlet Hood   Tree Bracket Fungus   Wood Ears
Penny Bun   Orange Peel Fungus   Panther Cap
Gemmed Amarita   Ruby Bolete   Jelly Ear
Deadly Nightshade   Porcelain Fungus
Stinking Dapperling   Brown Roll Rim   Rosy Bonnet
Dead Man's Fingers   Yellow Swamp Russala
Scarlet Elfcup   **The Sickener**   Poison Pie
Blue Roundhead   Beefsteak Fungus
Prunes and Custard   Deadly Fibre Cap   White Brain
Hedgehog fungus   **Stag's Horn Fingers**
Common Earthball   Bleeding Tooth Fungus
False Deathcap   King Alfred's Cakes   Earthstar
Silky Piggyback   Purple Jellydisc   Saffron Webcap
Starfish Fungus   Snakeskin Grisette   **Puffball**
Mousepee Pinkgill   Twig Parachute

Chapter 4 Interdependence

Stag Beetle   Variable Damselfly   **Spiked   Shieldbug**
Green Tiger Beetle   14-spot Ladybird   Forest Bug
Black Darter   Common Green Grasshopper   Glow-worm
Devil's Coach-horse   **Bloody-nosed Beetle**
Orange Ladybird   White-lipped Snail   Froghopper
Speckled Bush-Cricket   Common Backswimmer
Red-headed Cardinal Beetle   Hairy Dragonfly
Emerald Damselfly   Common Sexton Beetle   Yellow Slug
Brown-lipped Snail   Common Water-measurer
Death Watch Beetle   Green Tortoise Beetle
Whirligig Beetle   Hornet Robber-fly   Earwig
Leafhopper   Long-winged Conehead   Saucer Bug
Marmalade Fly   Common Hawker   Pond Skater
Banded Demoiselle   Field Grasshopper   Wasp
Water Scorpion   Coppery Click Beetle   Woodlouse
Wolf Spider   Black Garden Ant   Garden Spider
Carder Bee   Water Boatman   Yellow Meadow Ant
Hairy-footed Flower Bee   Brown Centipede

CHAPTER 5
ADAPTATION

Big idea: *Living things that are better adapted to their environment are most likely to survive; those not able to respond sufficiently to changes in their environment may become extinct.*

Part 1: Subject knowledge

This part sets out subject knowledge teachers require to support children's learning towards the big idea. The ideas presented go beyond the requirements of the National Curriculum, and hence provide teachers with levels of subject knowledge which enable them to meet the needs of children with different interests and abilities.

The topics include:
- Learning from experience
- Thinking and talking with scientific ideas
- Woodland habitats
- Adaptation and evolution
- Darwin's theory of natural selection
- The tree of life
- Biodiversity and classification

Part 2: Working towards the big idea

Each topic aims to move children's understanding further towards the big idea. The journey begins when children examine how micro-habitats in the school grounds provide for the basic needs of invertebrates (minibeasts) that live there. Children then focus their attention on the behaviour of different types of birds and how they are adapted to their habitats. Looking at the bigger picture, children discover how living things are found in certain environments because they have features that enable them to survive there. Children build on

Chapter 5 Adaptation

their understanding of adaptation to explore how living things which are better adapted to their environment are most likely to survive, while those not able to respond sufficiently to changes in their environment may become extinct.

The topics are:

- Habitats (5–7 years)
- Adaptation (7–9 years)
- Adaptation and evolution (9–11 years)

Part 1: Subject knowledge

Learning from experience

Children are natural explorers. Through enquiry activities they can discover where different animals and plants live in the school grounds. They can talk about what the animals eat, how they keep safe from predators and why they are suited to their habitats. In conversation with their teacher, they discover how different habitats provide for the basic needs of animals and plants that live there and begin to understand how living things depend on each other.

Thinking and talking with scientific ideas

As children learn to think and talk with scientific ideas, they are able to begin to see the bigger picture and explore how living things are adapted to the environment in which they live. Understanding adaptation enables children to focus their attention on the physical characteristics of living things and to work out how particular traits help them survive in their habitats. For example, it is not only the shape of a bird's beak which makes it suited to its habitat. Most birds that live in the woodland are perching birds, so are suited to living in trees and bushes. Perching birds share the same kinds of foot, with three toes pointing forward and one backward. Hence their feet are adapted to gripping a perch such as a branch on a tree. Different kinds of perching birds have their own particular shaped beak, depending on what they eat and how they search for food. Once children adopt the idea of adaptation as their own, they can use it to make sense of the fragility of the natural world. They then start to understand the dangers wildlife face from habitat loss due to human activity, and why loss of habitat may lead to extinction.

Woodland habitats

Woodlands are very special homes for a great diversity of living things, with a wide range of habitats for children to explore. Children learn how each level of the woodland, from soil to canopy, has inhabitants suited to their environment. Just like the floors in a house, different levels in the woodland provide different services for the inhabitants.

Taking a tour of a woodland, we can start by looking underneath the floorboards into the basement or cellar. Here we see the roots, which are the foundations on which trees and other plants are built. The roots also provide the plumbing system, able to pump vast quantities of water to the ever-thirsty trees. The basement is also a source of food for invertebrates such as worms and the animals which prey on them. It also provides a home for burrowing animals such as badgers, keeping the hibernators warm and safe throughout the winter.

Like many homes the ground floor is used the most. It is often untidy, being covered in leaf litter much of the time, but when carpeted in wildflowers can be breathtakingly beautiful. The ground floor is home for a wide variety of animals such as hedgehogs, mice, deer and a large range of invertebrates. It also provides a plentiful supply of food for birds, foxes, badgers, weasels, stoats and squirrels.

The first floor is not so busy. This is the level in the woodland made up of young trees and shrubs, which provide homes for insects and other invertebrates to feed and lay their eggs. Some birds build their nests in the first floor, keeping their young safe from predators which live on the ground.

The canopy is the equivalent to the roof or attic in a house. It provides shelter from the weather for both animals and fragile plants. Each species is adapted to where it lives in the wood, and the canopy helps maintain a microclimate which suits all its inhabitants living below.

Finally, we cannot have a house over four levels without an interconnecting staircase. In the woodland the trunks and branches of the trees not only provide pathways between levels, but also provide accommodation for animals such as owls and squirrels and a multitude of invertebrates.

Adaptation and evolution

Adaptation is the way living things change over time to suit their environment. Adaptation to their environment happens because of the small differences which occur in offspring as a result of reproduction. Offspring are not identical to each other or with their parents, resulting in some individuals being better suited to their environment than others are.

Here in the UK, adaptation is going on in our own back gardens. As areas of natural grassland and woodland continue to decline, birds and other animals which normally live there are finding their way to our gardens in search of food and materials. As a result, research has discovered that the great tit has been evolving by adapting its beak for bird feeders. Research published in *Wildlife* magazine reveals that great tits in the UK have evolved to grow longer beaks than their European counterparts have, where bird feeders in gardens are not as popular. Although the research is not definitive, it found that the birds with longer beaks were more successful at reproducing, providing evidence of natural selection at work in the UK.

Like many other animals, great tits produce more offspring than can survive. Large numbers die due to lack of food, disease and predation. In time of food shortages, the size of the beak can make a difference in the competition for the available food. In harsh winters, those tits with longer beaks will be more able to access food from garden feeders, and hence are more likely to survive and pass on their favourable characteristics to their offspring. Tits with smaller beaks are more likely to die before reproducing, so later populations of tits will contain more of the better-adapted birds with longer beaks. This is the way nature selects those birds which are best suited to survive, and which eventually may evolve into a new species. Researchers estimate that the beak length of the British bird has become longer between the 1970s and the present day, which is a really short length of time and is indicative of how quickly animals can evolve.

The great tits exemplify how natural selection acts as a refiner or shaper of organisms, such that living things become better suited over time for a particular way of life. Eventually they can become so well suited to that way of life that they cannot survive in any other way. The term scientists use for this process is 'adaptation', and they describe living things as being 'adapted' for a particular environment, habitat or way of life.

Darwin's theory of natural selection

The story of Darwin's finches is often used to illustrate how animals adapt to different environments. When he visited the Galapagos Islands in 1836, Darwin collected specimens of birds which inhabited the different islands. He first thought they were finches, blackbirds and wrens. He later discovered that they were in fact all types of finches, with different shapes and sizes of beaks. Darwin hypothesised that all the birds had evolved from one species that had arrived in the islands from the mainland of South America. Over time, these finches populated the islands, and their beaks evolved to suit the different types of food available. For example, the small tree finches have distinctive short curved beaks which they use to feed on insects, while the large ground finches have large, short beaks for cracking large seeds and nuts.

Darwin's genius was to work out that the finches changed over time as a result of competition for food and other resources. Imagine the advantage a long pointed beak may provide to pick seeds out of cactus fruits. Clearly, immigrant birds with longer beaks would have an advantage when competing for food and then pass on their advantageous feature to their offspring. As the numbers of long-beaked birds increases, the birds with shorter beaks find it harder to survive and are more likely to die before reproducing. Therefore, later generations will contain more of the long-beaked birds, which are better adapted to the environment on the island. Over time, these changes can accumulate to the point where the survivors, the long-beaked birds, have become a different species to the original immigrants through natural selection. This means that the long-beaked birds can successfully breed with each other, but cannot interbreed with other species to produce offspring that can reproduce.

Darwin's finches are still helping our understanding of evolution. In more recent years, Peter and Rosemary Grant were able to observe evolution in action by studying the development of two rival species located on the isle of Daphne. Up until 1982 the medium ground finch was well established on the island. Its beak was suited to cracking large nuts. Then the large ground finch arrived from a neighbouring island and was able to out-compete the smaller finches for the large nuts. Over the years the researchers found that the medium ground finches adapted to their new environment by developing smaller beaks more suited to the smaller nuts, which were ignored by the invading larger finches.

The tree of life

Evolution by natural selection is one of science's most significant discoveries. It is a big idea which has revolutionised our understanding of the natural world and our place in it. Life began billions years ago with simple single-celled organisms which have evolved into the diverse range of animals, plants and other living things which populate the planet today.

Dixon, D. (2018) When the Whales Walked. London: Quarto Publishing.

Chapter 5 **Adaptation**

To help explain the origins of the earth's rich biodiversity, Darwin described evolution in terms of a branching tree-like structure representing the evolutionary links between living things. We know today that the *tree of life* metaphor has its limitations, and that the relationships between living things may be more accurately pictured by a web than a tree. Having said that, the tree of life is still a powerful image through which to illustrate evolutionary history.

Topics in this chapter focus on the evolution of mammals and birds after the demise of the dinosaurs. Using the simplified tree of life, we can see how birds trace their ancestry back to the dinosaurs, which themselves evolved from early forms of reptiles. The tree also shows how early forms of mammals existed at the same time as dinosaurs and how they diversified after the dinosaurs became extinct.

Biodiversity and classification

The term 'biodiversity' describes the rich variety of life which makes up the natural world. It is possible to talk about the biodiversity of a single habitat, a region or even the planet. Biodiversity is simply the diversity of life in an area and is often measured by the number of different species of plants, animals and other living things that can be found there.

To help make sense of the rich diversity of plants and animals, scientists classify them into groups and subgroups by identifying similarities and differences between them. For example, within the broad group of animals we call birds, there are families which have similar characteristics. The tit family are small birds with plain or colourful plumages, stout legs and strong feet, and have short triangular bills. In the UK there are six kinds or species of tit; each are similar, yet have their own distinct characteristics. The blue tit with its colourful mix of blue, yellow, white and green makes it one of our most striking and easily identifiable garden visitors. Tits are social animals and can often be seen feeding in mixed species flocks. That is why we often notice different types of tits in our gardens.

When we talk about a kind of animal or plant, we are often referring to a species. Living things which belong to the same species have similar physical characteristics and are able to breed more of the same kind. However, living things which belong to different species cannot interbreed to produce fertile offspring.

Part 2: Working towards the big idea

Models of good practice

Topic: Habitats

Age group: 5–7 years

Learning goals

Children take a step towards the big idea when they explore the diversity of animals and plants that can be found in garden habitats. The topic starts by exploring children's attitudes to different types of minibeasts and focusses their attention on the need to safeguard their wellbeing. Further activities help children understand that animals live in places called habitats, which provide for their basic needs such as food, water and shelter. A key activity is for children to turn a small piece of ground into a wildlife area designed to attract butterflies.

Working scientifically

In this topic children will:

- use a variety of methods to find the answers to simple questions;
- observe closely using simple equipment;
- use their observations and ideas to suggest answers to questions;
- gather and record data to help answer questions.

Health and safety

Refer to the relevant safety codes in the ASE publication *Be Safe!* (2011) when planning to teach the activities in this topic. Also visit the RSPCA website for notes on a wildlife code of conduct. Children should wear protective gloves when searching vegetation for minibeasts. Warn children not to put anything in their mouths and not to damage plants.

Exploring children's ideas

The children will likely have experience of a range of common garden animals including birds and different types of invertebrates (minibeasts). Use images and video clips from the web to explore children's attitudes to a range of different invertebrates such as worms, bees, snails, beetles etc. Find out what children like about them and whether some invertebrates trouble them. List all the things about the animals that children like and dislike.

Story-telling: a day in the life of a minibeast

Children imagine that they are tiny, about the size of minibeasts, and live in a garden. Working in groups children create their own narratives which describe what they do all day. Encourage them to think about what they would eat and drink, and how they would keep safe. What would they be afraid of? Children share their stories and compare them with how they think minibeasts survive in garden settings. Do they think minibeasts may be afraid of them?

Role play: behaving like minibeasts

Create an area in the classroom for role play. Ask children to imagine that the area is a garden full of trees, flowers, bushes and other garden things. Children are the minibeasts who live in the garden. Groups take turns to use the space to behave like minibeasts. The other children try to work out what they are doing. Challenge the 'minibeasts' to react to different scenarios; for example, when a bird lands nearby looking for food or when the weather is very hot, cold or wet. What will they do when a person digs up all the plants? Encourage each group to discuss and justify their minibeast's behaviour.

Wildlife code

Talk about how vulnerable minibeasts are in the garden. Discuss how we need to treat them and other animals with care. Listen to children's ideas about how they should behave towards all living things in the garden, including plants, minibeasts and other animals. Display the main ideas in the form of a wildlife code.

Where do minibeasts live?

Start this enquiry by showing children pictures/video clips of different types of animals such as snails, ants, spiders, worms, beetles, woodlice, bees, butterflies and others which they might find in the school grounds (or a local park). Working in groups, children discuss where they think these small animals may be found. Do they live in the car park, playground, the sports field, grassed areas, bushed areas, flower beds, trees or somewhere else? Encourage them to justify their ideas. If you have a compost heap, make sure you put that on the list.

Working in supervised groups children explore areas of the school grounds looking for minibeasts. Encourage them to look carefully beneath leaf debris, logs, stones and other objects. Talk about the different types of plants in the garden, and help children search for bugs on their stems

Chapter 5 Adaptation

and leaves. Provide them with appropriate tools to search in leaf litter and to dig for worms in previously worked soil. With luck they may get a visit from the local robin with an eye for an easy meal. An adult could spray mustard powder mixed with water on grassy areas to encourage worms to come to the surface and use sweep nets in long grass to capture hidden creatures. While searching for minibeasts remind children of their wildlife code, and return the creatures to their habitats as soon as possible.

Photograph or video different areas to record the findings. Where appropriate use magnifiers to see things close up, and use picture cards or electronic devices to identify and compare minibeasts. Back in the classroom children share their experiences and use the photographs and video clips to help create a display showing where different kinds of minibeasts can be found.

Things to talk about

Encourage children to describe the different places where minibeasts live. Talk about where they live and how their habitats help them survive. Working in supported groups, children choose a minibeast to talk about. Provide each group with a picture/photograph of the animal and ask them to discuss the following questions:

- Where does the minibeast get its food?
- Where does the minibeast get its water?
- What might eat the minibeast?
- How does the minibeast keep safe?
- Is there a better place in the school garden/grounds for the minibeast to live?

Encourage children to listen to each other, provide reasons for their answers and share ideas. Each group presents its responses to the rest of the class. Focus discussion on the reasons children give for their answers and address misconceptions.

Information resources

- Buglife: www.buglife.org.uk/
- Invertebrates: www.bbc.com/bitesize/clips/z7d9wmn

- Magnificent minibeasts: www.bbc.com/bitesize/clips/zwwndxs
- Nature detectives: www.woodlandtrust.org.uk/naturedetectives/

Working on scientific understanding

Children work on their understanding of a habitat as a place where animals can find the things they need to live, such as food, water and shelter. Ask children to talk about the habitats where minibeasts live in the school grounds. Use the following talking points to scaffold children's thinking. Adjust the talking points depending on the minibeasts the children discovered in the school.

Talking points: true, false or not sure?

- Bees live near flowers because they like their colours.
- Woodlice live under stones and logs to keep dry when it rains.
- Snails live near plants because they eat their leaves.
- Worms live in soil to hide from birds.
- Spiders make webs to sleep safe at night.

Children work collaboratively to answer the talking points. Point out there may be more than one reason why minibeasts live in a particular place. Bring groups together to share ideas. Examine children's reasoning and address misconceptions. Start using the term 'habitat' to describe the place where an animal lives. Talk about particular habitats and how they provide the animals that live there with the things they need to survive (food, water and shelter).

How are woodlice suited to their habitat?

Woodlice are fascinating animals which are easy to find hiding under rocks and leaf litter and in compost heaps. Woodlice are not insects; they are crustaceans which are related to crabs and shrimps.

Before collecting woodlice, each group should set up a home for them in the classroom which provides for their basic needs. Talk about how woodlice feed on dead vegetation, such as rotting leaves and grass. They get all the water they need by sucking up moisture from the damp vegetation. Children set up mini-habitats in containers using decaying vegetation from the school grounds (or the local park). They should keep the vegetation damp and secure the container with a top with holes in it.

Working in small groups, children closely study the structure of a woodlouse and the way it moves. Put the woodlouse in a see-through plastic box with enough room to move. Keep it damp and remind children of the wildlife code. They use magnifying lenses to study it closely and make sketches to record its different parts. Encourage them to look closely at its armoured, segmented body and to count its legs. Does it have a head? Does it have any eyes? Encourage them to speculate about how its physical characteristics helps it keep safe. Do they think where they found their woodlice is a good habitat for them to live in? Encourage children to give reasons for their answers.

Groups present their findings to the class and talk about why they think woodlice are suited to living in their habitats. Encourage them to give reasons for why they sometimes curl up into a ball.

Show children pictures of their predators, such as centipedes, toads, shrews and spiders. Children speculate about how woodlice try to keep themselves safe. Children return the woodlice to where they found them and draw simple annotated pictures of their habitats.

Story-telling: my favourite minibeast

Ask children to tell a story about their favourite minibeast. Encourage them to describe the habitat where it lives, why it likes living there and any other animals which might share its habitat. Children work in groups and compare their stories with the rest of the class. Talk to them about their stories to assess their progress towards the learning goals.

Information resources

- Woodlouse information: https://walthamforest.gov.uk/sites/default/files/Woodlice%20fact%20sheet.pdf
- Woodlouse profile: www.rhs.org.uk/advice/profile?pid=723
- Woodlouse profile: www.wildlifetrusts.org/wildlife-explorer/invertebrates/crustacea-centipedes-and-millipedes/common-woodlouse

The bigger picture

Children make use of their understanding of habitats to explore how areas of the school grounds can be made more attractive to butterflies. Ask them what they like about butterflies and where they normally see them. Where would they expect to find caterpillars? Do they know what butterflies eat, and what their caterpillars eat? What do they know about the life cycle of a butterfly? Encourage them to speculate about how the school grounds could be made more butterfly friendly.

Life cycle of a butterfly

Use illustrated books and video clips to tell children the story of the life cycle of a butterfly. Talk about how butterflies produce their young (caterpillars) by laying eggs on the underneath of leaves for the caterpillars to eat. Caterpillars can be fussy eaters, and some will only eat certain plants. Butterflies taste the leaves with their feet before laying the eggs to make sure they will make a tasty meal for the caterpillars when they hatch. Talk about how caterpillars are young butterflies, even though they do not look like their parents. After eating a lot and getting much bigger, the caterpillars change shape and grow wings inside a protective bag called a chrysalis. By the time a caterpillar emerges from its chrysalis, it has changed into an adult butterfly. Show children pictures of a red admiral and a peacock butterfly, and talk about how their caterpillars like to feed on nettles. Remind children how nettles can sting. Why do they think nettles provide a good habitat for caterpillars to grow into adult butterflies? Use their responses to assess their progress towards the learning goals.

Butterfly conservation

Butterfly Conservation is the UK wildlife charity dedicated to saving butterflies, moths and our environment. The charity provides advice and resources for schools aimed at inspiring children to take an interest in conserving butterfly and moth habitats.

> By sharing our knowledge and enthusiasm for butterflies and moths we hope to inspire a new generation of naturalists, volunteers and conservationists. Most of all, we hope that our education work will spark a childhood connection to nature that will last a lifetime, providing a wealth of benefits to children and wildlife alike.
>
> (Butterfly Conservation, 2019)

Butterfly Conservation is also involved in conserving hundreds of sites and reserves for butterflies and moths across the UK. Visit their website for activity ideas and find out about the reserves nearest to you.

In search of butterflies and other flying insects

Find out from your local branch of Butterfly Conservation the best places to find butterflies in your area, and arrange to go on a butterfly hunt. Choose a nice warm, sunny day in spring or early summer. Provide children with tick sheets to record the number of butterflies and other flying insects such as bees, hoverflies, moths and wasps that they see. Before the visit, spend time talking about insects and classify them using their common characteristics, such as number of legs and body parts. Compare insects to other kinds of minibeasts such as woodlice and worms.

During the visit, groups work closely with an adult to identify and record the different types of flying insects. Take photographs and talk about the plants which the butterflies and other insects visit. Focus children's attention on what the insects are doing, and talk about how flowers contain food (pollen and nectar) which the insects like to eat. Encourage children to look inside the flowers and to speculate about what the insects are feeding on. Point out that the food (nectar) that butterflies like is deep inside the flower. Safeguard children with allergies.

Most butterflies are on the wing during the sunniest and warmest part of the day, so reserve a time between midmorning and early afternoon for the butterfly hunt. Butterflies are sensitive to rapid movement, so warn children they need to move slowly and carefully or they will frighten them away. How many different types of butterflies can they find? Which plants are they visiting? Ask children to describe the butterflies and how they move. Do they go from flower to flower, or do they sometimes land on the leaves of plants? What might they be doing when they land on the leaves? Compare the movement of the bees with the butterflies. Which visit the most flowers?

Children search for caterpillars by looking carefully underneath the leaves of plants that butterflies visit. An adult can help children search to make sure they are not stung by hairy caterpillars, nettles or other harmful plants. Children should wear gloves while they are searching. Caterpillars may prove difficult to find, but children can also search for leaves which have been eaten by caterpillars. Talk about how butterflies taste the leaves with their feet to make sure they lay their eggs on the 'tastiest' plants for their caterpillars to eat. How do children taste their food? Have they ever tried tasting it with their feet?

Use magnifiers and take photographs to look closely at any caterpillars they find. Avoid touching the caterpillars. Focus their attention on the colour of the caterpillars, and discuss whether they are easy to see on the leaves. Talk about whether their colour helps them keep safe from predators such as birds. What do children know about camouflage? Do they know any other animals which use camouflage to keep safe?

Things to talk about

Back in school, children tell their butterfly hunt stories. Help them use the photographs to talk about the animals they found and the habitats in which they found them. Encourage children to describe a habitat in which adult butterflies and their caterpillars live. How does the habitat provide them with food and shelter? Did the habitat help keep them safe? Do they think butterflies are suited to their habitats? Use the photographs and anecdotes from the children's stories to publish a blog of the butterfly hunt on the school's chosen platform. Include the children when preparing the blog, and edit it so that it represents their voices. Use children's ideas to assess their progress towards the learning goals.

Design a butterfly

Show children a picture of a peacock butterfly and tell the story of why it has such large eyespots. Talk about how these spectacular eyes, on either side of the body, appear very threatening to predators such as small birds and mice. Ask children to look closely at the upside-down butterfly and ask them what it looks like. Do they think it looks like a bird with a big beak, such as an owl? Does it look scary enough to frighten small birds and mice which may want to eat the butterfly?

Children design their own butterfly to frighten predators. Start by providing children with the outline shape of a butterfly, and ask them to colour it and add markings designed to frighten predators. As they go along, ask them to explain where the butterfly would live, and how the markings will help keep it safe. Children could also design a butterfly which uses camouflage to keep safe. Use the activities to assess children's progress towards the learning goals.

Modelling: how a butterfly gets its food

Butterflies eat by sucking up nectar and other liquids through their proboscis, which is a tube-like appendage, similar to a straw. Children create models of flowers by pasting paper petals onto the outside of a small paper cup. Partly fill the cup with a sweet liquid to represent the nectar. Children use bendy straws to model how butterflies drink nectar from flowers.

Encouraging butterflies into the school garden

By choosing nectar-rich plants for butterflies and the right food for their caterpillars, you can excite children's imaginations with a colourful display of plants and magnificent flying insects. Develop an instant garden in early spring by using mature plants. Children can help prepare the soil and maintain the beds.

Children need to be aware that adult butterflies and their caterpillars eat different parts of a plant. Butterflies feed on nectar inside flowers, while caterpillars feed on the leaves of plants. Some caterpillars feed on a variety of plants, while others are specialist feeders. To attract butterflies, children need to create habitats with the right type of plants for both the adult butterflies and their caterpillars. Easy-to-grow plants that provide food for adult butterflies and moths include lavender, honeysuckle, catmint, verbena, primrose, thyme, oxeye daisies, forget-me-nots, marjoram and most other plants which are rich in nectar. When it comes to plants caterpillars like to eat, you may want to consider nasturtiums, garlic mustard, lady's smock, buckthorn, fuchsias, thistles, common comfrey, common bird's-foot-trefoil and nettles.

Monitor the wildlife

Children monitor the growth of the plants and the variety of wildlife that visit the habitat throughout the spring and summer terms. Take photographs and publish them week by week as part of a classroom display, so children can see how the habitat changes. As well as identifying the different types of butterflies, they can record the types of bees, hoverflies and other minibeasts which feed there. They can also look out for birds and small mammals. Set up a wildlife camera to monitor the area; you never know what visitors there may be when you are not looking. More ideas for creating a wildlife garden can be found in Chapter 8.

Information resources

- Butterfly Conservation website: https://butterfly-conservation.org/
- Find a reserve: https://butterfly-conservation.org/our-work/reserves
- In your area: https://butterfly-conservation.org/in-your-area
- Minibeast identification key: https://schoolgardening.rhs.org.uk/Resources/Info-Sheet/Mini-Beast-Identification-Key
- Munching caterpillars: https://munchingcaterpillars.org/resources/
- The life cycle of a butterfly: www.bbc.com/bitesize/clips/zxcmp39

Topic: Adaptation

Age group: 7–9 years

Learning goals

Children make progress towards the big idea by engaging with the work of the RSPB and by creating habitats for birds and other wildlife in the school grounds. The topic provides opportunities for children to learn about the behaviour of different types of birds and how they are suited (adapted) to their habitats. Looking at the bigger picture, children discover how living things are found in certain environments because they have features that enable them to survive there and how changes to their environment can pose dangers which may lead to their extinction.

Working scientifically

In this topic children will:

- use scientific enquiries to answer questions;
- make systematic observations using a range of equipment;
- gather, classify and present data to help answer questions;
- report on findings from enquiries in appropriate ways;

Chapter 5 Adaptation

- use results to draw conclusions and make predictions;
- use scientific evidence to answer questions or to support their findings.

Health and safety

Refer to the relevant safety codes in the ASE publication *Be Safe!* (2011) when planning to teach the activities in this topic. Children should wear protective gloves when searching for invertebrates in the woodland. Stress safety, hygiene and the protection of the environment.

Exploring children's ideas

The Royal Society for the Protection of Birds (RSPB) is the largest nature conservation charity in the UK. Its mission is to protect birds and other wildlife which are at risk, by providing homes (habitats) in which they can thrive.

> Our birds and wildlife are increasingly vulnerable in a rapidly-changing world. Together, we can create bigger, better, more joined-up spaces to save our wildlife, and our shared home.
>
> (RSPB, 2019)

In this topic, children have opportunities to engage in a citizen science project organised by the RSPB, and to redesign areas of the school grounds to make them more bird-friendly.

Big Garden Birdwatch

Introduce children to the *Big Garden Birdwatch* organised annually by the RSPB. It started out as an event for children back in 1979, when the RSPB joined forces with BBC's *Blue Peter* to call on children to let them know what birds they saw in their garden. Taking part in the Big Garden Birdwatch provides children with opportunities to get involved with an exciting national citizen science project. This is real science, for a real purpose. Describing his love of the project, the TV presenter Chris Packham stated:

> There's no doubt in my mind that the RSPB's Big Garden Birdwatch is one of the greatest pieces of citizen science that's done anywhere on earth – so to play a tiny role in that is always a privilege.

There is a lot of information about the project and how to take part on the RSPB website.

Which areas in the school grounds are the most bird-friendly?

In preparation for the Birdwatch project, children survey the school grounds to find the most bird-friendly places. Encourage children to talk about birds they have seen in the school grounds or at home. Listen to their stories, and list the ones which they can name. Why do they think birds would want to visit their school? What are the birds looking for?

Provide children with a simple map or list of the key areas around your school which they can investigate. Working in supervised groups, children explore each area in turn to determine which is best suited to attract birds. To assess an area's suitability, children award one point for each of the following criteria:

- Is there food in the area for birds to eat?
- Is there water in the area for birds drink?
- Is there shelter in the area to keep birds safe?
- Are there places for birds to build their nests?

Use information sources to identify any birds. Talk about the best way for the children to record their findings. Photographs or video recordings would work well. Back in the classroom children share and discuss their data, and arrive at a consensus for the most bird-friendly areas in the school. Encourage the children to justify their choices and to explain why some areas are not suited to birds. Post the words 'food', 'water', 'shelter' and 'nesting sites' prominently in the classroom to remind children of the key features of a bird-friendly garden.

Design a bird-friendly garden

Working in groups, children use information sources to research the needs of the birds they want to attract and design a garden which suits their needs. Groups produce illustrations of their designs and justify their suitability using the previous points system for assessing different areas of the school grounds.

Garden birds are very active and rarely sit still for very long, especially if they see children wandering about. To observe birds such as tits, robins and finches children need to be hidden away, out of both sight and hearing of the birds. There are a number of ways this can be achieved:

- Build a hide close enough to the bird-friendly area so children can observe the birds.
- Build a bird-friendly area close enough to the classroom so children can see the birds through a window.
- Monitor the bird-friendly area using a wildlife camera.

An advantage of setting up your garden close to the classroom is that children can more easily monitor its use by different types of birds. If it is very close to the classroom window you may want to hang a netted curtain so that children can see out without alarming the birds. Being close to the classroom makes it easier to set up a wildlife camera to record the birds who visit early in the morning and late at night.

Based on their design ideas children talk about how they can turn a small area of ground into a bird-friendly garden. Use suitable resources such as online video clips, pictures and photographs to help children develop their ideas. Talk about providing a bird bath, feeders, bird tables, bird boxes and plants which birds like. Water is essential, so think of creating a small pond using a shallow container. Also set up micro-habitats such log piles and piles of leaf litter which provide homes for worms, woodlice, beetles and other invertebrates which birds like to eat. Plants provide food in the form of seeds, berries, fruits and nectar, and they also attract insects and other invertebrates for birds to eat. Grow plants for moths. Blue tits, great tits, robins and many other garden birds feed moth caterpillars to their young. Build the area close to a tree or large shrubs which provide shelter during bad weather or at night and which can provide natural nesting sites during spring. Use ideas from the RSPB website to help design the garden.

Children play a part in choosing the plants, preparing the soil, planting and maintenance. Once the area is set up, children monitor the health of the plants and record the birds and other wildlife it attracts. Children collect data throughout the year and publish results in the school magazine or on the school's blogging platform. The Big Garden Birdwatch is a long-term project which can be taken on by successive groups of children. Each year the bird-friendly area can be expanded and improved and other wildlife areas created. Try to make citizen science and wildlife conservation exciting and inspiring parts of the school science curriculum.

Children's favourite birds

Talk to the children about their favourite birds. Groups use information sources to produce case studies of different birds which include their songs, which children can try to imitate. A wide range of bird songs can be found on the RSPB website. Explain that the case studies should illustrate how the birds are suited to their habitats. Groups present their studies to the rest of the class. Use the presentations to assess children's progress towards the learning goals.

Information sources

- Bird-friendly garden: www.britishbirdlovers.co.uk/a-bird-friendly-garden
- Bird-friendly plants: www.britishbirdlovers.co.uk/planting-for-birds/buy-bird-friendly-plants
- Big Garden Birdwatch: www.rspb.org.uk/get-involved/activities/birdwatch/
- Bird identifier: www.rspb.org.uk/birds-and-wildlife/wildlife-guides/identify-a-bird/
- Birdsong: www.bl.uk/the-language-of-birds/articles/the-purpose-of-birdsong
- Garden birdwatch: www.bto.org/volunteer-surveys/gbw
- How to attract birds to your garden: www.youtube.com/watch?v=jH0425VzERs
- Urban bird fact files: www.bbc.com/bitesize/clips/zyftn39
- What do urban birds eat: www.bbc.com/bitesize/clips/zbx2tfr
- Wildlife garden: www.rspb.org.uk/get-involved/activities/give-nature-a-home-in-your-garden/

Working on scientific understanding

In this part, children progress from exploring the habitats of birds to bigger ideas about classification and adaptation. They learn that birds and other animals are found in certain environments because they have features that enable them to survive there. In other words, they are adapted to the habitat in which they live. Start by asking children to describe a bird. Is a bat a type of bird?

Talking points: true, false or not sure?

- Birds are the only animals that have feathers.
- Birds are the only animals that can fly.
- Birds are the only animals that have wings.
- Birds are the only animals that lay eggs.
- Birds are the only animals that have beaks and no teeth.
- Birds are the only animals that have scaly legs.
- Birds are the only animals that have four toes on their feet.
- Birds are the only animals to build nests.

Working in groups, children discuss the talking points and try to decide the main features that characterise a bird. Children share and justify their ideas with the class, and together decide on the characteristics that best describe a bird. Talk about how birds are warm-blooded vertebrate animals, just like themselves. This means they have a backbone and they use food to create their own body heat. Help children put their ideas together to compose their own definition of a bird.

How are birds adapted to their habitats?

The most likely visitors to the school garden are starlings, house sparrows, blackbirds, blue and great tits, robins, greenfinches and pigeons. Using information sources, children discover how the physical characteristics of the birds make them suited to garden habitats, parks and woodland.

- How are their beaks suited to what they eat?
- How are their feet suited to their habitat?
- How is their body size suited to their habitat?
- How does the colour of their plumage help them survive?
- How does having eyes on the sides of their heads help birds survive?

Encourage children to work out from the shape of their beaks what the different types of birds eat. Groups share their responses to the questions, and establish why the birds are suited to their habitats. Challenge children to think about whether penguins would be suited to living in woodland. Ask them to justify their ideas. Discuss the habitats which best suit penguins.

Bird design

Challenge the children to design a bird that lives on a remote, sandy island with no trees and populated by large, spiny cacti plants. Children must explain how the physical characteristics of the bird enable it to survive. Use the activity to assess children's progress towards the learning goals.

Hot seating: describing birds

The teacher starts by describing key features of her/his favourite bird. Children try to work out the type of bird. Individuals or pairs of children can then take up the hot seat and challenge the rest of the class to identify the bird which they describe. Use this activity to focus children's attention on characteristics such as the size of the bird, its plumage and the shape and size of beaks and feet. Talk about what distinguishes birds from other types of animals, and what distinguishes one type of bird from another. Encourage children to speculate about the reasons why there are so many different types of birds. Focus discussion on ideas about adaptation and how different birds are suited to the environments in which they live.

Things to talk about

Bring children together to reflect on their understanding of how garden birds are adapted to their environment. Draw children's attention to the fact that most birds that visit our gardens are perching birds. In other words, they are suited to living in trees and bushes. Perching birds share the same kind of foot, with three toes pointed forward and one backward. Their feet are well suited (adapted) to gripping a perch such as a branch of a tree. Although their feet are similar, the shape and the size of their beaks vary, depending on what they eat and how they search for their food. Children tell their own stories of bird life in the woodland, in which they describe the similarities and differences between various kinds of birds. They can prepare by using suitable information sources to ensure their stories are consistent with the science.

Class science magazine

Groups write illustrated articles for the class science magazine or blog on the following topics:

- How birds are adapted to living in forests.
- How birds of prey are adapted to hunting.
- How water birds are adapted to living on water.
- How flightless birds are adapted to living on the ground.
- How penguins and other birds are adapted to living in the Antarctic.

Children choose their own catchy titles. All articles are reviewed by the class and the teacher before publication. Edits should be negotiated through reasoned argument. Use this activity and children's story-telling to assess their progress towards the learning goals.

Information sources

- A-Z of birds: www.rspb.org.uk/birds-and-wildlife/wildlife-guides/bird-a-z/
- Beak adaptations: www.scientificamerican.com/article/best-adapted-beaks-bring-science-home/
- Birds: www.thoughtco.com/facts-about-birds-4069408

- Bird facts: www.rspb.org.uk/fun-and-learning/for-kids/facts-about-nature/facts-about-birds/what-do-wild-birds-eat/
- Common garden birds: www.gardenbird.co.uk/garden-birds
- Desert birds: www.dailymail.co.uk/news/article-2236849/A-place-sun-Desert-birds-use-inside-cactus-home.html
- Perching birds: www.arkive.org/ft/perching-birds

The bigger picture

Children develop their understanding of adaptation further by exploring how different kinds of animals are suited to woodland habitats. Start by taking children on an imaginary trip to a woodland. Ask them to list all the animals they would expect to find there. Classify them in terms of vertebrates and invertebrates. Explain how vertebrates have a backbone inside their body, while invertebrates do not. Birds are the most common vertebrates seen in woodlands, while worms, spiders, bees, beetles, woodlice and snails are just a few of the invertebrates. Children use information sources to discover more about vertebrates and invertebrates which they are likely to find in a woodland.

Taking a tour of a woodland

Visit the Woodland Trust or other conservation trust website to find a woodland closest to your school. Start the tour by talking about how woodlands are very special homes for a great diversity of living things, with a wide range of habitats. Explain how each level of the woodland from soil to canopy has inhabitants suited to their environment. Just like the floors in a house, different levels in the woodland contribute to the habitat by providing different services for the inhabitants. Use ideas from Part 1 to develop a narrative about the levels of accommodation the woodland provides for its inhabitants:

The basement (underground)

Both vertebrates and invertebrates can be found living underground. Children *carefully* excavate around the base of a tree to discover worms, beetles, ants and other types of invertebrates in the soil. They should also look out for signs of badgers, moles, rabbits and mice which build their homes in the woodland 'basement'.

Ground floor

Children look out for ground-feeding birds and small mammals. In some woodlands they may be lucky enough to spot larger mammals such as foxes or deer. The ground floor of the woodland provides a rich habitat for many kinds of invertebrates. Children search under logs and leaf litter and use sweep nets to find creatures hiding in long grass.

First floor

The first floor of the woodland is made up of young trees and shrubs which provide homes for invertebrates to feed and lay their eggs. Some birds build their nests in the first floor, keeping

their young safe from predators which live on the ground. Children search the first floor by checking foliage for invertebrates and looking out for birds and small mammals. Teach children shaking techniques to collect invertebrates in white sheets. Do not disturb nesting birds.

The loft (canopy)

Provide children with binoculars so they can identify different types of birds and other animals in the canopy of trees. Look out for nests, and encourage children to spend time watching what the birds are doing.

Staircase (trunks and branches)

Provide children with magnifiers to inspect the bark of trees to discover invertebrates which hide in cracks and small holes. Look out for larger holes which can provide nesting sites for bees, small mammals and birds.

How are wildlife in the woodland adapted to their habitat?

Children examine the invertebrates closely using magnifiers, and classify them according to their number of legs and body parts. What features make the invertebrates suited to living in the micro-habitat in which they were found? To answer the question children focus on body shape and size, presence of antennae, compound eyes, types and number of legs and whether they can fly. Explore how patterns and colours of exoskeletons can help with camouflage and even mimicry of objects such as leaves and sticks found in its habitat. Children speculate about how these features help them survive in their habitat. More than 90% of all animal species are invertebrates. Challenge groups to speculate about why invertebrates are so successful.

Back in the classroom

Groups present their findings to the rest of the class. They talk about the creatures they discovered and explain why they think they are suited to their habitats. Children use information sources to profile a woodland vertebrate and an invertebrate of their choosing. They present their ideas on an illustrated poster which describes how they are adapted to their habitat. Take photographs of the posters, and publish them on the school website. Use the posters to assess children's progress towards the learning goals.

Things to talk about

Compare birds with other types of vertebrates such as mammals, reptiles, amphibians and fish. Provide children with images of vertebrates which live in gardens and woodland, such as a woodpecker (bird), squirrel (mammal), a snake (reptile) and a frog (amphibian). What are their similarities and differences? Working in groups, children use information sources to discover the features which distinguish birds, mammals, reptiles and amphibians.

Places of Poetry

Places of Poetry is a community arts project which encourages people to write poems about the places that inspire them. The poems can be published on the Places of Poetry website by pinning them to the relevant sites on a digital map of England and Wales. Visit the website to enjoy some of the poems published in 2019. Children write their own poems inspired by their tour of the woodland with an emphasis on adaptation. If the project is still running, they can publish their poems on the Places of Poetry website.

Children design their own arthropod

The most common types of invertebrates are the arthropods. An arthropod is an invertebrate with an exoskeleton, segmented body and paired jointed legs. Examples of arthropods which children may find in woodlands are insects (beetles, butterflies, bees etc.), as well as spiders, woodlice, centipedes and millipedes.

Children design a new kind of arthropod which lives in a garden habitat. The habitat could be a pond, a tree or some other area of the garden. Criteria for the design are:

- The arthropod must have features or behaviours which distinguish it from other arthropods.
- The arthropod must have features which enable it to survive in its habitat.

Children work collaboratively in pairs to design and construct a model of their arthropod. They present and justify their designs to the class. They should justify their design according to the established criteria. It is expected that children will use information sources to research common kinds of arthropods to inform their designs. Use the activity to assess children's progress towards the learning goals.

Why are hedgehogs in danger of extinction?

Hedgehogs are mammals and they are in trouble. The numbers have declined from over 30 million in the 1950s to less than 1.5 million now. A third of our hedgehogs have been lost since the turn of the millennium and, if the decline continues, this fascinating nocturnal nomad will disappear forever from our gardens.

Working in groups, children use information sources to discover why hedgehogs are suited to living in our gardens. What do they eat? Where do they go during the day? How do they survive the winter? Children find out about a hedgehog's habitat and lifestyle and why they are in danger of extinction. Talk about how urbanisation serves to rob hedgehogs of their natural habitats. By destroying hedges and other green spaces, hedgehogs are denied the safe routes they need to search for food. The plight of the hedgehog clearly illustrates how rapid changes to natural environments pose dangers to wildlife, which may lead to their extinction.

Hedgehog Street

Hedgehog Street is a campaign organised by the British Hedgehog Preservation Society (BHPS) with the purpose of reversing the decline in the hedgehog population. The campaign is about recruiting *Hedgehog Champions* who care enough to take action to help save these loveable spiny creatures.

There is a lot that can be done, even if your school does not have a garden. Start by viewing the video clip *Hedgehog Close*, produced by the British Hedgehog Preservation Society. Discuss the video and talk about whether the school grounds are hedgehog-friendly. Groups visit the BHPS website where they can find wide-ranging information about hedgehogs and free resources explaining why they are in trouble and what can be done to help save them. Turn your school grounds into a highway for hedgehogs, and start your own campaign to persuade parents to join their children in becoming Hedgehog Champions.

Information sources

- Adaptation: www.bbc.com/bitesize/clips/zbp6n39
- Badgers: www.woodlandtrust.org.uk/blog/2019/08/badgers-what-do-they-eat-and-other-facts/
- Birds in Antarctica: www.wildfoottravel.com/antarctica/information/wildlife-plants/birds
- British Hedgehog Preservation Society: www.britishhedgehogs.org.uk/
- Find a wood near you: www.woodlandtrust.org.uk/visiting-woods/
- Hedgehog Close: www.britishhedgehogs.org.uk/hedgehog-close-film
- Hedgehog facts: www.natgeokids.com/uk/discover/animals/general-animals/hedgehog-facts/
- Hedgehog facts: http://britishhedgehogs.org.uk/leaflets/L9-Basic-Facts.pdf
- Minibeast discovery pack: https://bbsrc.ukri.org/engagement/schools/keystage1-2/minibeast/
- People's Trust for Endangered Species: https://ptes.org/campaigns/hedgehogs/

- Places of Poetry: https://www.placesofpoetry.org.uk/
- Why hedgehogs are in trouble: www.bbc.co.uk/blogs/natureuk/2011/11/why-hedgehogs-are-in-trouble-a.shtml

Topic: Adaptation and Evolution

Age group: 9–11

Learning goals

Children make progress towards the big idea by examining how adaptation led to the evolution of garden birds and mammals after the extinction of the dinosaurs. They learn how living things which are better adapted to their environment are most likely to survive, while those not able to respond sufficiently to changes in their environment may become extinct. Children investigate the resources woodlands provide for birds. They focus their attention on the importance of conserving trees for wildlife, and also for their own benefit. Opportunities are provided for children to take part in citizen science projects organised by the Woodland Trust to track the effects of weather and climate change on birds near the school. There are also opportunities to contribute to a project organised by the People's Trust for Endangered Species, which is designed to understand and protect mammals which share our green spaces.

Working scientifically

In this topic children will:

- plan scientific enquiries to answer questions;
- record data appropriately;
- report and present findings from enquiries in oral and written forms;
- identify scientific evidence that has been used to support or refute ideas or arguments.

Health and safety

Refer to the relevant safety codes in the ASE publication *Be Safe!* (2011) when planning to teach the activities in this topic. Children should wear protective gloves when searching for invertebrates and signs of mammals in the woodland and other green spaces. Stress safety, hygiene and the protection of the environment. When using bird feeders safeguard children with nut allergies.

Exploring children's ideas

Set the scene for the topic by asking children when they last saw dinosaurs roaming around the school grounds or the local park. Listen to their ideas, and show children pictures of common garden 'dinosaurs' such as pigeons, robins and blackbirds. Talk about how birds evolved from bird-like dinosaurs which lived millions of years ago.

Chapter 5 **Adaptation**

Fossil evidence for the evolution of birds

Working in groups, children use information sources to discover the fossil evidence which suggests that birds are descended from avian dinosaurs. Children explore the fossil record to find out how birds evolved. They start with archaeopteryx from the Jurassic period, and compare this bird-like dinosaur with the crow-sized confuciusornis from the Cretaceous period. Encourage children to focus their attention on how the physical features of the bird-like dinosaurs changed over time until they evolved into true birds, which we see in our gardens today.

The extinction of the dinosaurs

Start by showing children pictures of different types of dinosaurs and find out what they know about them. What facts do they know? Because of the fossil records, we know that dinosaurs lived all over the earth, including North America, South America, Australia, Europe, Asia, Africa and even Antarctica. There were many different types; some lived on the ground, others were able to fly and some lived in the seas. Dinosaurs roamed the earth for 180 million years, and became extinct 65 million years ago. Although the reason for their extinction is still debated, scientists think that it could have been due to earth's collision with a giant asteroid.

Allow children to speculate about how the collision would have changed the environment in which the dinosaurs lived, and why they were unable to adapt. Working in groups, children use information sources to study the habitats and feeding relationships of commonly known dinosaurs. Encourage each group to choose a different dinosaur. Children debate how the dinosaur would have been affected by the change in climate caused by an asteroid collision. How could the collision cause the climate to change? Do children think the asteroid theory can account for such mass extinction? Explore their reasoning. Groups present the results of their enquiries and argue whether they support the collision theory. How else could dinosaurs have become extinct?

Why did birds manage to survive the mass extinction?

Avian dinosaurs survived the great extinction and evolved into the birds we see today. Encourage children to speculate about why small bird-like dinosaurs survived, while the huge dinosaurs became extinct. Suggest to children that birds managed to survive the mass extinction because they were able to adapt to changes in their environment. Why were birds able to adapt, while the large dinosaurs perished?

Present the following ideas for children to debate:

- Birds survived because they were small and light, and hence did not need vast amounts of food to eat – unlike some of the gigantic dinosaurs.
- Like many birds today they would eat almost anything. We know that there were many kinds of insects and other invertebrates living on the earth at that time, including many of the minibeasts we find in our gardens today. On the other hand, most of the large dinosaurs had specialised diets.
- The birds could fly long distances in search of food – whereas the big, heavy dinosaurs had to trudge along on foot.
- Being small, birds were able to breed faster than the larger dinosaurs, hence having more offspring helped them survive.

Groups discuss the ideas and argue whether they think the statements are justified. They can use information sources to support their arguments, using specific examples of birds and dinosaurs.

In search of evidence to support a theory

Birds at the time of the mass extinction may have survived because they were omnivores. Like today's birds, they were able to eat a wide variety of plants and small animals. Flowering plants began to develop at this time, with species similar to modern magnolias and other colourful plants covering the landscape. The increases in the numbers of flowering plants was helped by evolving insects such as wasps, ants and beetles. Besides pollinating the plants, these insects provided food for new species of birds to flourish. Birds could also feed on the seeds and fruits produced by the flowering plants.

Children set up experiments to test the theory that one reason birds survived the mass extinction was because they have such a varied diet. In the school grounds children can set up various feeding stations using different types of foods. Before choosing the foods, visit the RSPB website to make sure they are safe for birds to eat. Keep the feeding stations clean and filled with fresh food. Children predict which foods will be most popular and the time of the year when the stations will be in most demand. Children plan the enquiry so they are able to test their predictions and find answers to the following questions:

- Which kinds of birds use the feeders?
- Which time(s) of the year do they use them most?
- Which kinds of birds are fussy eaters?
- Which kinds of birds are not fussy eaters?
- Which foods will birds not eat?
- Do birds mainly use the feeders when their natural sources of food are scarce?
- What reliable conclusions can be formed about the feeding habitats of birds?

Use wildlife cameras to help record the different types of birds that visit the feeders in the school grounds, and also use window feeders which can be attached to the classroom windows so children can watch the birds feeding up close. Window feeders can be purchased from the RSPB website.

Children debate whether the findings of the enquiry provide evidence for why birds survived the mass extinction. Report the findings in your school science magazine or on your school blogging platform.

Spring visit to the woodland

The older the tree the more important it is to wildlife. Ancient and veteran trees are those in the mature stage of life which have important features including hollowing and deadwood. Cavities and decaying wood provide habitats for a diverse range of wildlife including bats, birds, invertebrates and fungi. Rot holes provide homes for brown long-eared bats, while tawny owls use large holes to build their nests. Hollows created in old trees also make a great habitat for barbastelle bats, which roost deep inside in winter. Hornets also make nests in hollow trees. Visit the Woodland Trust website to discover more about notable, ancient and veteran trees and to use their map to find out where they can be found closest to your school.

Organise a visit to the woodland in search of old and notable trees and to survey the bird life that visit them. Before you go, show children pictures of ancient and veteran trees and point out the characteristics which attract wildlife. A tree is likely to be old if has a wider trunk than is normal for its species and has lots of deadwood, crevices and holes. In other words, it is likely to be old if it looks old.

Working in supervised groups, children search the wood in a quest to find the oldest-looking trees. When they find an old tree, children identify it and give it a huge hug. Encourage children to speculate about the age of the tree and to think of it as a resource for us, as well as for birds and other wildlife. Talk about how trees contribute to our wellbeing by providing oxygen, improving air quality, regulating the climate, fighting climate change, conserving water, preserving soil and reducing noise pollution.

Groups sit quietly and using binoculars observe the birds and other wildlife which inhabit the tree and surrounding vegetation. Remind children of the four levels in the woodland described in Part 1. Is there more going on in the canopy or closer to the ground? Use sound recorders to record the different bird sounds. Take notebooks and pencils so children can sketch their tree, highlighting the features which are useful for wildlife.

Food, shelter and nesting sites

Encourage children to speculate about how different types of birds would use the tree for food, shelter and nesting. Help children examine the bark and leaves for bugs. Shake low-lying branches and catch the creatures which fall down in a white sheet. Children carefully search beneath the leaf litter and any fallen branches at the base of the tree for seeds and invertebrates. Children take photographs to record what birds would find to eat in their tree. Birds such as great tits, blue tits, robins, chaffinches and other small birds feed on insects, caterpillars, worms, spiders and other invertebrates. They also feed on seeds and nuts, especially in winter.

Spring is breeding time for many kinds of birds. Children look out for signs of birds collecting nest materials and those starting to feed their young. Look out for birds with beaks full of worms and insects and for lots of movement to and from nest sites.

Back in the classroom

Children use their photographs to create a display of the woodland depicting the resources available to the birds. They can also create watercolour paintings of their chosen tree from their sketches. Compare the results of the investigation with information about the feeding habits of the birds from the RSPB website. Talk about how woodland birds are suited (adapted) to their habitat. What would happen to the birds if the woodland were destroyed?

Talking points: true, false or not sure?

- If the woodland were destroyed the birds could not survive.
- If the woodland were destroyed the birds would soon find another place to live.

- Because birds can fly they have a better chance of surviving the destruction of the woodland than other woodland animals.
- If the woodland were destroyed the birds would quickly adapt to living in different types of habitat.

Children use the talking points to help them predict what would happen to bird populations in the UK if our woodlands continue to be destroyed. Also talk about the effects of habitat destruction on mammals, reptiles and amphibians which live in the woodland. Groups choose an animal such as a hedgehog, snake or frog, and use information sources to discover how it is suited to its habitat. They use the information to predict how the destruction of its habitat would affect its chances of survival. How quickly could it adapt to a different habitat? Use outcomes from these activities to assess children's progress towards the learning goals.

Nature's Calendar Project

Children can help scientists from the Woodland Trust track the effects of weather and climate change on different kinds of birds. As part of their *Nature's Calendar Project* the Woodland Trust wants volunteers to record when they first see different types of birds feeding their young. By comparing the data with previous years, scientists are able to track the effects of weather and climate change on the breeding habitats of the birds. This will enable scientists to work out which birds are best adapting to the changes in their environment caused by climate change.

> Our climate is changing. Climate change will produce some winners which are well adapted to climate change and some losers which cannot adapt quickly enough. Long-term monitoring of species like blackbird will help scientists to gain a greater understanding of this issue, and provide policymakers with hard evidence.
>
> (Woodland Trust Website)

Visit the Woodland Trust website and join the Nature's Calendar Project. Find out what they want you to record and the best time to look out for birds first feeding their young. Blackbirds, for example, tend to start feeding their young from mid-March to May. The timing of the blackbird breeding season is affected by the weather. Warmer weather in spring can cause the birds to start breeding earlier. The danger is, if they start breeding too soon, there may not be the food available to feed their young.

Children can research birds commonly seen in the school grounds, parks, hedgerows and green areas near the school. Use the Woodland Trust website to find out when they normally start to breed. At the first signs of spring, children start to look out for signs of birds collecting nest materials and those starting to feed their young. As they did in the woodland, children look out for birds with beaks full of worms and insects and lots of movement to and from nest sites. During spring, continually monitor the school grounds and organise regular visits to the local park and other green areas to record bird activity.

To share their findings with the scientists, children log on to the Woodland Trust website information page. The Trust is not monitoring all woodland birds, so children should keep their own records for the birds that live near the school. Children who repeat the survey in future years can use the records to discover whether the birds' breeding habits are changing. Each year publish the outcomes of the survey on the school's blogging platform.

How do school grounds compare with woodland habitats?

Children explore the resources which are available to birds in the school grounds. Groups record seeds, fruits and invertebrates which are available for birds to eat and possible shelter and nesting sites. Compare the resources available in the school grounds with those provided by woodland habitats. Ask children to look at the two habitats from a bird's point of view. Where would they prefer to live, and why? Encourage children to speculate about why woodland birds have adapted to life in our gardens. How can the school grounds be improved to attract a greater diversity of birds? Ideas about how to create a woodland edge habitat can be found in Chapter 8. Also visit the RSPB website.

Information sources

- Ancient trees: www.woodlandtrust.org.uk/visiting-woods/trees-woods-and-wildlife/woodland-habitats/ancient-trees/
- Avian dinosaurs: www.livescience.com/15737-avian-ancestors-dinosaurs-learned-fly.html
- A-Z of birds: www.rspb.org.uk/birds-and-wildlife/wildlife-guides/bird-a-z/
- Birds are dinosaurs: www.nhm.ac.uk/discover/why-are-birds-the-only-surviving-dinosaurs.html
- Bird feeders: www.rspb.org.uk/birds-and-wildlife/advice/how-you-can-help-birds/feeding-birds/safe-food-for-birds/
- Dinosaur fossils: www.theguardian.com/science/lost-worlds/2013/jun/05/dinosaurs-fossils
- Evolution of birds: www.scientificamerican.com/article/how-dinosaurs-shrank-and-became-birds/
- Great tit evolution: www.sheffield.ac.uk/news/nr/great-tits-adapt-beaks-to-bird-feeders-1.739657
- Nature's Calendar Project: https://naturescalendar.woodlandtrust.org.uk/
- RSPB: www.rspb.org.uk/
- Why birds survived: www.nhm.ac.uk/discover/why-are-birds-the-only-surviving-dinosaurs.html

Working on scientific understanding

In this part, children work on their understanding of how animals adapt to changes in their environment and how adaptation can lead to evolution. Large dinosaurs became extinct because they could not adapt to sudden changes in their environment. Many smaller animals, such as birds and mammals, did survive because they were more able to access the limited resources which were available after the great collision.

Things to talk about

Reflect on the ideas children explored in the first part of the topic. Show children a video clip which depicts the story of why the dinosaurs became extinct. Focus on how the debris from the collision with the asteroid blocked out the sun. Listen to children's ideas about how this would have affected the plants. Establish that many plants would have struggled to survive.

Chapter 5 Adaptation

Case study the demise of tyrannosaurus rex, which was one of the largest meat-eating animals ever to walk the earth. This enormous predator had long legs, a powerful tail and a huge head with strong jaws and serrated teeth that were perfect for slicing through flesh. Tyrannosaurus rex mainly preyed on plant-eating dinosaurs, such as the triceratops. Children research the feeding habits of tyrannosaurus rex and other meat-eating dinosaurs, and create a food web which includes producers, primary, secondary and tertiary consumers. They can start with a simple food chain which includes tyrannosaurus rex, and develop it into a food web including different types of plants, herbivorous dinosaurs and carnivorous dinosaurs.

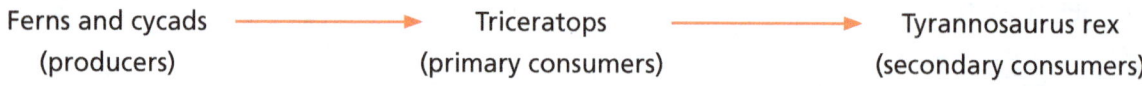

Ferns and cycads	Triceratops	Tyrannosaurus rex
(producers)	(primary consumers)	(secondary consumers)

Children present and discuss their food webs with the rest of the class. Encourage them to discuss what would have happened to the primary and secondary consumers if the food supply provided by the producers was dramatically reduced when the debris from the asteroid collision blocked out the sun. Debate why these very large dinosaurs would have found it difficult to adapt to these sudden changes in their environment.

Ask children to speculate about what happened after the extinction of the dinosaurs. Talk about how dinosaurs dominated the earth with little competition from birds and other animals for the available food resources. In the wake of their extinction, birds and other animals were able to take advantage of the available resources and slowly evolved to produce the great diversity of animals which populate the earth today. Being able to fly, birds were quick to populate all corners of the world, and different species evolved as they adapted to their new environments.

How have new species of birds evolved?

By exploring the work of Charles Darwin, children can identify and make sense of evidence that has been used to support his theory of evolution by natural selection. Focus their attention on the evolution of finches on the Galapagos Islands. Children use information sources to discover how each island has its own particular species of finch, distinguished by the shape and size of their beaks. Use ideas from Part 1 to speculate about how the different species could have evolved from one species of finch which had earlier arrived on the islands from the South American mainland.

Talk about how evolutionary biologists Rosemary and Peter Grant have been studying the Galapagos finches. Remarkably, they found that the finches have continued to evolve, resulting in the establishment of new species which differ from Darwin's finches in body size, song and other characteristics. There is a lot of information on the web about their work.

Groups use findings from Rosemary and Peter Grant's research, together with Darwin's discoveries, to illustrate how adaptation can lead to evolution. Ask children to identify a particular type of finch, and encourage them to speculate about how the species evolved through natural selection. Groups display their ideas on a poster, which can be presented to the rest of the class. Use the posters to create a classroom display. Use ideas from Part 1 to discuss Darwin's theory of evolution by natural selection.

Evolution in the school garden

We do not have to go to the Galapagos Islands to see evolution in action; we can see it happening in our school gardens. Use ideas from Part 1 to introduce children to the research which has shown that the great tit has been evolving by adapting its beak for bird feeders.

Encourage children to speculate about how the widespread use of bird feeders could lead to great tits evolving longer beaks. Children model the advantages of long, thin beaks, using bird feeders and different sizes of tweezers to access the food. Challenge children to design beaks which are perfectly adapted to bird feeders. Take care to safeguard children with nut allergies.

Drama: Darwin's modern-day bulldogs

Today, Charles Darwin is remembered as one of our greatest scientists. However, he was not always universally popular. When he first published his ideas about evolution he created a lot of controversy, as his theory seemed to directly challenge the Bible.

Darwin was very sensitive to criticism, which brought on depression. He was often in poor health, and when the storm broke after the publication of *The Origins of Species*, it was left to T.H. Huxley to defend and champion Darwin's ideas. Huxley earned himself the nickname *Darwin's Bulldog* because of the enthusiastic way he was prepared to defend Darwin's ideas.

Talk about how Darwin disliked arguments and was upset by the criticism he received from fellow scientists and theologians. Discuss the role Huxley played in championing Darwin's theory of evolution. Ask children to take on the role of Darwin's bulldogs and, like Huxley, present an enthusiastic and passionate argument for evolution. Working in groups, children use information sources to research their arguments, and then present it in the style of a televised interview. Each member of the group takes on a different role. The roles include the interviewee (Huxley), the interviewer (Wilberforce), the camera operator, the producer and the script editor. Video the presentations, and if appropriate, publish edited versions on the school's social media platform. Use this activity to assess children's progress towards the learning goals.

Chapter 5 Adaptation

Information sources

- Charles Darwin: https://kids.kiddle.co/Charles_Darwin
- Darwin online: http://darwin-online.org.uk/
- Dinosaur facts: www.activewild.com/dinosaur-facts-for-kids-students-and-adults/
- Why dinosaurs became extinct: https://easyscienceforkids.com/why-dinosaurs-became-extinct-video-for-kids-2/

The bigger picture

Had dinosaurs not been wiped out 65 million years ago, many of the mammals we see today, including ourselves, may not have existed. It was because of the mass extinction that mammals were able to evolve and dominate the land.

Things to talk about

Discuss how the demise of the dinosaurs provided opportunities for mammals to evolve. Without the dinosaurs, mammals had less competition for resources.

It is thought that the first true mammals were shrew-like in appearance. These early mammals were small, nocturnal, hairy and warm-blooded, and probably laid eggs. They ate insects and, in contrast to the huge dinosaurs, these early mammals were just 10 centimetres long. Being small and feeding at night they could survive amongst the dinosaurs. Once the dinosaurs were wiped out more of the food and other resources were available to the mammals. As a result the small mammals were able to thrive and gradually evolved into larger herbivorous and carnivorous mammals. Children debate why mammals were able to survive the great asteroid collision.

Talking points: true, false or not sure?

- Mammals survived because they were warm-blooded.
- Mammals survived because they were covered in fur.
- Mammals survived because they were small.
- Nocturnal mammals had the best chance to survive.
- It was the small mammals that could hide in holes in the ground that survived.
- Mammals that climb trees had the best chance of surviving.
- It was the mammals with the best sense of sight that survived.
- Mammals with superior hearing survived best.
- Herbivorous mammals survived best.
- Small mammals that ate invertebrates survived best.
- Omnivorous mammals survived best.

Groups discuss the talking points and decide on the features which helped mammals survive the mass extinction. Groups share and debate their ideas. Focus on what happened after the demise of the dinosaurs. How would the mammals benefit from the extinction of the dinosaurs?

Chapter 5 Adaptation

Hypothesising about how mammals evolved

The fossil records suggest that even though small mammals existed long before the dinosaurs died off, these warm-blooded creatures did not diversify until the dominant dinosaurs were out of the way and the environment had recovered from the asteroid impact.

These early mammals were hairy, nocturnal shrew-like creatures which mainly ate insects. Like today's shrews, we can presume that being nocturnal helped the early mammals avoid predators, but after the dinosaurs were wiped out the mammals had more opportunities to search for food during the day. Shrews have poor eyesight, which is a disadvantage for hunting during the day. However, some individuals would have had slightly better eyesight than others had, and hence an advantage in the competition for sources food. More food means they can grow bigger and out-compete other mammals with poorer eyesight. Because offspring are not identical to their parents, or each other, inherited characteristics can be enhanced as they are passed from generation to generation. This means that the eyesight of some of these early shrews could have progressively improved through the generations until new species of mammals that hunted in the daytime were created. Today, after 65 million years of evolution there are more than 5,000 mammal species, varying in size from the 1.5-gram bumblebee bat to the 190-tonne blue whale. Provide children with the story-line and encourage them to create their own rich narratives of how mammals developed after the extinction of the dinosaurs.

The age of the giant mammals

After the demise of the dinosaurs mammals evolved and diversified by adapting to the changes in their environment caused by the great collision. In some cases, mammals took on the shape of the dinosaurs which they replaced. For example, compare the body shape of a giraffe and a brachiosaurus. Like the brachiosaurus, the giraffe evolved a long neck and teeth which are perfectly suited for stripping vegetation from trees. Children use information sources to compare the physical characteristics of a range of giant mammals, living and extinct, with similar-looking dinosaurs. Children compare the habitats in which they lived and the types of foods which they ate. Encourage children to think of possible reasons for their similarities. Discuss children's ideas and assess their progress towards the learning goals.

Chapter 5 Adaptation

Mammal detectives

During the 65 million years since the mass extinction of the dinosaurs, the early mammals have evolved into the diverse range of mammals we find on the earth today. They have evolved differently depending on their environment. In this enquiry children set out to find evidence of the mammals that live in their local green spaces, such as the school grounds, parks and woodland. For example, they can look for evidence of hedgehogs, foxes, mice, rabbits, shrews, moles, bats and rats.

Some of these animals might be tricky to find, especially in built-up areas. However, if there are small mammals living in your school grounds it is likely they will leave some clue to their identity. To find evidence children need to do some research on the mammals to learn about their habitats, the shape of their paw prints, what their faeces looks like and what they eat. Also, encourage children to talk about how the mammals have evolved to suit their habitats. How do their characteristics enable them to survive?

Groups decide what evidence they are looking for with regard to each mammal, and plan how to collect it. Most mammals are creatures of habit and use regular paths and runs. Often these follow hedgerows, fences and walls, which provide cover and are often the easiest routes to take. Some animals can be identified from their undisturbed tracks, from their poo or their left-over meals. Baited footprint tunnels along their runs can be used to record their footprints. Information about how to make footprint tunnels for hedgehogs and other mammals can be found on the web.

Mammals found in gardens are typically nocturnal, or active around sunrise or sunset. The best way to see them is to set up wildlife cameras. Once you have discovered the mammals that visit the school ground you can extend your search to other places such as parks, woodland, churchyards and cemeteries, playing fields, golf courses, allotments and rivers banks. Churchyards can be excellent habitats for wildlife. They are quiet and undisturbed and hence provide a haven for all kinds of mammals. Children take photographs and publish the results of their enquiry in the school science magazine, or on the school website or blogging platform.

The People's Trust for Endangered Species (PTES)

Take part in the PTES annual *Living with Mammals Survey* and help scientists to understand and protect the mammals which share our green spaces.

> Towns and cities are home to a surprising number of wild mammals: from pygmy shrews and pipistrelle bats, the weight of a twenty-pence coin, to heavyweights, such

> as badgers and deer. Whether in a garden, allotment, a local park or churchyard, telling us what you see builds a bigger picture of the wildlife on our doorstep. It can tell us when a species is in trouble. Without the help of thousands of wildlife watchers, we wouldn't have known hedgehog numbers had fallen by a third in urban areas in less than 20 years and acted to help them.
>
> (PTES website, 2019)

Visit the PTES website to register to take part in the survey, which usually runs from April to June. All you have to do is record the mammals that you see each week and any signs they might leave behind, such as droppings or footprints. You can chose any green space to survey, be it the school grounds or a local park. Children can also look out for mammals in their gardens at home. In fact, you can survey any green space within 200 metres of a building. Printed packs which include full instructions, survey forms and a simple *Spotting Wild Mammals Guide* are available on the website. Children share their sightings on the PTES website.

Why scientists like dinosaur poo

Show children pictures of dinosaur poo. There are lots of examples on the web. Ask them why scientists get excited when they find dinosaur poo. Explain how scientists can discover what dinosaurs ate by studying their poo, and hence whether they were plant-eaters, carnivores or omnivores. They can also discover the kinds of animals and plants which populated the earth at the same time as the dinosaurs. Children use information sources to find out which of today's animals and plants lived at the same time as the dinosaurs. Groups share their findings.

Why were snails able to survive the mass extinction?

Scientists have long known that snails shared the same habitat as dinosaurs and have found snail fossils within the dung of plant-eating dinosaurs. It is thought that the snails made their way into the poo pats after they were deposited. Dinosaur pats provided warm, damp and food-rich mini-habitats that snails could easily exploit. Remind them that snails are detritivores. They are part of nature's recycling system.

Start the enquiry by asking children to list the features which they think may have enabled snails to survive the great asteroid collision. Was it to do with their size and structure, or more to do with what they eat? Children hunt for snails in the school grounds or bring in snails which you have collected elsewhere. House the snails in a tank with food and water. Fresh lettuce and a small saucer of water should keep them happy. Make sure you put a top on your tank with small holes to let in the air. Groups study the snails using magnifiers. By placing them on sheets of clear Perspex they can see them move from underneath. When handling snails, children should use disposable gloves and take care not to harm the animals; their shells can be quite delicate. Children set up experiments to determine the range of plants and other foods snails will eat.

Each group decides on a list of questions which will help it work out why snails survived the mass extinction. Here are some examples:

- What are their preferred habitats?
- How would the asteroid event affect their habitats?
- Would any of their physical features help them survive?

- Are they specialised feeders or will they eat a wide range of foods?
- How would their eating habits help them survive?
- When are they active, during the night or day? Would this help them survive?
- Are snails able to hibernate and conserve their energy?
- Could the way they reproduce be a factor in their ability to adapt to changes in their environment?
- Do they have strategies to help them cope with extremes of weather?

Groups use information sources to find answers to their questions. Each group presents their arguments for why snails were able to survive. Use children's responses to assess their progress towards the learning goals.

The Tree of Life

Introduce children to Darwin's tree of life using ideas set out in Part 1 of the chapter. Explain how Darwin used the tree of life metaphor to represent the evolutionary links between living things, and to help explain the origins of the earth's rich biodiversity.

Use a copy of the simplified tree of life diagram to trace the ancestors of birds back to the dinosaurs and beyond to reptiles, amphibians and fish. Also show how early forms of mammals existed at the same time as dinosaurs, and how they diversified after the dinosaurs became extinct.

Children create a simple tree of life which links vertebrates found in gardens and woodlands back to a common ancestor. Use the tree to describe and compare the evolutionary relationships between the different animals. For example, are humans more closely related to mice than they are to birds? Are birds more closely related to bats or dinosaurs? Are frogs more closely related to humans than they are to snakes? A simple tree of life can raise a lot of fascinating questions. Challenge children to use information sources to find out where invertebrates, plants and fungi belong on the tree of life.

Biodiversity Blitz of the local park

BioBlitz the local park to survey its rich biodiversity and record what you discover on a customised tree of life. BioBlitz is a collaborative race against the clock to discover as many species of plants, animals and fungi as possible within a set location. It can be a whole school activity, including children, teachers, support staff, governors, parents and others who are part of the school community.

> A BioBlitz is an informal and fun way to create snapshot of the biodiversity of an area. It provides an opportunity for participants to learn together and share their expertise and enthusiasm for nature. This is a great way of breaking down barriers to engagement with science and raising awareness of the role of biological recording. It also gives the public an opportunity to contribute to a genuine scientific survey.
>
> Guide to Running a BioBlitz, 2013

A *Guide to Running a BioBlitz* is freely available on the Natural History Consortium website. The guide is designed to support the running of BioBlitzes and similar wildlife events anywhere there is wildlife, including urban and rural areas. It provides all the information teachers need to plan and manage a thorough wildlife survey in a chosen area, such as a public park.

BioBlitzes work best when supported by scientific experts. Contact local wildlife trusts, museums, universities and nature groups to find volunteers willing to support your school. Share the data collected from your survey on the National Biodiversity Network Gateway, so scientists throughout the UK can have access to your findings. Also, publish the outcomes of your BioBlitz on the school's blogging platform.

Information sources

- Bird watching: www.stem.org.uk/resources/elibrary/resource/31004/bird-watching-schools
- Conservation advice: https://ptes.org/get-informed/publications/guidance-leaflets/
- Footprint tunnel: https://ipswichhedgehogs.wordpress.com/2017/08/04/how-to-make-a-hedgehog-footprint-tunnel/
- Guide to Running a BioBlitz: www.bnhc.org.uk/wp-content/uploads/2014/04/BioBlitz-Guide-2013.pdf
- How adaptation works: www.rspb.org.uk/birds-and-wildlife/natures-home-magazine/birds-and-wildlife-articles/how-do-birds-survive/how-adaptation-works
- Mammal ancestors: www.sciencemag.org/news/2013/02/ancestor-all-placental-mammals-revealed
- Natural History Museum BioBlitzes: www.nhm.ac.uk/take-part/citizen-science/bioblitz.html
- People's Trust for Endangered Species: https://ptes.org/get-involved/surveys/garden/living-with-mammals/spotting-urban-mammals/
- Shrew facts: www.softschools.com/facts/animals/shrew_facts/107/
- Snail facts: www.snail-world.com/snail-facts/
- Tracking tunnels: https://ptes.org/wp-content/uploads/2015/06/Guidance-for-detecting-hedgehogs-using-tracking-tunnels.pdf
- The British Hedgehog Preservation Society: www.britishhedgehogs.org.uk/

Further reading

Websites

- Charles Darwin: www.nhm.ac.uk/discover/museum-highlights-charles-darwin.html
- Darwin's Finches: www.nationalgeographic.org/thisday/sep15/darwin-explores-galapagos-islands/
- Great Tit Evolution: www.sheffield.ac.uk/news/nr/great-tits-adapt-beaks-to-bird-feeders-1.739657
- Natural Selection: www.darwinproject.ac.uk/commentary/evolution/natural-selection
- What Is Evolution? www.bbc.co.uk/bitesize/articles/z9qs4qt
- Woodland Trust: www.woodlandtrust.org.uk/visiting-woods/trees-woods-and-wildlife/british-trees/

Books

- Bright, M. and Carpentier, M. (2019) *Darwin's Tree of Life*, London: Wayland.
- Dixon, D. (2018) *When the Whales Walked*, London: Quarto Publishing.
- Green, J. and McElfatrick, C. (2019) *The Magic and Mystery of Trees*, London: DK.
- Loxley, P. (2018) *Practical Ideas for Teaching Primary Science: Inspiring Learning and Enjoyment*, Abingdon: Routledge.
- Loxley, P., Dawes, L., Nicholls, L. and Dores, B. (2018) *Teaching Primary Science: Promoting Enjoyment and Developing Understanding*, Abingdon: Routledge.
- Radeva, S. (2019) *Charles Darwin's: On the Origin of Species*, London: Penguin.
- Scott, K. (2017) *The Story of Life: Evolution*, London: Big Picture Press.
- Scott, K. and Willis, K. (2016) *Botanicum*, London: Big Picture Press.

ASE Journals

- Primary Science 132 (March–April 2014) *Insects: Little Things That Run the World* by Luke Tilley.
- Primary Science 139 (September–October 2015) *Why Are There Still Apes in Apes Have Changed into People?* by Terry Russel and Linda McGuigan.
- Primary Science 140 (November–December 2015) *Introducing Evolution into the Curriculum* by Stuart Scrase.
- Primary Science 156 (January–February 2019) *Teaching and Learning About Evolution: A Developmental Overview* by Terry Russel and Linda McGuigan.

Red Admiral   Painted Lady   Marbled White
Clouded Yellow   Six-spotted burnet
Small Copper   **Elephant hawk-moth**
Grayling   Silver-studded blue
Brown Hairstreak   ORANGE TIP   Peacock
Dingy skipper   Tortoiseshell   Cinnabar
Camberwell beauty   Chalk Hill blue
Brimstone   Garden tiger moth   Bee moth
Leopard moth   Diamond back   Gatekeeper
Death's-head hawk moth   Brown Argus
Apple-leaf skeletonizer   Common clothes moth
Parsnip moth   Grizzled skipper   Wax moth
Pearl bordered fritillary   Garden pebble moth
Red-belted clearwing   Scalloped hook-tip
Chocolate tip   Fruit-tree tortrix   Hornet moth
Ghost moth   Meadow dwarf   Purple emperor
Chimney sweeper   Lunar hornet moth

Blackbird   Blue tit   Cuckoo   Swallow
Song thrush   Sparrowhawk   Rook   Green Woodpecker
Spotted Flycatcher   Swift   Jay   Yellowhammer
Tawny Owl   Turtle Dove   Starling   Kingfisher   Wren
Brambling   Fieldfare   Red Kite   House Martin
Wood Warbler   Tree Creeper   Marsh Harrier
Raven   Bullfinch   Kestrel   Chiff Chaff
Long-eared Owl   Nightingale   Robin   Siskin
Nuthatch   Long-tailed tit   Magpie   Coal tit
Snow Bunting   Jackdaw   Collared dove
Sparrow   Waxwing   Great Spotted Woodpecker
Marsh tit   Song thrush   Barn owl   Rock dove
Pheasant   Partridge   Goshawk   Willow tit
Wood Pigeon   Long-tailed tit   Sand Martin
Little Owl   Buzzard   Osprey   Willow Warbler
Pied Flycatcher   Greenfinch   Hawfinch
Linnet   Common Crossbill   Reed Bunting
Nightjar   Goldcrest   Skylark   Garden Warbler

CHAPTER 6
INHERITANCE

Big idea: *Living things produce offspring of the same kind, but normally offspring vary and are not identical to their parents. Small differences that occur during reproduction may over time lead to evolution.*

Part 1: Subject knowledge

This part sets out subject knowledge teachers require to support children's learning towards the big idea. The ideas presented go beyond the requirements of the National Curriculum, and hence provide teachers with levels of subject knowledge which enable them to meet the needs of children with different interests and abilities.

The topics include:

- Learning from first-hand experience
- Thinking and talking with scientific ideas
- Pollination, fertilisation and seed dispersal
- Inheritance and diversity
- Selective breeding of plants
- Asexual reproduction

Part 2: Working towards the big idea

Each topic aims to move children's understanding further towards the big idea. The journey begins by exploring the diversity of plants and examining the conditions plants need to grow from seed. The ideas are moved forward when children learn about pollination and how seeds (offspring) are produced by sexual reproduction. Children work on their understanding of inheritance to learn how living things produce offspring of the same kind, but normally offspring vary and are not identical to their parents. Finally, children explore how small differences that occur during reproduction may over time lead to evolution.

Chapter 6 Inheritance

> **The topics are:**
> - Variety and growth (5–7 years)
> - Life cycles of plants (7–9 years)
> - Inheritance and evolution (9–11 years)

Part 1: Subject knowledge

Learning from first-hand experience

Plants and animals grow, produce offspring and eventually die. To produce offspring, flowering plants produce seeds which require the right conditions to grow into mature plants. Animals give birth to offspring which grow into adults. These are some of the ideas about reproduction children learn early on in their primary science education. They are ideas which match their everyday experiences. Through science activities children expand and enrich their understanding of the ideas in various contexts. For example, children explore the structure of plants and their flowers and learn how seeds are contained in fruits. They investigate different types of seeds and the conditions required for growing them. With a little guidance, there is a lot children can discover from first-hand experience. However, the ideas children discover for themselves only provide them with fleeting insights into the wonders of the natural world. To appreciate the bigger picture children need to learn to think with scientific ideas.

Thinking and talking with scientific ideas

When learning outdoors, there are lots of fascinating things happening which can be explained with the help of scientific ideas. For example, the narrative in Chapter 1 illustrates how children can engage more intimately with nature by thinking with scientific ideas. The inspiration for the story comes from watching the behaviour of bees and butterflies with regard to a sweet-smelling red rose. The insects ignore the highly perfumed and beautiful red rose in favour of the less striking verbenas and the foxgloves. When looked at it from a scientific point of view it is not surprising that the bees are not attracted to the red rose. Scientists have discovered that bees cannot see the colour red, and to the bee the rose looks much like the surrounding green foliage. However, bees are highly attracted to shades of purple, blue and yellow and look out for plants with single blossoms which are easiest to access, just like the flowers of the verbenas and the foxgloves.

What the insects are really looking for is the pollen and nectar inside the flower, which they take back to their nest or hive. Of course, the insects don't know that by collecting the pollen and nectar they are helping the plant reproduce. The flower is the plant's reproductive organ which

Chapter 6 Inheritance

contains both male and female cells called gametes. Sexual reproduction takes place when the male sex cells are transferred and combined with the female sex cells, resulting in the production of seeds capable of producing offspring. Sexual reproduction normally occurs between different plants of the same species. However, some plants are self-pollinating, meaning that male sex cells and female sex cells on the same plant can combine to reproduce fertile seeds.

Pollination, fertilisation and seed dispersal

Pollination and fertilisation together describe sexual reproduction in flowering plants. Pollination refers to the transfer of pollen (male sex cells) from the anther to the female part of the plant, the stigma. Pollination normally occurs with the help of wind or animals, such as insects and birds. These animals are called pollinators. Flowers that rely on pollinators produce nectar, and they are usually brightly coloured and scented in order to attract the pollinators. Flowers that are wind pollinated do not need to attract pollinators. They are usually small and insignificant. Their anthers and feathery stigmas hang outside the flower. This allows the wind to blow pollen from the anther and puts the stigma in a position to catch the pollen that is floating in the air. When the pollen lands on the stigma, a pollen tube goes down the style which enables male sex cells (pollen) to combine with the female sex cells (ovules), hence fertilisation takes place.

As a result of fertilisation a fruit is formed with seeds inside, each of which contains genetic information from the combination of the male and female sex cells. Plants disperse their seeds to prevent over-crowding. They do this in a range of different ways, depending on the habitats to which they have adapted. Animals play an important role in seed dispersal. Some plants, such as a burdock, produce fruits with hooks.

These hooks can stick to a passing animal's fur and drop off in a different place. Animals may eat fruits and the seeds can pass through their digestive systems undamaged and hence can be widely dispersed. Seeds such as peas are dispersed when the ripe pod 'explodes', shooting the seeds away from the plant. Some fruits, such as the horse chestnut, simply drop off the tree and roll away from the parent plant. In the right conditions, dispersed seeds are able to germinate and grow into a mature plant.

Inheritance and diversity

For over 140 million years animals have helped flowering plants to reproduce sexually. The first flowering plants appeared on earth when dinosaurs still existed. It is generally assumed that from the start the function of the flowers was to help the plant reproduce. When transporting pollen between plants, animals are in fact exporting the plant's genes. The seeds which are produced and the new plants which grow from them contain genes from each of their parents. This ensures that offspring inherit characteristics from both their parents and are not identical to either. Moreover, during reproduction random changes to the genetic material can happen which produce small differences in the offspring. These differences can result in some individuals being better suited to their environment than others and over time may lead to evolution.

To illustrate how inherited differences may lead to evolution, we can speculate about how plants may evolve longer roots. It could be argued that individuals which inherit the ability to grow longer roots may be able to out-compete others for water in time of drought. Possibly, those with shorter roots may not live long enough to reproduce, leaving the ones with the longer roots to access the limited amount of water and produce offspring with similar traits. In this way, populations of long-root plants can evolve. Over many generations, inherited differences may accumulate to the point where survivors have evolved into new kinds of plants.

Today there are over 400,000 types of flowering plants around the world, each with its own unique beauty. We only have to look in our gardens, woodlands and meadows to find a vast variety of colours, shapes and scents. Different types of plants have developed their own special ways of attracting pollinators. For example, some orchids produce pheromones to attract insects. Bee orchids are fascinating and beautiful plants with flowers that resemble a female bee. The petals also smell like female bees emitting an enticing fragrance. When male bees land on them, thinking they have found a mate, they are covered with pollen and consequently pollinate the next orchid they visit. The beauty of nature goes far deeper than just its appearance. Seeing nature with 'scientific eyes' can reveal its wondrous behaviour, as well as its aesthetic beauty.

Selective breeding of plants

Many of the plants we grow in our gardens have not evolved naturally; they have been produced by artificial means through selective breeding. Plant breeders take advantage of the changes produced in offspring due to sexual reproduction. For example, there are over 3,000 varieties of tulips which are a result of selective breeding techniques. To produce new varieties, breeders select parent plants with desirable traits and cross-pollinate them to produce hybrid offspring which inherit those traits. It may be possible to cross a tulip which has a bright yellow flower consisting of small single petals with a tulip with a more complex flower structure to produce a hybrid with bright yellow multi-layered flowers. The offspring of cross-pollinated plants inherit characteristics from both their parents. This has enabled plant breeders to develop the huge variety of tulips which are available today. This type of selective breeding is called hybridisation and is dependent on both parents passing genetic information onto their offspring.

Asexual reproduction

Plants do not always need partners to produce offspring. Often new plants can be regenerated from the vegetative parts of a parent plant, such as leaves, stems, roots, rhizomes, tubers and runners. A popular activity in primary schools is to grow a new plant from the top of a carrot. Normally the carrot top is placed in water and left to grow roots. Given the right conditions, a new young plant can then be grown to maturity.

Growing a new plant from part of a single parent is called cloning and is an example of asexual reproduction. Asexual reproduction occurs naturally in a wide range of plants and other living things, producing offspring (clones) which are genetically identical to their parent. The production of bulbs by daffodils and the propagation of strawberries by producing runners are examples of asexual reproduction.

Gardeners often take advantage of a plant's ability to reproduce asexually by taking cuttings. Growing from cuttings involves removing healthy non-flowering stems and planting them in damp compost. After a few weeks new roots develop and hence a new plant is produced which is a clone of its parent. Often we think of clones as being physically, as well as genetically, identical to their parents; however, this is not always the case. Sometimes gardeners find that daughter plants grown from cuttings or other parts of a plant are not identical. The reasons for this are complex, but scientists agree that the variation is caused by random changes or mutations to the plant's genetic material during the cloning process. Because these changes are not created in the sex cells, the variations are not passed on to their offspring.

Part 2: Working towards the big idea

Models of good practice

Topic: Variety and growth

Age group: 5–7 years

Learning goals

Children take a step towards the big idea by exploring plant diversity and by learning how to grow flowering plants from seeds to add colour to the school environment. There are close links between ideas in this topic and those set out in Chapter 4. Learning starts with children visiting the local park to identify and describe the structure of a variety of common flowering plants, including trees. In the school garden, learning is focussed on the growing cycle of flowering plants. Children explore the conditions plants need to grow and monitor the stages in their development from seed to the production of flowers, which eventually produce new seeds (offspring). In the final part of the topic, children are taken on a farm visit to explore the variety of life on the farm and to learn about the stages of development of the various farm animals. They also explore variations in the same kind of farm animals.

Scientific ways of working

In this topic children will:

- ask and seek answers to simple questions;
- observe closely and use simple equipment;
- design and perform appropriate tests;
- take measurements using scientific equipment;
- use their observations and ideas to suggest answers to questions;
- gather and record data to help answer questions.

Health and safety

Check whether the seeds you intend to sow have been treated with pesticides. Regard all plants and seeds to be hazardous; children should be warned not to put them in their mouths. As a general rule, children should be warned not to touch plants growing in green areas unless given permission by a supervising adult. When using plants in the classroom safeguard children with allergies. When planning to teach the activities in this topic refer to the relevant safety codes in the ASE publication *Be Safe!* (2011).

Exploring children's ideas

This topic starts in the local park in the autumn term where children are introduced to the different types of plants that grow there. Outside learning continues in the local park throughout the year, as children explore how the plants change from season to season. Activities focus children's attention on the variety of forms and colours of different types of plants, including trees.

Exploring the variety of plants in the local park

Take children on a guided tour of the local park to explore the variety of plant life. Prepare children for the tour by showing them pictures of the different types of plants they expect to see in the park. Include trees, woody plants (shrubs or bushes) and non-woody (herbaceous) plants. Young children never seem sure whether a tree is a plant, so spend some time talking about trees before the tour. Talk about how trees are like any other plant, but much bigger. They have stems which are called trunks, leaves on their branches, roots underneath the ground and some produce flowers, normally in spring.

While in the park children work in supervised groups. The first activity is for each group to choose a tree to adopt. Encourage children to give their tree a name and to speculate about its age, depending on its size. To get to know their trees, groups collect leaves, nuts, seeds, cones; they measure the width of the trunk and trace where its roots enter the ground. Talk about how trees can be identified by the shape of their leaves, and help children use information sources to identify their tree. Children listen to sounds made by their tree, touch and sense the texture of the bark and create simple bark rubbings. Take photographs of the different parts of the tree.

The colours in the park change depending on which time of the year you visit. Provide children with a card with all the colours of the rainbow, and ask groups to find plants in the park to match each of the colours. Supervised groups collect evidence of the range of colours by collecting leaves and fruits such as berries, nuts and seed pods and by taking photographs of the different flowering plants. As you tour the park focus children's attention on the different types of plants and talk about how they vary. Focus the discussion mainly on the shape and colour of their leaves and flowers. Before heading back to school, challenge children to find the largest and smallest plants in the park. Take photographs to record.

Chapter 6 Inheritance

Autumn colours

Back in the classroom, groups use their collections of leaves and other objects to produce a poster which illustrates the range of nature's colours. Did they find all the colours of the rainbow? What was the most common colour? What colours are missing? Groups talk about their posters and compare the shape and colour of the different leaves and the other objects they collected. Help children learn to recognise different types of trees. Display children's posters and photographs of the trees and other plants to illustrate the diversity of plants in the park.

Seasonal changes in the park

Arrange for the children to return to the park at different times during the year to experience the changes which take place from season to season. Before each visit, record the weather and ask children to speculate about the effects the weather might have on the plants in the park. On each visit children repeat the activities from the autumn term and collect evidence regarding:

- changes to their adopted trees;
- changes to the variety of flowering plants;
- changes to the colours in the park.

After each visit, add to the display to show how the plants in the park have altered in response to the seasonal changes in the weather. Identify deciduous and evergreen plants and compare their leaves. Talk about how winter days are too dark and cold for deciduous trees to grow, and that is why they lose their leaves. In spring, when there is more sunshine and the weather warms up, deciduous trees grow new leaves and produce flowers. At the end of the school year, groups use photographs of their adopted trees taken in autumn, winter, spring and summer to create a display showing how the trees in the park change throughout the seasons.

Working on scientific understanding

In this part children further develop their understanding of the structure of plants and have opportunities to grow their own flowering plants in the school garden.

Things to talk about

Start this part after their spring visit to the park. Recap the things children learnt from their visits in autumn, winter and spring visits to the park. Ask children to talk about when they think plants grow best. Are there more flowering plants in winter or spring? Create a display of different kinds of spring flowering plants to illustrate the diversity of spring colour.

Comparing the structure of flowers

Bring different kinds of flowering plants in pots to the classroom. Discuss the features which the plants have in common such as leaves, roots, stems and flowers. Then encourage children to talk about their differences, including their size, the shape and size of their leaves, and the shape and colour of their flowers.

Working in groups children compare the structure of different flowers. Be aware of children with allergies and sensitivities. Use commercial flowers with big petals. Children dissect the flowers to reveal their different parts. What is the same about the flowers? How are they different? Children use their own words to describe the form of the flowers. Do they look like bells or cups? Help children choose appropriate words. Talk about the different parts and compare the colours, shapes, numbers and sizes of their petals.

Design their own flowers

Challenge children to design their own flowers which are different from the ones they have been investigating. Children paint colourful illustrations and make models. Encourage children to describe and compare their flowers. Talk about similarities and differences. Show children pictures which illustrate the diversity of flowers which exist in nature. Ask children to describe the different forms.

Growing flowering plants from seed

Talk about how growing plants from seeds is an exciting experience. They are so small and unremarkable, yet can grow and produce the most beautiful flowers. Ask children to describe how flowers make them feel. What do they like best, their scents, shapes or colours? Listen to their stories and suggest they grow their own flowers to make the school grounds more colourful. Find out what children know about growing plants from seeds.

Provide children with a choice of different flowering plants which they could grow. Easy growing flowering plants include cornflowers, sunflowers, nigella, aquilegia, nasturtiums, marigolds, pansies and tobacco plants. It is often a good idea to sow seeds in pots indoors until they germinate and produce seedlings. This way children can explore the conditions which influence the early stages of growth and discover for themselves the best way to grow the seeds. Avoid using plastic when sowing the seeds. You can find lots of ideas for making eco-friendly pots on the web.

Prepare the outdoor beds in advance to make sure the condition of the soil is right for the plants and is soft enough to be worked by the children. Plant outdoors when the weather is right. Children can continue to experiment with different growing conditions. Organise a watering and weeding regime and monitor the growth of the plants. Take measurements and photographs and make sketches at regular intervals until the plants start to flower. Children record the progress of their plants in their diaries. Display photographs showing the changes in the plants at regular intervals. Every week, provide time for children to talk about how their plants have changed. Encourage them to speculate about reasons for the changes and probe their understanding of the conditions plants need to grow. When the plants produce seeds, talk about the life cycles of the plants and how the seeds can be used to grow new plants. With support, children produce their own illustrated guides to growing flowering plants. Use the activity to assess their progress towards the learning goals.

Wheelbarrow gardening

Use old wheelbarrows as containers to grow flowering plants. Use the space creatively to produce themed designs and colourful patterns. Help children plant their seedlings and use objects such as stones, shells, small logs and twigs to add interest to the garden. Help children paint floral designs on the stones and shells.

Weeding opportunities

Weeds are plants that we don't want to grow or are growing in the wrong place. Turn weeding activities into learning opportunities by encouraging the children to carefully remove the weeds so that they can be studied in the classroom. Groups use magnifiers to study the structure of the different types of weeds. Compare the form of their leaves and flowers and the structure of the roots. Encourage children to talk about the structure of the plants and assess their use of appropriate language. Ask children to speculate about where the weeds came from. Use their responses to help assess their progress towards the learning goals.

Information sources

- What does a plant need to grow? www.bbc.com/bitesize/articles/zxxsyrd
- What are the parts of a plant? www.bbc.com/bitesize/articles/z3wpsbk
- From a seed to a flower: www.youtube.com/watch?v=dJjNh2pMSB8
- How to sow seeds outdoors: www.rhs.org.uk/advice/profile?PID=206
- RHS school gardening: www.rhs.org.uk/education-learning/gardening-children-schools
- What plants can you find outside: www.bbc.com/bitesize/articles/zw2y34j

The bigger picture

In this part, the children's attention is turned towards reproduction in animals to reinforce parallel ideas about inheritance. Start by asking them to explain the difference between plants and animals. Working in groups, children use pictures of plants and animals to compare differences and similarities. Groups present their ideas to the class. Listen to their reasoning and summarise the main differences between plants and animals.

Things to talk about

Ask the children to talk about themselves. How have they grown and changed since they were babies? Listen to their stories and list all the things they can do now which they could not do when they were babies. Ask them to talk about their pets. Focus on cats and dogs. Do they have more things in common with their pets or with plants? Listen to their ideas and talk about some of the things humans and animals (mammals) have in common.

How do farm animals change as they grow up?

Young children can benefit enormously from visiting a working farm, especially if they live in an urban area. Farm visits provide a range of stimulating, hands-on experiences of farming and the countryside, which support the curriculum and also help children appreciate where their food comes from. To find a farm to visit, go to the *Visit My Farm* and *Food for Life* websites. These websites also provide resources to help you plan your visit.

Plan the visit so children can find out how animals on the farm are raised from birth and how they grow, change and are kept healthy. They can also explore individual differences between animals of the same kind. For example, are all sheep the same? If not, how do they differ?

Visit the farm in spring when there are likely to be newborn lambs and other young animals to see. Before the visit, organise key questions for the farmer to answer about the stages in the development of particular animals and variation in the same kind of animals. Compare the animals with the way the children have changed from birth. For example, lambs are able to stand up and walk quickly after they are born. Do the children know how long it took them to learn to walk?

Children ask questions about the different animals on the farm.
They can find out:

- How the young animals are born.
- How the animals feed their offspring.
- When young animals start to grow teeth.
- How long young animals are dependent on their mothers.
- What the different animals on the farm eat.
- How long it takes for young animals to grow into adults.
- Whether young animals look like their parents.
- Individual differences between farm animals.

Encourage the farmer to talk about differences between the same kinds animals. Are all sheep or cattle the same? Can he/she recognise individual animals? Take photographs of the farm animals to create a display back in the classroom.

Children's stories: life on the farm

Back in the classroom, use the photographs to talk about the trip to the farm and listen to children's stories about what they learnt. Compare stages in the development of animals to stages in a child's development. Use photographs to illustrate similarities and differences between various farm animals. For example, compare chickens to sheep and sheep to cattle. Also, talk about variations in the same kind of farm animals. Are sheep all the same? Are lambs identical to their parents? Illustrate differences in animals of the same kind.

Children tell stories in words and pictures which feature the variety of life on the farm. Discuss children's stories and assess their progress towards the learning goals.

Information sources

- Countryside Classroom: www.countrysideclassroom.org.uk/
- Country Trust: www.countrytrust.org.uk/
- Farm Discovery: www.countrytrust.org.uk/what-we-do/farm-discovery-homepage
- Farms to visit: www.countrysideclassroom.org.uk/places
- Food for Life: www.foodforlife.org.uk/schools/what-can-you-do/visit-a-farm
- Growth and Change: www.bbc.com/bitesize/clips/z4tmhyc
- Variation in plants: www.bbc.com/bitesize/clips/zn89wmn
- Visit my Farm: http://visitmyfarm.org/

Topic: Life cycles of plants

Age group: 7–9 years

Learning goals

Children make progress towards the big idea by exploring the life cycle of plants and discovering how they have evolved to attract pollinators. Initially, children explore how flowering plants produce fruits which contain seeds and investigate how the seeds are dispersed. Children work on their understanding of the nature of seeds and how they germinate to produce offspring. To help see the bigger picture, children focus their attention on pollination and the symbiotic relationships flowering plants have with their pollinators. This part provides opportunities for children to talk about the life cycle of flowering plants in ways which enable them to see how plants and animals are dependent on each other for their survival.

Working scientifically

In this topic children will:

- ask questions and use scientific enquiries to answer them;
- set up enquiries including comparative and fair testing;
- make systematic and careful observations using a range of equipment;
- record findings using scientific language, drawings and labelled diagrams;
- report findings from enquiries using oral and written explanations, as well as displays, articles and blogs;
- use results to draw conclusions and make predictions.

Health and safety

Regard all plants and seeds to be hazardous; children should be warned not to put them in their mouths. As a general rule, children should be warned not to touch plants growing in green areas unless given permission by a supervising adult. Children should wear protective gloves when collecting seeds and fruits. Stress safety, hygiene and the protection of the environment. Safeguard children with pollen allergies. When planning to teach the activities in this topic refer to the relevant safety codes in the ASE publication *Be Safe!* (2011).

Exploring children's ideas

This topic starts in autumn and provides opportunities for children to talk about life cycles of flowering plants in ways which enable them to see how plants and animals are dependent on each other for their survival.

Chapter 6 Inheritance

Things to talk about

Start by talking about autumn as a time of change when the weather gets colder and plants and animals prepare themselves for the winter. In the hedgerows, parks, woodlands and gardens the leaves on trees and other plants change colour, taking on rich shades of golds, browns, coppers, bronzes and reds. At the same time, fruits are ready to harvest and their seeds are distributed in a range of ingenious ways.

Ask children to describe what autumn means to them. How does it differ from other seasons? What are the signs that autumn has begun? Listen to the children's stories. Show children the Woodland Trust video clip: *A year in the life of a horse chestnut tree*. Discuss how the tree changes from season to season.

Autumn seed safari

Take children on an autumn safari to collect fruits and seeds from the school grounds, a local park, woodland and hedgerows. Look on the Wildlife Trust and Woodland Trust websites to find a local wildlife reserve near you. Children collect acorns, conkers, hazel nuts, berries, sycamore seeds and any other fruits which they *find on the ground*. Select areas where children can sit down, and with the help of magnifiers sketch some of the fruits on the plants. They can also take photographs.

Autumn is conker time. Children sketch the familiar spikey outer case, with the hard conker nut inside. Encourage children to speculate about why the outer case is so spiky and what is contained inside the hard nut.

The sultana game

Listen to what children know about squirrels. Talk about how squirrels bury acorns and other nuts in autumn, so they can dig them up in winter when food is scarce. The problem for the squirrels is that they often forget where they buried them, so in effect they are accidently planting new oak trees.

To understand the problems squirrels face when trying to retrieve the buried nuts, children play the sultana game. Ask them to imagine they are squirrels. Where would they bury an acorn so it would not be found by other animals? Give each child a sultana to represent an acorn or hazel nut. Within a defined area on the safari, ask the children to independently bury their food so it is safely hidden. Do not mention that you will ask them to find it again later.

Take the children to another area to continue exploring, recording and collecting different types of berries, nuts and seeds. Before returning to school, take children back to the area where they buried their sultanas and ask them to find the one they buried. Several are likely not to be able to find it. Talk about how the same thing happens with the squirrels, and how difficult it may be for them to find food which they buried weeks before. Discuss how squirrels play a part in dispersing seeds and hence help new trees to grow. Which other ways can the different types of woodland seeds inside nuts and fruits be dispersed? Full details of similar activities can be found on the SAPS website.

Design their own seeds

Back in the classroom children use magnifiers to help them carefully sketch and describe the characteristics of the different types of fruits, nuts, seed pods and seeds which they collected. Are they small or big? Are they soft and juicy, or hard and dry? Are they bright and colourful? Do they have wings or parachute, or maybe spikes and hooks? Encourage children to speculate about how their structure helps their dispersal. Seeds are mainly dispersed by wind or animals. Children design their own plants with seeds that can be transported long distances by the wind. Use children's designs, together with the things collected from the safari, to create a display depicting seed dispersal.

Things to talk about

Talk about how flowering plants produce fruits, which contain seeds. Given the right conditions, these seeds can grow into plants. Not all fruits are the same. Some plants produce soft fruits such as apples, blackberries and strawberries. Other plants produce dry fruits with a seed contained in a hard outer shell. Seeds contained in a hard outer shell, such as acorns (oaknuts) and conkers (chestnuts), are types of nuts.

When is a vegetable a fruit?

Bring in a range of fruit and vegetables such as apples, pears, passion fruits, pomegranates, peaches, plums, avocados, cucumber, peppers, pumpkins, tomatoes and peas in a pod. Ask children to speculate about which of the fruit and vegetables contain seeds. Can they predict their size and number? Children carefully dissect them to discover that some contain a number of seeds, while others may have only one. Point out that, from a scientific point of view, they are all fruits because each one contains at least one seed. Any part of a plant which contains a seed is a fruit. Vegetables are other edible plant parts, such as their leaves, roots and stems. Children compare the shop-bought fruits with the ones found in the woodland.

What conditions do acorns and conkers require to grow?

Acorns and conkers are easy to grow if treated in the correct way. The best nuts to plant are those which have recently fallen from their parent tree and have not had time to dry out. A good test is to place them in a jar of water. Healthy nuts will sink to the bottom, while dried out ones will float. To make the nuts germinate, children need to reconstruct the conditions that suit the seeds in the wild. Both types of trees are adapted to cold winters and warm springs and summers. Children in the UK can reproduce these conditions both naturally and artificially.

Plant the nuts outside before the end of November. Plant them about 2 cm deep, in pots filled with potting compost. Water the compost so that it is damp, and place pots in the school garden where they will be exposed to rain and cold throughout the winter months. Stand the pots on bricks so that excess water can drain away. By mid to late spring the plants should have germinated and can be potted on into larger pots, where there is room to grow into saplings. Children compare their saplings with mature trees. How are the offspring similar to their parents? Are there any differences?

With climate change, winters in the UK are becoming increasingly unpredictable, so children may want to help 'fix' the conditions which suit the acorns and conkers. They can do this by putting the nuts in a refrigerator for two or three months before planting them out in pots in the spring. Wipe them with paper towels to make sure they are dry, and put them in sealed plastic bags or containers before placing them in the cool part of the fridge. In early spring sow the seeds in pots and germinate on a classroom window sill or outside in the garden.

Compare the growth of the plants grown in natural conditions with those grown artificially. Talk about how different types of plants are suited (adapted) to particular conditions. If the conditions change, then the plants struggle to grow. Children can plant acorns and conkers in conditions which do not suit them, to see if they grow. For example, they could plant some nuts in pots in November and leave them near a radiator throughout the winter. It will be interesting to see if the seeds will germinate in these warmer conditions.

Children choose a healthy sapling to plant out in the school grounds. They can give their sapling a name, similar to how they would name a pet. They look after the tree and monitor its growth for the next few years, knowing it will still be growing by the time they have their own children. Children report their findings in the form of a science magazine article or blog entitled 'Do acorns and conkers need a helping hand?'

Design a plant with very unusual fruits

Ask children to imagine they are plant scientists who explore the world in search of new types of plants. On an expedition deep into the Amazon rainforest, they find an unknown plant with very unusual fruits. The plant grows along the banks of a fast flowing river. The challenge is to design the plant and give it a name. The design includes a drawing of the structure of the plant and its fruit. Working in groups children try out different ideas until they agree on a design. They then make a model of the fruit and use it to explain how the plant's seeds are dispersed. Ask them to provide reasons for their designs, and challenge them to think of other ways plants along the river could disperse their seeds. Ask them to talk about why plants produce lots of seeds and then disperse them. Use outcomes of the design challenge to assess children's progress towards the learning goals.

Working on scientific understanding

In this part, children work on their understanding of the nature of seeds and how they germinate to produce offspring.

Things to talk about

Focus children's attention on the nature of seeds. Encourage them to visualise a seed as a capsule which contains food and a tiny plant (embryo) waiting for the right conditions to grow. Talk about how the embryo requires water and the right temperature to germinate. The seed contains enough food for the embryo to produce a young seedling, with a stem, leaves and root. Ask children to speculate about what happens next. How does the seedling grow into a mature plant? Respond to their ideas, and talk about how the seedling uses air, light and water and nutrients from the ground to produce its own food, which it uses to grow into a mature plant. Refer to Chapter 4, if children need to learn about the conditions plants need to grow.

Talk about how mature plants produce flowers, which in turn produce seeds which are dispersed when the cycle starts again. Show children a BBC video clip of the life cycle of a plant and discuss the different stages. Encourage children to talk in detail about the life cycles of oak and horse chestnut trees. Focus talk on whether seeds are living or non-living. Listen and discuss children's ideas.

Talking points: true false or not sure?

- Living things move, so seeds must be dead.
- Seeds are not dead because they have never lived.

- Seeds are best described as non-living things.
- Seeds are dead but they become alive when planted in soil.
- Living things grow, so seeds are dead until they start to grow.
- Inside the seed there is a tiny plant which is alive.
- Seeds are dormant, which is not the same thing as dead.

Children work collaboratively in groups to respond to the talking points. Each group presents and justifies their ideas to the rest of the class. Focus the discussion on the meaning of dead, as opposed to non-living or never lived. Can dead things come back to life? What is the difference between something being dead or dormant? Talk about how there is a tiny living plant inside the seed, just waiting for the right conditions to grow.

What are the best conditions for germination?

Children germinate a number of large seeds such as beans and peas on damp cotton wool. At different times they dissect the seeds to see how the embryo grows into a seedling. Explain how the tiny plant inside the seed needs water and how it uses the food stored inside the seed to grow. Use the term 'germination'. Children devise their own tests to discover the best temperature conditions to germinate the beans and peas.

The world's best flier

The humble dandelion is one of the most successful plants found in our gardens. If we are not vigilant, then it will establish its offspring all over the garden. We find it growing in lawns, flower beds, vegetable patches and even cracks in the paths. Left alone, it would take much of the space intended for the plants we want to grow. So why is it so successful at reproducing that it can be found in practically every garden in the UK?

Dandelions are able to spread so easily because their seeds use an extremely efficient form of flight. The fruits have parachute-shaped bristles, enabling them to travel distances of 1 km or more propelled by the wind. Scientists believe the dandelion seeds have a claim to be one of the natural world's best fliers.

Children use magnifiers to investigate the structure of the dandelion seed and design tests to discover how far they can fly in the school grounds. Groups make their own working models of a seed that is propelled by the wind. They can test their models in different wind conditions using a multi-speed fan. How do their models compare with the real thing?

Things to talk about

Talk about the advantages of producing seeds which are able to travel long distances. Ask children to speculate about what will happen to most of the dandelion seeds. Talk about how seeds need space to germinate and grow and water, light and nutrients to develop into healthy plants. They need to compete with other plants for these resources, and by spreading their seeds over a large area it is likely some of them will find suitable places to grow. As with all living things, plants compete which each other to survive. If they are successful they will live and reproduce, if not they will die. The flying ability of the dandelion's fruits make them well suited to urban environments.

Plants grow in unusual places

Ask the children to describe the most unusual places they have found plants growing. It may be a crack in a pavement or perhaps on a decaying piece of wood. Take them out to search for weeds which are growing around the school in unusual places. Ask children to speculate how they got there. Children take photographs to record their findings. Set children a homework to find plants growing in unusual places near their homes, and ask them to take photographs. Back in the classroom children use information sources to identify the plants and find out how their seeds are dispersed. Create a display entitled 'plants grow in the weirdest places'. Discuss children's findings and use their ideas to assess progress towards the learning goals.

Information sources

- A year in the life of a horse chestnut tree: www.woodlandtrust.org.uk/visiting-woods/trees-woods-and-wildlife/british-trees/common-non-native-trees/horse-chestnut/
- Dandelion seeds: www.bbc.com/bitesize/clips/zs9c87h
- Horse chestnut tree: www.countryliving.com/uk/homes-interiors/gardens/a657/fact-file-horse-chestnut-tree/
- How plants produce seeds: www.bbc.com/bitesize/clips/zfx76sg
- Nuts and seeds: www.woodlandtrust.org.uk/blog/2017/07/difference-between-nuts-and-seeds/
- Root and shoot growth www.bbc.com/bitesize/clips/zb4rkqt
- Seed dispersal: www.bbc.com/bitesize/clips/znvfb9q
- The life cycle of a dandelion: www.bbc.com/bitesize/clips/zs9c87h
- What are stages of a plant's life cycle? www.bbc.com/bitesize/articles/zyv3jty
- What is the life cycle of a plant? www.bbc.com/bitesize/articles/z2vdjxs
- Wildlife reserve near you. www.wildlifetrusts.org/nature-reserves

Chapter 6 Inheritance

The bigger picture

In this part, children explore the symbiotic relationships flowering plants have with their pollinators and come to understand pollination as a key part of the process through which flowering plants produce their offspring.

Things to talk about

Start by describing spring as the time when plants produce many of their flowers and when bees, butterflies and other insects are out feeding on the flowers. Talk about how flowering plants reproduce sexually, which involves transferring pollen from the male part of a plant onto the female part of another plant. This process is called pollination and is carried out with the help of animals such as bees and butterflies or with the help of the wind. As a result of pollination the flower wilts and seeds are formed which are capable of producing new plants (offspring).

Using magnifiers, groups explore flowers with large reproductive parts such as tulips, daffodils and gladioli to discover the male and female parts. Ask children to speculate about why bees and other insects are attracted to flowers, and how they manage to transfer pollen from the male anthers to the female stigma. Children should wear protective gloves and aprons when handling the flowers. Avoid using plants which may release large amounts of pollen, and safeguard children with allergies.

Spring flower safari

Take children back to the places they visited on their autumn safari to see how they have changed. Take photographs of any trees with catkins such as oak, birch, hazel and pussy (grey and goat) willow. Children use magnifiers to explore the structure of the catkins. Talk about how trees with catkins mainly depend on the wind for pollination. Safeguard children with allergies.

In May, the horse chestnut trees will be flowering in the park. Children look out for their magnificent pink and white flowers. Set up areas where children can sit down, and with the help of magnifiers, sketch some of the flowers on the trees. They can also take photographs. Encourage groups to search areas around the trees to discover seedlings which have recently germinated from last autumn's conkers.

Assign different areas of the park or woodland to different supervised groups, and ask them to survey the variety of flowering plants and insects visiting the flowers. Use a wildlife identification app on a tablet or mobile to help identify the various types of plants and insects. Do not forget the wildflowers, including weeds. Many parks let designated areas grow wild to encourage wildflowers to flourish. Look out for bluebells, early purple orchids, wood anemones, common dog violets, red campions, wood sorrel, garlic  mustard, lords and ladies, yellow archangel and the stunning white flowers of the wild garlic. Groups sit quietly close to drifts of flowers and take note of all the 'visitors', especially butterflies and bees.

Children's drawings

Children use magnifiers to look inside the different types of flowers. Do all the flowers have the same basic structure? How do they differ? How do the catkins differ from the other flowers? Each child chooses a flower and creates a line drawing of its structure, including all the internal parts they can see with their magnifiers. Help children to identify the pollen-coated anthers and the stigma. Safeguard children with allergies.

Things to talk about

Back in the classroom, listen to children's stories about what they learnt from the safari. Encourage them to describe the insects which were visiting the flowers. Talk about how these plants entice bees and other pollinators to climb inside their flowers with the offer of a meal of nectar and pollen. In the case of the bees, to reach the nectar they have to push past the male anthers of the flower, collecting pollen as they go. Off they fly to another flower and pollinate it by rubbing against the female stigma, coating it with the sticky pollen. When the pollen lands on the stigma, it grows a tube down the style to fertilise the seeds, which are then capable of growing into new plants.

Talk about the plants that are wind-pollinated, such as the grasses and trees with catkins such as oak, birch, hazel and pussy (grey and goat) willow. These plants do not need to attract pollinators and hence their flowers can often be small and seem insignificant. They may not be pleasing on the eye, but when it comes to the process of pollination they are perfectly suited to the job which they have evolved to do. The anthers and feathery stigmas of wind-pollinated flowers hang outside the flower. This allows the wind to blow pollen from the anther and puts the stigma in a position to catch the pollen that is carried by the air. Use drawings and photographs from the safari, along with video clips from the web, to illustrate the different ways flowering plants are pollinated. Explain how the pollen is used to create a fertile seed. After a flower is fertilised, it produces fruits which contain seeds for the next generation of plants. Remind children about the various types of fruits and the different ways seeds are distributed.

Design your own flower

Ask children to imagine they are big, hairy, long-tongued bumblebees looking for a meal. What sort of plants would they be attracted to? Does it help to have a long tongue? Remind them of the problems their size may cause when trying to get nectar out of a flower. Also point out that bees cannot see the colour red, so they need to bear that in mind when designing their flower. Working in groups, children design and make 3D models of a flower especially designed to attract bumblebees. They make scale models of bumblebees out of modelling material to demonstrate how the bees will access the nectar and pollinate the plant. Children compare their design with flowers known to attract bumblebees. There are lots of examples on the web. Children present and justify their designs to the rest of the class. Probe their understanding of pollination and assess their progress towards the learning goals.

Story-telling: the life cycle of the bumblebee

Bumblebees are social insects. They live in a colony with one queen and her female workers, who all happen to be her daughters. Bumblebee colonies do not normally survive the British winter. Each year a new colony is formed by a queen which has mated in the summer and has hibernated throughout the winter. Starting a new colony is fraught with danger, and many queens do not survive long enough to produce any offspring.

Children use information sources to help tell the story of the life cycle of the bumblebee. Like much of our wildlife, bumblebees are struggling to survive due to loss of habitat. Encourage children to find out why bumblebee populations are on the decline and to feature their struggle for survival as part of their narrative. Children first present their story in poster form, with illustrations taken from the web. They can later use the ideas, and their imaginations, to craft a short story about the perils faced by a queen bee. Encourage them to write their stories from the bee's point of view.

Visit to a wildflower meadow

Wildflower meadows contain native grasses and wildflowers, which provide habitats for a wide variety of insects, birds and other animals. Bees and butterflies are attracted by the open nature of the wildflowers, which makes it easy for them to access the nectar and pollen. Visit your local Wildlife Trust website to discover the reserves near you where wildflowers grow. The best time to visit is often in late May and early June, although wildflowers can be found right through the summer. Download information about the reserve and discuss with the children which flowers, butterflies and bees they are likely to see. Talk about how the grasses are wind-pollinated.

In preparation for their visit, groups use information sources to create their own field notebooks with pictures and information about the different types of flowers, grasses, butterflies

and bees which they expect to see. They should also leave room to record the variety of birds, insects and other animals which share the habitat. Children use their notebooks to help audit the diversity of the flora and fauna in the meadow. Take magnifiers and cameras for children to observe and record the wildflowers and other wildlife. They can make sketches of the grasses and flowers, with close attention to their reproductive parts.

Floral formulae

To encourage close observation of the wildflowers, children can create a floral formula for each kind of plant. By counting the sepals (S), petals (P), anthers (A) and carpels (C) they can make up a floral formula such as S3 P6 A12 C1. Children use their formulae to compare the different types of flowers. Creating a formula for some flowers can be challenging because of the large number of parts. In this case encourage children to make approximations. If need be, use a smartphone wildflower identification app to help children identify and analyse the flowers. Creating plant formulae helps to focus children's attention on the 'real' structure of flowers. The standardised image of a flower with one central carpel, surrounded by stamens can, in some cases, be misleading. Some flowers have multiple carpels, and others consist of clusters of small flowers appearing as a single bloom.

Botanical art

Back in the classroom children use their photographs and drawings to create botanical illustrations of their favourite wildflowers. Explain that botanical paintings are not diagrams; they are works of art which faithfully capture the colours and form of a plant. Use images from the Kew collection to illustrate the scientific and aesthetic nature of botanical art.

Set up the classroom as an art gallery to display the children's illustrations. Ask them to explain the purpose of each part of the flower. Use the activity to assess their progress towards the learning goals. Use colour copies of children's paintings to publish a book on local wildflowers.

Information sources

- Bee facts: www.woodlandtrust.org.uk/naturedetectives/blogs/nature-detectives-blog/2018/03/bee-facts-for-kids/
- Buglife: www.buglife.org.uk/activities-for-you/children-and-schools
- Bumblebee nests: www.bumblebeeconservation.org/bumblebee-nests/
- Grow wild: www.growwilduk.com/
- How do flowering plants reproduce? www.bbc.com/bitesize/articles/zqbcxfr
- Kew collection of botanical art: https://prints.kew.org/collections
- Lifecycle of bumblebee: www.bumblebeeconservation.org/lifecycle/
- Pollinator identification chart: www.buglife.org.uk/sites/default/files/Pollinator%20identification%20chart.pdf
- School activities: www.bumblebeeconservation.org/fun-and-learning/activity-sheets/
- Solitary bees: www.growwilduk.com/wildflowers/bees-pollinators/take-crash-course-solitary-bees
- Why are bees attracted to flowers? www.bbc.com/bitesize/articles/zx4ktv4
- www.buzzaboutbees.net/bee-life-cycle.html

Topic: Inheritance and evolution

Age group: 9–11 years

Learning goals

Children make progress towards the big idea by exploring how plants produce offspring either sexually or asexually, and they come to recognise how plants change over time. Initially, children work on their understanding of how new varieties of tulips have been developed by artificially cross-pollinating selected plants with desirable features. By exploring how new varieties of tulips are produced, children can begin to understand how offspring inherit physical characteristics and why they are not identical to their parents. To help see the bigger picture, children build on their understanding of inheritance to explore how the small differences that occur during reproduction may lead to evolution.

Working scientifically

In this topic children will:

- plan scientific enquiries to answer questions;
- collect data to answer their questions;

- take accurate measurements using scientific equipment;
- make and test predictions based on scientific theories;
- report and present findings from enquiries, including conclusions in oral and written forms.

Health and safety

Regard all plants, seeds and bulbs to be hazardous. As a general rule, children should be warned not to touch plants growing in green areas unless given permission by a supervising adult. Children should wear protective gloves when handling tulips and other types of bulbs as they can have irritants. Stress safety, hygiene and the protection of the environment. When planning to teach the activities in this topic refer to the relevant safety codes in the ASE publication *Be Safe!* (2011).

Exploring children's ideas

Tulips are popular bulbs and grown in gardens in many parts of the world. There are over 3,000 varieties, which are divided into 15 groups based on the flower type, size and blooming period for the tulip. Tulips are easy to grow and come in so many different colours. They can be planted in autumn to create a diverse range of colour around the school in spring. Children can explore first-hand the variation in the blooms from different tulips.

Ask children what they know about tulips. How are they grown and what do they look like? Can they think of a word which best describes the shape of a tulip flower?

How do tulips vary?

The tulip originates from Central Asia and first arrived in the Netherlands in the 16th century. It is from these wild Asian tulips that all the 3,000 commercial varieties have been artificially developed by plant breeders. Children use information sources to explore the different varieties of tulips. Using pictures from the web and other sources, they compare the wide variation in their blooms. Group the different varieties according to the shape of their flowers.

Children choose a range of varieties to plant out in the garden, using beds and containers. Grow some in pots so they can be brought into the classroom for children to study in spring. There is information about growing tulips on the RHS website.

What are the best conditions for growing tulips?

Before planting out the bulbs, children raise questions to examine the conditions tulips need to grow. Remind them that plants need light, water and nutrients to grow strong and healthy. Focus their attention on the types of nutrients tulips need to grow healthy flowers. Groups research the best compost and organic fertilisers for growing tulips. They then plan investigations to find out how effective the fertilisers are by devising controlled experiments. When the tulips grow in spring children collect data to answer their questions.

Chapter 6 Inheritance

Are tulip bulbs just big seeds?

Children compare the structures of a tulip bulb and a broad bean. In advance, soak the beans in water to make them easier to dissect. Children should wear protective gloves and take care when handling and dissecting bulbs and seeds.

Things to consider:

- Similarities and differences of internal structures.
- Evidence of an embryo (baby plant).

Chapter 6 **Inheritance**

- Evidence of any leaves or roots.
- Evidence of how a new plant would grow.
- Evidence of stored food for new plant to grow.

Children produce detailed drawings of their findings and draw pictures depicting how they imagine new plants would grow from both the bean and the bulb. What conclusions do they draw? Is a bulb just an oversized seed? If not, what is it? Remind them that seeds are produced by flowers. How are bulbs produced? Groups discuss these questions and use information sources to seek answers. Groups then come together to share their responses.

Things to talk about

Help children talk about and compare their seeds and bulbs. Inside the seed there is food and an embryo, which is a tiny undeveloped plant. In the right conditions the embryo is able to use the food to grow and develop. Once it has developed its first leaves and roots, it is able to produce its own food, which it can use to grow into a mature plant. Talk about what the children observed inside the bulb. Point out that inside a bulb is a fully formed plant, waiting to grow. The plant inside the bulb already has the parts it needs to grow into a mature plant; it is just waiting for the right growing conditions. Help children identify the modified leaves which store the food it needs, the central shoot with its leaves and flower bud, and the roots waiting to grow.

Art, history and science: tulip books

In the 17th century when Holland was in the grip of 'tulip mania', paintings of tulips were very popular, mainly because the real things were enormously expensive to buy. The extraordinary price of tulips meant most people could not afford to buy them, and the next best thing was to buy a painting or, better still, a book full of beautiful pictures.

Children use information sources to research the origins of the tulip and how greed led to 'tulip mania' in Holland in the 17th century. Working in groups children produce modern versions of the tulip books which were so popular in Holland, by creating their own paintings of the different types of tulips grown in the school garden. They paint the tulips in their own style or that of their favourite artist, but the main thing is to portray the elegance and beauty of these wonderful flowers and to illustrate their variety. Children can study the works of artists such as Judith Leyster, Paul Cézanne, Pierre Renoir, Claude Monet and modern-day artists who have been inspired by the tulip's beauty.

Information sources

- Heritage tulips project: https://dutchoils.com/dutch-heritage-tulip-paintings/
- Judith Leyster: https://mydailyartdisplay.wordpress.com/2013/12/03/judith-leyster-and-tulip-madness/
- Tulip types: www.gardenia.net/plant-variety/tulip-types

Working on scientific understanding

In this part, children work on their understanding of how different varieties of tulips have been developed by cross-pollinating selected plants with desirable features. By exploring how new varieties of tulips are produced, they can begin to understand how offspring inherit physical characteristics and why they are not identical to their parents.

Selective breeding

Talk with the children about the tulips they planted in the garden. How are they similar? How are they different? Talk about the colour and form of the flowers of each variety. Also compare the leaves. Compare the tulips with other flowering plants in the garden. Discuss how many of the plants we grow in our gardens have not evolved naturally, and how many of the different varieties have been produced by artificial means through selective breeding. Use ideas from Part 1 to explain how gardeners select plants with desirable traits and cross-pollinate them to produce hybrids which inherit those traits.

Discuss how flowering plants rely on pollination to reproduce; this involves the pollen from the male part of one parent plant being transferred onto the female part of the second parent plant. The offspring of cross-pollinated plants inherit characteristics from both their parents; this has enabled plant breeders to develop the huge variety of tulips which are available today. More about selective breeding can be found in Chapter 7.

Design a new tulip variety

There is a lot of information on the web about plant breeding. Groups can research how different varieties of flowering plants are produced by crossing parent plants to produce hybrids with desirable features. Tell them the story of how tulip growers for centuries searched for the elusive black tulip. Since the 16th century, growers have tried to cultivate a black tulip, and until this day they have not succeeded. The darkest tulip was cultivated at the end of the 20th century and goes by the name of the *Paul Scherer*. Although sometimes described as a black tulip, the colour is most accurately described as a very dark purple. The search for the Holy Grail of tulips continues!

Challenge children to design a new variety of tulip. It must be realistic and based on existing varieties which can be found on the web. They start by drawing pictures of their ideal tulip, including colour, size and shape of the petals, as well as the structure of the flower. They can search the web for the two most suitable parents to produce their ideal tulip. The final drawing of the offspring must be based on a combination of characteristics of the parents. Groups explain and justify their choice of parents and the structure of their ideal tulip variety to the class. Use the activity to assess children's progress towards the learning goals.

How do heirloom tulips compare with hybrids?

Heirloom tulips are plants which occur naturally in the wild, and they are described as the uncut diamonds of tulips. They can also be referred to as heritage or species tulips. Heirloom tulips are the uncultivated descendants of tulips which evolved naturally in their native habitats in Europe, Asia and Africa. Compared to the modern-day hybrids, heirloom tulips are mostly small, some tiny, yet have a raw beauty and can be relied on to return each year and to produce offspring. Hybrids are more flashy, but not so reliable. Children use information sources to research the different heirloom tulips and compare them with ones that have been hybridised. Groups share their findings with the rest of the class. Talk about the extent to which selective breeding has changed the tulip. Discuss the advantages and disadvantages of planting heirloom tulips.

Growing heirloom tulips

Groups can grow heirloom tulips in appropriately prepared beds, lawns or containers which can be left to perform year after year. In the right growing conditions, heirloom tulips flower each year and provide an ever-increasing number of offspring which children can enjoy and study for some years to come. Use information sources to choose and learn how to grow heirloom tulips.

Exploring asexual reproduction

Although tulips can reproduce by producing seeds, they also reproduce by producing bulblets which develop underground. After flowering, tulips store food in their bulbs for the next year's growth. The parent bulb also produces bulblets, which normally take two years to develop before the offspring are ready to flower. Children can research how plants that are grown from bulbs reproduce asexually without the need for pollination. In early autumn, children can carefully dig up bulbs around the school to see which have formed bulblets. They can also grow different types of bulbs in pots and monitor their progress periodically over the year to discover how they grow and how they reproduce by forming bulblets. Be careful to choose non-hybridized bulbs which are able to reproduce.

Plants can also reproduce asexually from cuttings, which involves removing parts of the plant and growing them in suitable conditions. Cuttings are normally taken from non-flowering shoots, which can be grown in pots until they form roots and are ready to be planted out. It is often advisable to propagate hybridised plants from cuttings, as the offspring are more true to the parent than from seed. Common garden plants which are suitable to propagate from cuttings include penstemon and verbena. Purchase healthy plants from your local nursery, and take cuttings in spring and early summer. Compare offspring with their parent plant. Visit the RHS website for information about other ways plants can be reproduced asexually.

Chapter 6 Inheritance

Information sources

- Taking cuttings: https://schoolgardening.rhs.org.uk/resources/sequence-card/how-to-take-semi-ripe-cuttings
- The black tulip: www.amsterdamtulipmuseum.com/en/faq/tulips/do-black-tulips-exist/
- www.bulbs4u.co.uk/product/heritage-tulip-absalon-1780/

The bigger picture

Evolution is the scientific theory of how living things gradually change and develop over time to produce new species. Like all living things, evolution in plants is largely driven by natural selection, whereby the plants best suited to survive in their environment pass their useful traits to the next generation. Today, there are about 375,000 known species of plants worldwide, all of which are uniquely suited to the environment in which they live. In this part, children build on their understanding of inheritance to explore how the small differences that occur during reproduction may lead to evolution.

Things to talk about

The selective breeding or hybridisation of tulips and other plants are examples of artificial selection, which is the process by which people intervene in the evolution of certain plants and animals. Point out that natural selection is nature's unplanned way of creating new varieties and species of plants and animals. Use ideas from Part 1 to talk about how small differences which occur during reproduction may lead to evolution by natural selection. Speculate about how plants may evolve longer roots. Children use information sources to explore desert plants which have evolved vast root systems to help them survive. Groups can also explore other characteristics of desert plants which enable them to survive.

Copycats: an evolution game

Divide the class into two large groups, A and B, with up to 16 children in each group. Give members of each group a piece of drawing paper with a number on it from 1–16. Explain that you are going to give the first member of each group a simple line drawing of a flowering plant, and you want them to copy it as accurately as possible. They will only have two minutes. The children then pass on their copy to the next child who will have 2 minutes to copy it, and so on. The copying continues until everyone in the group has had a turn. When they have finished, collect all the numbered copies and compare the final copies with the originals. How do the final copies vary from the originals? What are the main differences? How do the final copies of the two groups vary? (Copycats is based on a similar activity which can be found on the SAPS website).

Use the copycat drawings as an analogy to explain how plants can evolve. Talk about how every time plants reproduce, their offspring are slightly different. Over many generations the plants may change so much they become a new kind of plant, therefore increasing the diversity of the plant kingdom. Diversity means that plants are able to thrive in the many varied environments of the world. Working in groups, children use information sources to discover the plants which have evolved in deserts, mountains, rivers, rain forests, oceans, the tundra and the Antarctic regions.

Chapter 6 Inheritance

Each group presents their findings to the rest of the class. Encourage groups to talk about how the plants they researched are adapted to suit their environments. Discuss how adaptation to different environments has led to the evolution of the great diversity of plants which populate all corners of the earth.

Rooting out the weeds

Use weeding activities in the school garden as opportunities for children to compare the root systems of different kinds of plants, including grasses. Which kinds of weeds have long, thick taproots, and which have short, thin fibrous ones. How do roots differ amongst the same kinds of plants? Compare the roots of plants growing in different parts of the garden. Collect and display the different types of weeds.

Talking points: true, false or not sure?

- Plants inherit their root structure.
- The root structure depends on the soil in which the plant grows.
- The root structure depends on the size of the plant.
- The root structure depends on the climate in which the plant grows.

Working in groups, children try to reach agreement on their responses to the talking points. Then, as a whole-class activity, groups compare their responses and share their reasoning. Probe children's thinking and assess their progress towards the learning goals.

Botanical art: Venus flytrap

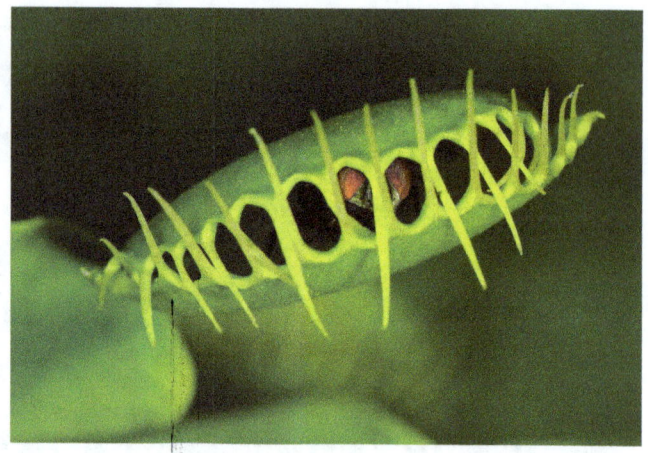

Charles Darwin was fascinated by the way different plants evolved to suit the environments in which they live. He was especially fascinated by carnivorous or insectivorous plants, as he called them. Chapter 7 describes the correspondence Darwin had with an American scientist called Mary Treat concerning the experiments he did with insect-eating plants.

Venus flytrap and other carnivorous plants can be purchased from plant nurseries. Talk about how they naturally grow in wet, sandy soil which lacks the nutrients the plants need to grow strong and healthy. To acquire the nutrients they need, carnivorous plants trap and digest insects. Children use pencil and watercolour to create accurate, botanical illustrations of the carnivorous plants. Display the artwork, and talk about the features of each of the plants which enable them to survive in their environment. Children use information sources to find out how they reproduce, and speculate about how they might evolve in the future if insects become scarce. Use this activity to help assess children's learning towards the learning goals.

Population survey of British wildflowers

Wildflowers are normally found growing in meadows, woodlands, hedgerows and other areas undisturbed by human activity. Wildflowers are uncultivated plants which have naturally evolved to suit the places where they grow. For example, bluebells are suited to living in woodland because they grow and flower in early spring. This enables them to take advantage of the spring rain and sunshine to reproduce before the trees produce their leaves and block out much of the sun's light.

Wildflowers are often herbaceous plants, meaning that once they have flowered and shed their seeds, the stem withers, falls off and rots into the ground. In order to produce the next generation, annual wildflowers produce large amounts of seeds which survive in the soil until the conditions are right for germination. Contact your local Wildlife Trust, Woodland Trust, National Trust, Plant Life or other conservation organisation to find out where wildflowers grow naturally in your area. Habitats vary from marshy pasture and mountain landscape to traditional wildflower meadows.

In late spring or summer, organise a trip to a wildflower area so children can record the diversity of wildflowers. Children record the different types of plants and compare their size, flowers structures and colours. Focus their attention on competition. What resources are the plants competing for? Children carry out a population survey by counting the different types of wildflowers in a measured area. Different groups can survey different areas. Which types of wildflowers are the most successful? Are there any common characteristics amongst the most successful plants? Which are the most common pollinators? Are the same pollinators attracted to all the flowers, or are some flowers more popular than others? Which flower colours do pollinators like best? Does the structure of the flower influence which pollinators it attracts?

Back in the classroom, display and discuss the outcomes of the enquiry. What conclusions can children draw from their surveys? Talk about the physical traits inherited by the wildflowers which make them suited to their environment. Did children discover any individual differences between the same kinds of plants?

Children use information sources to discover more about the different types of wildflowers they recorded. They explore the structure and life cycles of each of the plants and find out how they are adapted to the area in which they live. Using photographs from their fieldwork, groups report their findings in the form of a blog which can be published on the school's social media platform.

The Great British Wildflower Hunt (GBWH)

Join in on the *Great British Wildflower Hunt* and help Plantlife in their quest to protect the wildflowers that light up our towns and countryside. Plantlife provide spotter sheets to help children identify wildflowers around the town, in woods and in the countryside. To take part, sign up on their website and download all the resources.

Plantlife are keen to help primary schools improve children's knowledge of the 'nature on their doorstep'. To do this they provide a wide range of support, including:

- providing resources for teachers and education professionals;
- delivering workshops in schools;
- delivering training workshops for teachers and other education professionals.

Have children visit the Plantlife website to see what they can do to support science education in your school. Bringing in experts will help foster respect for science and interest in the activities.

Growing wildflowers

Children can grow wildflower plants from seeds in the school garden. There is a wide range of seed mixes commercially available to suit different areas in the garden. For example, there are woodland mixes which can be grown under trees, and meadow or field flowers which can be grown in sunny areas of the garden. You can buy mixtures of wildflower seeds which have been selected to attract pollinators. The Royal Botanical Gardens website 'Grow wild' is a good source of information for growing wildflowers. Make sure the conditions of the soil are right for the seeds you want to grow.

How do wildflowers respond to conditions which do not suit them?

Wildflowers are naturally adapted to living in environments which suit them. Some grow best in shady woodland, while others thrive in open meadows where they can soak up the direct sun.

In this investigation children grow wildflowers in conditions which do not suit them, and compare their growth with those grown in more favourable conditions. For example, some groups can grow woodland seeds in both shady and sunny conditions, while other groups grow meadow seeds in both the shade and the sun. All other growing conditions should be controlled by following the instructions on the seed package. Encourage children to make and justify predictions about the effects the different conditions are likely to have on the growth of the seeds. Compare rates of growth, size, population density and number of flowers. Are there any kinds of wildflowers which grow well in both shade and sun? Children draw conclusions and speculate about the features of individual plants which may affect their growth in different conditions.

Competition for space to grow

Children plan investigations to explore the influence competition for space has on the growth of wildflowers. How much space do wildflowers need to grow well? Can they thrive with very limited space, or do they need room to grow? Children plan their own investigations, which involve sowing seed mixes ever more densely in controlled conditions. Use the recommended sowing rate as a control and sow some areas more sparsely and others more densely. While planning the enquiry, encourage children to speculate about the outcomes. Ask them to justify their ideas. Children can compare the results of the experiments with their predictions. Compare the plants which grow most vigorously with those that seem to struggle, and draw conclusions for reasons why.

Based on the results of the two wildflower enquiries, can children find any evidence to support the theory that offspring which inherit traits which are most suited to their environment are the ones which are most likely to survive? Publish the outcomes of their enquiries in the school science magazine. Use the enquiries to assess children progress towards the learning goals.

Information sources

- Grow wild: www.growwilduk.com/
- Growing wildflowers: www.growwilduk.com/wildflowers/how-grow-wildflowersSpotter sheets: www.plantlife.org.uk/uk/discover-wild-plants-nature/spotter-sheets
- School Resources: www.plantlife.org.uk/uk/discover-wild-plants-nature/learning-and-volunteering/schools
- The Great British Wildflower Hunt: www.plantlife.org.uk/wildflowerhunt/
- Wildflowers: www.growwilduk.com/wildflowers/learn-about-wildflowers/whats-wildflower

Further reading

Books

- Cubey, J. (2019) *RHS Plant Finder 2019*, Woking: RHS Publications.
- Fiona Waters, F. and Preston-Gannon, F. (2018) *I Am the Seed That Grew the Tree: A Nature Poem for Every Day of the Year*, London: National Trust.
- Watts, A. (2011) *Every Nursery Needs a Garden*, Abingdon: Routledge.

ASE journals

- Primary Science 122 (March–April 2012) *Visit a Farm? Surely Not!* By Bill Graham.
- Primary Science 126 (January–February 2013) *Something Beginning with B . . .* by Chris Deaves.
- Primary Science 134 (September–October 2014) *Research into Inheritance and Evolution* (with Dr Who's help!) by Terry Russel and Linda McGuigan.
- Primary Science 137 (March–April 2015) *Why Clone a Sheep When They All Look the Same Anyway?* By Terry Russell and Linda McGuigan.
- Primary Science 138 (May–June 2015) *Effective Strategies for Teaching Evolution: The Primary Evolution Project* by Chris Hatcher.
- Primary Science 144 (September–October 2016) *Teaching Science Down on the Farm* by Debbie Hicks.

Chapter 6 Inheritance

Lady Fern   Stork's Bill   Foxglove   Groundsel
Buttercup   Garlic Mustard   Dyer's Greenweed
Cuckoo Flower   Thrift   Marsh Hair Moss   Ivy
Lesser Celandine   Yorkshire Fog   Wood Anemone
Creeping Jenny   Common Ragwort   Hemlock
Cow Parsley   Bluebell   Wood Sorrel   Timothy
Perennial Rye   Viper's Bugloss   Marsh Violet
Campion   Shepherd's Purse   Yellow Rattle
Cornflower   Common Mallow   Plantain   Bugle
Cowslip   Harebell   Germander Speedwell
Devil's Bit Scabious   Quaking Grass   Bracken
Meadow Saffron   Crested Dog's Tail   Vetch
Maidenhair Spleenwort   Adder's Tongue
Creeping bent   Meadow Crane's bill   Poppy
Common Mouse-ear   Stitchwort   Wavy Hair Grass
Deadly Nightshade   White Bryony   Coltsfoot
Cotton Grass   Traveller's Joy   Forget-me-not
Snowdrop   Primrose   Oxeye Daisy   Ragwort

Chapter 6 Inheritance

Birch Willow Sycamore Hornbeam
Crab Apple Douglas Fir Blackthorn
Beech Sweet Chestnut Norway Spruce
Aspen Laburnum Copper Beech Elm
Walnut Hawthorn Cedar of Lebanon Oak
Bird Cherry Whitebeam Maple Hazel
Plymouth Pear Horse Chestnut Holm Oak
Scots Pine London Plane European Larch
Conifer Lime Holly Hardwood
Poplar Evergreen Rowan Juniper
Yew Lawson Cypress Alder Ash
Stone Pine Softwood Sessile Oak
Field Elm Midland Hawthorn Wild Cherry
Black Walnut Holm Oak Field Maple
Huntingdon Elm Broadleaf Wych Elm
Deciduous Western Hemlock Apple

CHAPTER 7
FOLLOWING IN DARWIN'S FOOTSTEPS

Big idea: *An explanation is not a guess. Scientific explanations are subject to rigorous testing and supported with reliable evidence before they are trusted.*

Part 1: Subject knowledge

This part presents ideas about science which enable teachers to assist children when working towards understanding the big idea. The ideas presented go beyond the requirements of the National Curriculum, and hence provide teachers with levels of subject knowledge which enable them to meet the needs of children with different interests and abilities.

The topics include:

- Introduction
- Darwin the family man
- Darwin the gentleman scientist
- Darwin's theory of evolution
- Jean-Baptiste Lamarck's theory of evolution
- Darwin's correspondents
- Darwin's scientific women

Part 2: Working towards the big idea

Each topic aims to move children's understanding further towards the big idea. The journey starts when children begin to find things out about the natural world by asking questions and doing something to discover the answers. By following in Darwin's footsteps, children engage with the collaborative nature of science and learn that a scientific explanation requires evidence to back it up. By engaging with Darwin's science, children learn to appreciate the value of rigorous testing, so that the evidence produced to support a theory is reliable.

> ### The topics are:
> - Finding things out (5–7 years)
> - Scientific explanations (7–9 years)
> - Darwin's science (9–11 years)

Part 1: Subject knowledge

Introduction

Darwin was a great scientist who spent his life striving to explain and understand the rich diversity of animals and plants that live on the earth. By studying his work children learn about the collaborative and rigorous nature of his science. Children also learn how science is based on the assumption that there are reasons (causes) for why things happen in the natural world, which can be discovered through scientific ways of thinking and working.

Darwin the family man

Darwin was born in 1809, into a middle-class and privileged family. His father was a doctor, and his mother was the daughter of Josiah Wedgwood, the founder of the famous pottery company. His mother died when Darwin was only 8 years old. His grandfather Erasmus was a surgeon and a well-known naturalist and poet. Erasmus was a radical thinker, who published his own ideas on evolution at the end of the 18th century, years before Darwin was born. His grandfather's ideas about evolution were criticised by Darwin as being too vague and having little or no scientific facts to back up the arguments.

At the end of January 1839 Darwin married his cousin Emma Wedgwood, and over the years they had 10 children. As with many families of the time, not all the children survived into adulthood. Anne died when she was 10 years old, Mary only lived for a few weeks and Charles was just 2 years old when he died. Whenever his children were ill, Darwin refused to work and devoted himself to their welfare.

Family life was very important to Darwin. Like most parents he enjoyed his family and had strong relationships with his children. As a gentleman scientist he worked from home. His wife, children and servants all contributed in their own ways to his research and writing. When they were young, Darwin observed the development of his children as part of his research into the expression of emotions in humans and animals. Darwin recorded his son William's development from the day he was born in December 1839 until the autumn of 1844. He also recorded the development of his daughters Anne and Henrietta but in less detail. He recorded all types of behaviours including the onset of frowning and smiling and how they used their eyes to express their emotions. In later years Emma took over the observations focussing on the children's development of logical thought and language. More about Darwin's relationship with his wife and children can be found on the *Darwin Project* website.

Darwin the gentleman scientist

As mentioned earlier, Darwin could be described as a gentleman scientist. By the 1840s, collecting and recording plants and animals was popular amongst wealthy middle-class gentlemen, who had the resources and time to devote themselves to science. Darwin was himself a great collector. As a schoolboy he collected insects and shells, and during his time at Cambridge University, when he wasn't drinking, playing cards or shooting, he collected beetles. He was elated to have an illustration of a rare beetle he discovered published in a catalogue of British insects. His interest in beetles led him to develop a wider interest in studying nature and to develop a friendship with John Henslow, a professor of botany at Cambridge. It was due to his friendship with Professor Henslow that Darwin was invited to join the expedition to South America aboard the *Beagle*.

The idea that living things evolved over time was not a new idea when Darwin set out on his voyage aboard the *Beagle* in 1831. Many scientists of his time accepted that livings things had changed over time, as evidenced by the fossil remains of animals which existed long ago. The exotic animals and plants which Darwin discovered on the expedition served to persuade him that evolution must be the reason for the great diversity of living things on the planet. The thing he did not understand was why and how evolution came about. Finding evidence to explain the causes of evolution became his lifetime work. After more than 20 years of collecting evidence, Darwin finally published his famous book, *On the Origin of Species*, which explained all his ideas. The book meticulously lays out the argument and evidence for his theory of evolution by natural selection.

Darwin's theory of evolution

Even before Darwin's time, fossil hunting was very popular, and the fossils which collectors found provided clear evidence that animals and plants changed over time. Like his grandfather,

many naturalists before Darwin speculated about the causes of evolution. Do animals change over time due to the laws of nature, or was the nature of evolution more divine? Darwin was never convinced by the old arguments, dismissing them as too theoretical. They left him 'much disappointed, the proportion of speculation being so large to the given facts' (Boulter, 2008, p 5).

Experimentation was the tool with which Darwin constructed his science, which was built on sound evidential foundations to support his theories. He was always quick to criticise theories which he thought did not fit with available evidence, and he tore to pieces arguments that did not stand up to scrutiny. About a best-selling book called *Vestiges of the Natural History of Creation*, published in 1844, he wrote that the author's 'geology strikes me as bad and his zoology far worse'.

Darwin's great achievement was his theory of evolution by natural selection, which explains how living things gradually change over time to form new species. Darwin worked on his theory for over 20 years before he felt confident enough to publish it. He spent much of that time exploring how different plants and animals are adapted to their environments and the struggles they have to survive. He found that individuals within the same species show a wide range of physical traits, some of which are better suited to their environment than others are. Those better-suited individuals are more likely to survive and reproduce, hence are able to pass on their traits to the next generation. Through this process which Darwin called natural selection, survivors continue to develop the traits which enable them to survive; these can accumulate over many generations to the extent they become a new species.

Jean-Baptiste Lamarck's theory of evolution

Because of the greatness of Darwin's achievements, they can easily overshadow the important work done by other scientists of his time. For example, Jean-Baptiste Lamarck (1744–1829) devised a theory which explained how animals acquired certain characteristics. Lamarck proposed that the giraffe evolved from a creature with a shorter neck. He argued that through repeatedly stretching their necks to reach leaves higher up in the trees, giraffes are able to make their necks longer, and when they reproduce they pass on this neck-stretching ability to their offspring. Over generations, this neck stretching resulted in their necks getting progressively longer.

Although Lamarck's ideas were not correct, he had at least proposed a mechanism by which species could evolve. Darwin was not impressed, but Lamarck had provided a stepping stone in the search for a theory of evolution. Scientists do not work in isolation; they learn from and build on the work of previous generations. Criticism heaped on Lamarck and other scientists made Darwin determined to ensure that his arguments were seen to be backed up by reliable evidence, so that he could not be accused of too much speculation.

Darwin's correspondents

Darwin wrote to hundreds of correspondents, and his letters and notebooks show us how he worked. Many of his observations and experiments were carried out in his own garden and surrounding woodland. Darwin took long walks in the countryside where he could observe the local wildlife. His ways of working were similar to the way children perform investigations in school; they included observations, identification, recording, collecting, making comparisons, testing, reflective thinking and creative thinking.

Darwin wrote and received over 15,000 letters in his lifetime, corresponding with amateur and professional naturalists from Britain and around the world. Darwin used his correspondents to discuss ideas, gather information and send him specimens, all of which he used in developing and supporting his theories. From his correspondence it seems that Darwin was convinced of the theory of evolution by the time he returned home from his voyage on the *Beagle*. He spent most of the next 20 years collecting evidence to support his argument that evolution occurred through the process of natural selection. Although Darwin spent much of his time thinking and experimenting in his garden at home and corresponding with other scientists, he also spent time exchanging letters with gardeners and animal breeders to find out how desirable traits from selected individual plants and animals could be passed on to the next generation. He even bred his own pigeons in order to test his ideas. Darwin's knowledge of animal and plant breeding played an important part in shaping his thinking, and he used examples of pigeon breeding to demonstrate the feasibility of his theory about natural selection. Information about some of the most significant or well known of his correspondents can be found on the *Darwin Correspondence Project* website.

Darwin's scientific women

In Darwin's day, women did not have the same opportunities for education and employment as did men. On the whole, they were expected to become wives and mothers and run the family home. It was believed that women were poorly suited for education and not capable of working in demanding professions. Regardless, some highly motivated women managed to beat the odds and worked as doctors, explorers, political activists, writers and naturalists. One of these women was Lady Florence Dixie, who was a war correspondent and political activist. She was also a naturalist and wrote to Darwin about the animals she had observed on a trip to Patagonia.

Lady Florence wrote a utopian novel entitled *Gloriana*, in which a young girl dreams of the day women are no longer second-class citizens and are able to vote and have a career. She makes a vow to her mother that someday she will turn her dream into reality. Some years later, she starts a revolution to free women from oppression. The book espouses her belief that nature provides women with the same intellectual abilities as men, and it was only because men at the time deliberately set out to deny women an education that they were unable to take up the same careers. In the book she writes:

> Nature has unmistakeably given to woman a greater brain power. This is at once perceivable in childhood . . . Yet man deliberately sets himself to stunt that early evidence of mental capacity, by laying down the law that woman's education shall be on a lower level than that of man's . . . I maintain to honourable gentlemen that this procedure is arbitrary and cruel, and false to Nature.

Darwin wasn't concerned whether his correspondents were men or women, as long as he could trust their science. Darwin exchanged numerous letters with an American scientist called Mary Treat. Mary was an accomplished scientist who made her living by writing books and science articles for popular magazines. She also carried out experiments for leading scientists, including Darwin. He was clearly impressed by Mary's scientific ability, and publicly acknowledged and praised her work. After she sent him her observations on butterflies, he commented:

> Your observations and experiments on the sexes of butterflies are by far the best, as far as is known to me, which have ever been made.

Darwin encouraged Mary to publish her results in an academic journal. In reply, she pointed out that she did not have any income, other than what she could earn from publishing her work. Therefore, she had to publish her work in popular magazines which would pay for her articles. She wrote back to Darwin:

> You may wonder at my selecting a literary magazine rather than a scientific one, but I am wholly dependent on my own exertions and must go where they pay best.

Darwin, like other gentlemen scientists, was able to devote his time to science and did not need to worry about making a living. Most women in Darwin's time were wholly reliant on the wealth of their husbands, which made independent women scientists like Mary Treat all the more remarkable. She not only had to battle against the prevailing prejudice against women scientists, she also had to struggle to make a living.

Chapter 7 Following in Darwin's footsteps

The women who corresponded with Darwin provide fascinating insights into science, and also into the inequalities that existed in society at the time. Prejudices against women can still exist in science today, especially with regard to subjects such as engineering and physics. By learning about the achievements of women like Mary Treat, Florence Dixie, Lidia Becker, Marianne North, Clémence Royer, Antoinette Brown Blackwell, Mary Elizabeth Barber and Elizabeth Garrett, children may be inspired to follow their footsteps. Information about Darwin's women can be found on the *Darwin Correspondence Project* website.

Part 2: Working towards the big idea

Models of good practice

Topic: Finding things out

Age group: 5–7 years

Learning goals

Children take a step towards the big idea when they learn that they can find things out about the natural world by asking questions and doing something to discover the answers. They start following in Darwin's footsteps by carrying out simple tests to answer questions about earthworms. Children's attention is focussed on the advantages of working together and sharing ideas when trying to find things out. When working on scientific understanding, children learn the story of how Darwin travelled halfway around the world in search of unknown animals and plants. Children become part of the story by searching for 'unknown' minibeasts that live hidden in the school grounds. The picture of Darwin's science is further developed when children learn how he collected plant specimens and sent them home. Children engage with the story by responsibly collecting parts of plants from a local park and creating simple herbariums.

Working scientifically

In this topic children will:

- carry out enquiries to answer questions;
- observe closely and form simple tests;
- use their findings to answer questions;
- collect and record data to answer questions.

Health and safety

Children should wear protective gloves when handling earthworms. They should also wear gloves when searching for minibeasts and collecting parts of plants from the ground. Warn children not to put anything in their mouths and not to damage plants. When planning to teach the activities in this topic, refer to the relevant safety codes in the ASE publication *Be Safe!* (2011).

Exploring children's ideas

Use the picture story book *Ada Twist, Scientist* by Andrea Beaty to set the scene for this topic. This is a story of a little girl who is fascinated by the world around her and has a passion for finding out how things work. Her desire to find out is inspired by her experiences, which produce a multitude of questions which she is determined to answer. As the story tells us, Ada Twist had all the traits of a great scientist.

Following in Ada Twist's footsteps

Talk about Ada's passion for asking questions and how asking questions is important for finding things out. Ask children whether they think Ada asked the right questions when she was trying to find the source of the terrible stink. What questions would they ask? Children imagine there is a terrible stink in the school grounds. What questions would they ask to find the cause of the smell?

In her wisdom, Ada asked these two challenging questions:

- How does the nose know there is something to smell?
- And, does it still stink if there's no nose to tell?

Ask children whether they know what a smell looks like and how it gets up their nose. Do they think they could smell a stink without a nose? Listen to their ideas, and ask them how they can find out whether they can smell smelly things without using their nose. Provide them with smelly things to smell, and let them test out their ideas. Ask children to justify their answers. How do they know they are right?

Following in Darwin's footsteps

Ask children whether they know any animals which do not have a nose. Focus their attention on earthworms. Charles Darwin was fascinated by earthworms, and children can follow in his footsteps by carrying out their own experiments on their behaviour. Children need to collect earthworms from the garden and keep them safe in suitable conditions in the classroom until they are returned outside. Encourage children to speculate where they expect to find earthworms, and let them search in those places to find out if they were right.

Working in groups, children use magnifiers to make sketches of their worms and to discover whether they have a nose. Encourage children to speculate whether their worms are able to smell stinky things. With support, groups devise ways of testing whether their worms have a sense of smell. Talk about their findings and help them draw conclusions.

Encourage children to ask and find answers to other questions about earthworms. For example:

- Do earthworms have eyes?
- Do earthworms have ears?

- Are earthworms sensitive to being touched?
- Do earthworms have a mouth?

With support, groups closely observe earthworms to answer their questions. Children describe what they discovered and speculate about how worms are able to live in their underground habitat.

Collaborative learning

Talk about how scientists often help each other when they are trying to find answers to questions. Ask the children whether it was a good idea to work together when doing the earthworm experiments. How were they able to help each other? What did they talk about? Did they listen to each other? Suggest they follow some rules when working together, so that they can help each other. Negotiate some rules and display them in the classroom. For more information about *effective talk*, refer Chapter 3.

Information sources

- *Ada Twist, Scientist* (2016) by Andrea Beaty, Abrams Books.

Working on scientific understanding

Introduce Charles Darwin by telling children a story of his adventures around the world to find new kinds of animals and plants. Use the NowYouKnowAbout YouTube video entitled *The Story of Charles Darwin*, which provides an animated account of his life. Show children images of the HMS *Beagle* from the web, and describe how Darwin travelled across the world. He was away from home for five years. Travelling on a sailing ship could be very dangerous, especially in stormy weather. Ask children to imagine what it would have been like aboard the *Beagle*. Would they like to go on an adventure to discover animals and plants like Darwin did? What do they imagine they might discover? Show children pictures of iguanas and giant tortoises which Darwin found on the Galapagos Islands.

Following in Darwin's footsteps

Talk about Darwin when he returned home to England, and how his adventures made him famous. Discuss his family life. Talk about how his wife and children helped him with his science experiments, which he carried out in the garden and surrounding countryside. He did not manage to discover large animals like iguanas and giant tortoises, but he did discover a lot about smaller animals such as worms, beetles and other insects.

Ask children to talk about the animals that live in the school grounds. Do they think there might be animals living there which they have never seen before? Where do they think they might be hiding? Working in small supervised groups, take children on an expedition to find 'undiscovered' animals. Start in the school grounds. Groups search for minibeasts (invertebrates) which they have never seen before. They search in soil, underneath leaf litter, underneath logs, on plants and trees and in the compost heap. Allow each group to collect an animal which they can study back in the classroom. Use small collecting jars to individually house the animals.

Back in the classroom remind children of the rules for group working. In groups, they decide what they want to find out about their animal. For example, does it have eyes, a nose and ears? How many legs does it have? Does it have feet? How many parts does it have to its body? Encourage children to think of their own questions. Children start by making sketches of their animal, and then use magnifiers to explore its anatomy. Encourage them to speculate about what it eats and how it keeps safe. Does its colour help it keep safe? Groups describe their animals to the rest of the class, and use identification apps or cards to help identify them. Take photographs of the minibeasts and create a display depicting what the children have learnt about them. Return the animals to the places where they were found.

Darwin searched for living things in different places and was interested to find out whether they were similar or different. Following in Darwin's footsteps, the search for 'unknown' minibeasts can be continued in other areas, such as a local park or other green space. Help children compare the animals they find in the different places. Encourage groups to talk about what they have learnt from their expeditions, and publish their photographs on the display. Use the activity to assess children's progress towards the learning goals.

Information sources

- Darwin gets a job on the *Beagle*: www.youtube.com/watch?v=GsJ77YnBh-A
- NowYouKnowAbout videos: www.youtube.com/user/nowyouknowabout/videos

The bigger picture

Darwin collected hundreds of plant specimens from places he visited on his expedition aboard the *Beagle*. He sent the plants back to the UK, so scientists could use them to add to their knowledge of the diversity of plants around the world. Darwin dried and pressed the specimens between layers of blotting paper and sent them securely back to England in strong wooden chests.

Children follow in the footsteps of Darwin by collecting interesting parts of plants from different areas of the local park. The purpose of the enquiry is to create a classroom display which provides evidence for the diversity of plants that grow the park. In preparation for the visit, ask children to speculate about the shapes, sizes and colours of plants they expect to find in the park. Do they expect they will all be the same? If not, how will the plants differ? Also, the activity provides opportunities for children to develop their observational, collecting and recording skills.

Organise the visit so that supervised groups survey different parts of the park. In their area, children look out for interesting plants, and collect parts that have *fallen onto the ground*. Children collect leaves, flowers, stems, fruits or seeds. Place the parts carefully in a paper bag, and write on it the name of the plant. Also, take photographs of the plant.

Back in the classroom, children create a record (herbarium) for each of their plants by sticking the parts collected to a sheet of cardboard, along with the name and a photograph of the plant. Help children identify their specimens, and talk about where the plants grew in the park. Were they growing out in the open, or near a wall, tree, bush or hedge? Compare plants growing in different areas. Draw a map of the park, and together with all the plant records create a large display showing where the specimens were collected. Talk with the children about the differences and similarities between the plants in the display. Introduce the words variety and diversity. Ask children what they learnt from their collections about the variety of plants in the park. Can they now answer the question about how the plants differ? Use the outcomes of this enquiry to assess children's progress towards the learning goals.

Plants that grow in the school grounds

Provide support to help children raise their own questions about the plants that grow in the school grounds. What would they like to find out? How would they find the answer? What samples would they collect? What records would they keep? Help groups plan and carry out their enquiries, and use the activity to assess children's progress towards the learning goals.

Information sources

- Darwin Project: www.darwinproject.ac.uk/learning/7-11/darwin-the-collector

Topic: Scientific explanations

Age group: 7–9 years

Learning goals

Children make progress towards the big idea by carrying out experiments similar to Darwin's through which they learn about the nature of scientific explanations. By following in his footsteps, they learn about the collaborative nature of science and how he set up experiments to help him explain things in nature that puzzled him. They also learn that an explanation is not a guess and, to be trusted, an explanation needs evidence to back it up. While children are working on their understanding of scientific explanations, there are also opportunities to further develop their knowledge of seed dispersal. Children discover more about Darwin's science by exploring the correspondence he had with Joseph Hooker, who was a trusted colleague and close friend of Darwin's.

Working scientifically

In this topic children will:

- plan scientific enquiries to answer questions;
- set up enquiries which include fair testing;
- make careful observations over a period of time;
- report findings from enquiries orally and in written form;
- draw conclusions, suggest improvements and raise further questions;
- seek scientific evidence to support a theory.

Health and safety

Check whether the seeds you intend to use have been treated with pesticides. Teach children never to eat the seeds and to treat all weeds as hazardous. They should wear protective gloves when handling the plants. Plan all gardening activities to include appropriately sized tools and equipment, as well as considerations of safety and hygiene. Refer to the relevant safety codes in the ASE publication *Be Safe!* (2011) when planning to teach the activities in this topic.

Exploring children's ideas

Start the topic by finding out what the children recall about Charles Darwin. Introduce Darwin as a family man and a scientist.

Darwin the family man

Working in groups, children use information sources to find out about Darwin the family man. Groups come together to present and discuss what they find out. Does it surprise them to discover that Darwin was a devoted family man? Do they think today's scientists have families? What do they think scientists do when they are not doing science? Talk about how scientists are ordinary men and women, who do all the things most people do when they are not at work.

Darwin the scientist

Working in groups, children use information sources to find out about Darwin the scientist. Listen to what children discover. Groups create maps showing the places Darwin visited on his

Chapter 7 Following in Darwin's footsteps

five-year voyage aboard the *Beagle* and create a display depicting the types of animals and plants which he discovered. Discuss how he was amazed and inspired by the rich diversity of living things which he found in different parts of the world.

After he returned home, Darwin married Emma Wedgwood and settled down in Down House in Kent. For the next 20 years he studied the hundreds of preserved specimens of animals, plants and fossils which he collected on his voyage. He spent much of his time performing experiments to find explanations for some of the puzzling things he experienced on his voyage. Darwin performed many of his experiments in his own garden. Most of his experiments required little more than a magnifying lens, a notebook or diary for recording observations and some basic garden equipment, and of course a lot of creative and analytical thinking.

Things to talk about

Talk about how, during his five-year journey around the world on the *Beagle*, Darwin discovered that similar animals and plants could be found living in different places. For example, he was fascinated to find that plants growing on the South American coast were similar to plants which he found growing on nearby islands. After he returned home, Darwin started to search for explanations for why similar plants could be found growing in distinctly different locations hundreds of miles apart. Encourage children to speculate about why similar plants can be found growing in different places.

Following in Darwin's footsteps

Darwin speculated that the similarity was due to seeds from the mainland being transported to the islands. A scientific explanation is not a guess, so Darwin was determined to find evidence that seeds could be transported across oceans and survive on nearby islands. In the 1850s he embarked on a series of experiments to demonstrate that a variety of dispersal methods was possible. He conducted several experiments to discover whether the seeds of common garden plants could survive and germinate after being soaked for long periods in salt water. Did they survive or perish? Challenge the children to find out for themselves.

Children follow in Darwin's footsteps by devising their own experiments to find out whether seeds could be transported across oceans and still germinate after being exposed to the extreme conditions involved. To be transported by the sea, the seeds would need to be able to float and to survive for weeks in saltwater.

Do seeds float in saltwater?

Children plan investigations to find the types of seeds that float best in saltwater. It is important to remember that seeds are found inside fruits, some with high levels of buoyancy. For example, passion fruits float really well, while other fruits such as avocados are not as buoyant. Provide children with a wide range of fruits, nuts and seeds to test. Safeguard against nut allergies.

How does saltwater affect the ability of seeds to germinate?

Darwin used cress, radish, cabbages, lettuces, carrots, celery and onion seed. Children can also use mustard seeds and mung beans which normally germinate in a few days. They plan investigations to see how exposure to saltwater affects their ability to germinate. Encourage children to speculate about how the length of time spent immersed in saltwater may influence germination. Do they think the amount of salt in the water would make a difference? What about the temperature of the water in which the seeds were soaked? Help them to think of all the variables which they need to take into account. Groups should grow some seeds in normal conditions to use as control experiments. Outcomes of the control and test experiments can be compared to discover the effects saltwater has on the seeds. Be warned, Darwin found many of his seeds 'smelt very badly' after a week in the water.

Sowing salty seeds

Children continue their investigation in the garden when they are growing spring vegetables and flowers. For example, they can store some of the seeds in saltwater and plant them out at weekly intervals during the spring season. Seeds which have not been soaked can be planted at the same times and their rates of growth compared. Talk about how tests are reliable if they produce the same outcomes when repeated. Do they think their results apply to all types of seeds?

What does the evidence tell us?

Darwin found that some of his seeds were able to grow after long periods in the salty water. Therefore, it may be possible that plants on the mainland could have spread to islands by floating in the sea. However, he was not entirely convinced, because he was concerned about their ability to float over such long distances. Children present the results of their experiments and talk about whether they provide support for Darwin's idea about seed dispersal. Is it possible that seeds can travel long distances in the sea and still be able to grow? Children can discuss other ways seeds are able to travel long distances.

Talking points: true, false or not sure?

- Seeds could be carried by the wind.
- Seeds could be carried by birds or other animals.
- Seeds could be carried by fish.
- Seeds could be carried by leaves.

Chapter 7 Following in Darwin's footsteps

- Seeds could be carried by driftwood.
- There is no explanation for how the seeds travelled across the sea.

Groups develop reasoned arguments for the most likely ways seeds could be dispersed over such long distances. Groups present and debate their ideas with the rest of the class. If they were scientists, what experiments would they do to find evidence to support their theories? Listen to children's ideas and assess their progress towards the learning goals.

Information sources

- Learning resources: www.darwinproject.ac.uk/learning/7-11
- Seeds in salty water: www.darwinproject.ac.uk/learning/universities/getting-know-darwins-science/biogeography

Working on scientific understanding

Talk about children's responses to the talking point, that *there is no explanation for how seeds travelled across the sea*. Survey the children to find out how many think this statement is true. Point out that scientists believe that there are always explanations or reasons for why things happen in nature; sometimes they are just hard to work out. Darwin was a great scientist because he was very good at working things out. Often he started to work out an explanation by speculating or hypothesising about what might be happening, as he did with the seed dispersal problem. He then did experiments to find evidence to support his ideas. Discuss the nature of a scientific explanation. Talk about how a scientific explanation is not a guess, and how it needs some evidence to back it up.

Darwin's weed garden

Darwin cleared a small patch of ground to observe what happened to the weeds which grew in it over a period of time. He was surprised at how many of the weeds which germinated in the patch did not survive beyond seedlings. In his book *On the Origin of Species*, he reflects on the struggle seeds have to survive.

> With plants there is a vast destruction of seeds, but, from some observations which I made, I believe that it is the seedlings which suffer most from germinating in ground already thickly stocked with other plants. Seedlings, also, are destroyed in vast numbers by various enemies; for instance, on a piece of ground three feet long and two wide, dug and cleared, and where there could be no choking from other plants, I marked all the seedlings of our native weeds as they came up, and out of the 357 no less than 295 were destroyed, chiefly by slugs and insects.

(p 67–8)

Following in Darwin's footsteps

Talk about how Darwin studied weeds in his garden at home, and how he was interested in finding out how many died off before they could grow into mature plants. Read the above extract from Darwin's book. Are children surprised that so few plants survived? Can they think of any other reasons why they did not survive?

Ask children what they know about weeds and where they come from. Point out that people do not plant weeds; they just grow without any help. Children follow in Darwin's footsteps to work out an explanation for where weeds come from. Working in groups, they start by creating a possible explanation (hypothesis). Groups then come together to share their ideas.

Encourage groups to justify their ideas. Why do they believe their theory is correct? How can they prove it? What experiments could they do? Working collaboratively children choose what they believe to be the most likely explanation. To test their ideas, groups clear selected areas of the school garden to allow weeds to grow. Each group should have their own metre square area. To test whether weeds come for airborne seeds, half of each area should be left open to the air, while the other half is covered by a homemade poly-tunnel to prevent seeds from the air getting into the soil. All areas need to be kept watered. Monitor the number and types of weeds in each area every week, and compare and compile the results. Each week, talk about the evidence collected and whether it supports their hypothesis. Talk about Darwin's observations. Did children find many of the young weeds (seedlings) were destroyed before they were able to grow into mature plants? Is this something they can explain?

The bigger picture

Although Darwin worked from home, he did not work alone. He collaborated by exchanging letters with many different people, including scientists, gardeners, pigeon breeders and beekeepers. He communicated with people all over the world. Some of his correspondents carried out similar experiments to his, which enabled them to compare results. Joseph Hooker was a botanist, who was a trusted colleague and close friend of Darwin's. Over his lifetime Darwin and Hooker exchanged 1,400 letters, on a wide range of subjects. Below are extracts from letters Darwin sent to Joseph Hooker about his saltwater and weed garden experiments.

Chapter 7 **Following in Darwin's footsteps**

Darwin's letters

7 Apr 1855

My dear Hooker

I wrote this morning to thank for the Rhododendrons.

   I have begun my seed-salting experiments, & I shd. be extremely much obliged if you would tell me what kinds you would expect to be most easily killed by sea-water . . . Secondly will you tell me, at a guess, how long an immersion in sea-water you shd. imagine wd. kill the more susceptible seeds? Should you expect a week's fair immersion wd. destroy any of them? . . .

Adios

C. Darwin

A week later on the 13th of April, Darwin sent another letter which acknowledged the help Hooker had given him. In the letter, Darwin describes some of his own precise methods of experimentation. He talks of the cress, radish, cabbage, lettuce, carrot, celery and onion seeds he has exposed to various temperatures and how they had germinated after being immersed in water for a week. He points out:

the water of nearly all & of the cress especially, smelt very badly, & the cress seed emitted a wonderful quantity of mucus . . . so as to cohere in a mass; but these seeds germinated & grew splendidly.

After discovering that seeds can survive in water for long periods, he turns his attention to how far they could travel in the ocean:

Today I replant the same seeds as above after 14 days immersion. As many sea-current go a mile an hour: even in a week they might be transported 168 miles: the Gulf-stream is said to go 50 & 60 miles a day.

The following extract is from one of a number of letters Darwin exchanged with Hooker on the subject of his weed garden:

12 Apr, 1857

My dear Hooker

   . . . I have been interested in my "weed garden" of 3x2 feet square: I mark each seedling as it appears, & I am astonished at number that come up. & still more at number killed by slugs &c. – Already 59 have been so killed; I expected a good many, but I had fancied that this was a less potent check than it seems to be; & I attributed almost exclusively to mere choking the destruction of seedlings. –

Children reply to Charles Darwin

Interpret Darwin's letters to Hooker to suit your children. Share the letters with the children as if he were writing to them. Children reply to his letters providing him with information from their own experiments. Encourage them to compare what they found out with what Darwin had to say on the subject. Copies of both Darwin's letters and the children's can be displayed in the classroom.

Drift seeds and drift fruits are the name given to seeds and fruits which are adapted to long-distance travel in seas and oceans. Some drift thousands of miles before finding a place to grow on a distant beach. Groups use information sources to research drift seeds and drift fruits and write to Darwin to tell him about their new discoveries. Add the letters to the display.

Darwin Correspondence Project

More information about Darwin's experiments and extracts from the letters he wrote can be found on the *Darwin Correspondence Project* website. The website provides a wide range of science activities based on his correspondence. There are fascinating experiments involving carnivorous plants which are guaranteed to excite the children's imaginations. The experiments lead children to question whether carnivorous plants would be better described as animals!

Collaborating with local primary schools

Collaboration is an important part of science. Working together, scientists can achieve more than working alone. Talk with other schools about the possibility of collaborating on science research projects. Children from local schools can meet up to discuss the type of projects they would like to do and to form research groups. Once the projects and groups have been established, children carry out their research activities in their own schools and share ideas within their groups by texting and video conferencing. Under the teachers' guidance, groups can also communicate using an appropriate social media platform.

Children in each research group can follow in Darwin's footsteps by collaborating in a quest for knowledge. Groups plan their own projects, do experiments similar to Darwin's, or even take part in national citizen science projects. Organise a science conference where all the research groups come together to present the outcomes of their research.

Information sources

- Darwin Correspondence Project: www.darwinproject.ac.uk
- Doing Darwin's experiments: www.darwinproject.ac.uk/learning/11-14/doing-darwins-experiments
- Key correspondents: www.darwinproject.ac.uk/commentary/key-correspondents
- Learning resources: www.darwinproject.ac.uk/learning/11-14

Chapter 7 Following in Darwin's footsteps

Topic: Darwin's science

Age group: 9–11 years

Learning goals

Children make progress towards the big idea by learning how Darwin designed experiments to collect evidence to support his theories. In this topic, children have opportunities to explore the rigorous nature of Darwin's science by exploring the work he did with earthworms and by examining the correspondence he had with his colleague, Mary Treat. Darwin made sure the experiments he carried out in support of his theories were meticulously planned, so that the evidence he produced was reliable and not open to criticism from other scientists.

Children follow in Darwin's footsteps by making predictions about the behaviour of earthworms and planning their own experiments to test their ideas. They consider the importance of fair testing and repeating results to make sure they are reliable. They work on their understanding of rigorous testing by considering letters exchanged by Darwin and Mary Treat, in which they discuss experiments carried out on insect-eating plants. By engaging with Darwin's correspondence, children learn to appreciate the value of rigorous testing, so that the evidence produced to support a theory is reliable. In the later part of the topic, children explore how Darwin used pigeon breeding as a model to help explain his theory of evolution. Children also learn about botanical art and carry out fieldwork to survey and classify different types of beetles and birds which live in their area.

Working scientifically

In this topic children will:

- plan scientific enquiries to test predictions;
- plan fair tests;
- report and present findings with the help of posters;
- reflect on the reliability of their findings by repeating tests, and comparing results with others;
- interpret data objectively;
- draw conclusions, suggest improvements and raise further questions;
- identify scientific evidence that has been used to support or refute ideas or arguments.

Health and safety

Children should wear protective gloves when searching for and handling worms, beetles and other invertebrates. Stress safety, hygiene and the protection of wildlife. When planning to teach the activities in this topic refer to the relevant safety codes in the ASE publication *Be Safe!* (2011).

Exploring children's ideas

In a previous topic, children explored the physical characteristics of earthworms. In this topic, children plan and carry out more meticulous tests to explore the ways earthworms respond to different types of stimuli.

Charles Darwin studied the behaviour of earthworms for most of his working life. His interest began shortly after his return from his *Beagle* voyage, and he was still talking about them in his letters only months before he died in March 1882. Darwin was fascinated by the behaviour of earthworms. He called them the most important animal in the history of the world, because they mix nutrients into the soil which plants need to grow strong and healthy.

Darwin experimented with different types of food and found that earthworms preferred wild cherry and carrots, and preferred raw fat to raw meat. He also tested the earthworm's sensitivity to light and heat by exposing them to different sources of light and by holding a poker heated to dull redness near some worms. In addition, he tested their sense of hearing by using a metal whistle and having his children play musical instruments to attract their attention. Darwin even shouted at the worms, while at the same time making sure his warm breath did not affect them. Through various means Darwin discovered that earthworms were extremely sensitive to vibrations. He was also curious to know whether earthworms were intelligent. Through his observations in the garden he noted that earthworms pulled leaves into the ground by their tips, which is the most the efficient way of doing it. What he wanted to find out was whether this behaviour involved decision-making or whether it was just accidental. He reasoned that if worms were able to make choices and decisions then they must have some level of intelligence.

Following in Darwin's footsteps

Children follow in Darwin's footsteps by devising and carrying out their own tests on the behaviour of worms. To carry out experiments children will need to collect earthworms from the garden and keep them in suitable conditions in the classroom until they are returned outside. Children devise their questions or choose from the following:

- Can earthworms hear sounds?
- Are earthworms sensitive to light?
- Do earthworms have a sense of smell?
- Do earthworms have a sense of touch?
- Are earthworms intelligent?
- Are earthworms sensitive to vibrations?
- What range of foods will earthworms eat?

Having decided on their questions, children should speculate about the answers. Encourage them to justify their predictions.

Designing tests which provide reliable evidence for the behaviour of earthworms requires some thinking about them. For example, how can it be proved that earthworms have some level of intelligence? Decision-making is a sign of intelligence, so children need to devise tests where the earthworms are provided with a choice. Repetition plays an important part in these kinds of experiments to show that the observed behaviours are linked to a cause and not just coincidental.

For example, if children want to test whether a worm has a sense of smell or touch, then they need to observe the same behaviour from the worm to the relevant stimuli on numerous occasions and control the experiment to make sure there is no other possible cause.

Analysis of data

Encourage children to think carefully about whether they can rely on the results of their tests to answer their question. Interpreting data objectively is an important part of any scientific investigation. Although it is satisfying when a theory is proved right, negative answers can prove to be just as valuable to scientists in their quest for knowledge. Outcomes are not always black or white, or right or wrong. Often investigations do not prove anything conclusively, but instead provide useful insights which help scientists to know whether they are on the right path and which help them decide what they need to do next.

When analysing their results groups can consider these questions:

- What did we learn from the experiment?
- How do we know whether the results are reliable?
- If we repeated the tests, can we be sure that we would get the same results?
- What have we learnt that we can rely on?
- Do we have sufficient reliable evidence to answer our question?
- What should we do next?

Children use information sources on the web to discover how Darwin conducted his experiments and to compare his results with theirs. Talk about how scientists often compare results from experiments they carried out independently. Ask children to explain why.

Conference on the behaviour of earthworms

Explain how science conferences provide opportunities for scientists with similar interests to come together to share their ideas. In conferences, ideas are exchanged in seminars which consist of a series of short presentations in which the scientists outline their research and present their findings. At the end of each presentation the audience is invited to ask questions.

Organise the classroom into the form of a seminar room so children can present the findings of their research into the behaviour of earthworms. Each group should describe their methods and present and justify their findings. The audience should be invited to ask questions which require the presenters to defend the reliability of their findings. Use the presentations to assess children's progress towards the learning goals.

OPAL Soil and Earthworm Survey

Visit the OPAL website and find out about how children can discover more about the world of worms and also help build a picture of the nature of soils across the UK. As Darwin pointed out, earthworms are extremely important and play a vital role in recycling plant nutrients and aerating the soil. By taking part in the survey, children will improve their knowledge of earthworms and the nature of the soils in which they live. Explain how they will be taking part in a national science project, run by professional scientists. This is real science in action.

The best time to do this survey is from March to September. Start by downloading the *Soil and Earthworm Survey Booklet*, the *Earthworm Identification Guide* and the *Soil Survey Recording Sheet*. Prepare by organising the equipment required, including pH strips, mustard, vinegar, a ruler, a spade and bin bags. Identify suitable areas for the survey in the school grounds, and do a risk assessment before children start work. All the information children need to carry out the survey can be found in the booklet. Outcomes of the survey are submitted by filling in an online form. In addition to the survey, there is a *Kids Zone* and other information and activities on the website.

Information sources

- Darwin on earthworms: www.darwinproject.ac.uk/earthworms
- Darwin's earthworm: http://darwin-online.org.uk/EditorialIntroductions/Chancellor_Earthworms.html
- Darwin's earthworms: www.sciencelearn.org.nz/resources/22-charles-darwin-and-earthworms
- Soil and Earthworm Survey: www.opalexplorenature.org/soilsurvey

Working on scientific understanding

Start by talking about the nature of science. Science is about finding explanations for the behaviour of things which are part of the natural world. Science can be as straightforward as finding out what causes rain or as complex as searching for an explanation for the creation of the universe. In Darwin's case he wanted to know what caused the great diversity of living things on the earth to evolve. This is a big question, which needed a big idea to answer it.

Use information about Darwin's correspondents in Part 1 to talk about how he spent much of his life searching for the causes of evolution. Point out that his ways of working were similar to the way children perform investigations in school; they included observations, identification, recording, collecting, making comparisons, testing, reflective thinking and creative thinking. Discuss how he also corresponded with other scientists to help him find an answer. His letters and notebooks show us how he worked.

Darwin's correspondence

Children discover the nature of Darwin's science by exploring letters which he exchanged with other scientists. Talk about how Darwin exchanged numerous letters with Mary Treat. Point out that Mary was an accomplished scientist who made her living by writing books and science articles for popular magazines. More information about Mary Treat is presented in Part 1, and children can find out more on the *Darwin Correspondence Project* website.

Chapter 7 Following in Darwin's footsteps

Share the following extracts from letters Darwin exchanged with Mary Treat to illustrate how Darwin collaborated with scientists in the UK and other parts of the world. In the first extract he mentions the *Drosera filiformis*, which is a small insect-eating plant commonly known as the thread-leaved sundew.

Down,
Beckenham, Kent.
Jan. 1. 1873

Dear Madam,

I am very much obliged for your kind letter; & should esteem it a great favour if during warm weather next summer you will observe two points for me in Drosera filiformis. Namely to place some flies within quarter of an inch of the apex of the leaf & observe whether it bends at all after an interval of a day or two. Secondly to rub with a clean needle a few of the glands with some little force, and to touch each gland half a dozen times; & then observe whether in the course of an hour or two the hairs or filaments bearing these glands become incurved. I am glad to hear that D. filiformis catches only small insects, as I suspected this. I have observed with care several other species of Drosera. . . .

With my best thanks
I remain Dear Madam

Yours very faithfully
Charles Darwin

Vineland, New Jersey.
28 July 1873

Mr. Darwin.

Dear Sir,

. . . I carefully removed strong plants away from atmospheric agitation, and found they would bend toward a struggling fly. I pinned living flies within a quarter of an inch of the leaf, in less than an hour the fly's legs would become entangled in the filaments. I then tried them three quarters of an inch from the leaves. The leaves bent perceptibly away from the light toward the flies, but did not reach them at this distance. I tried bits of raw beef with the same result. I could see no effect produced upon the glands by rubbing them with a needle; perhaps I did not understand just how you wished it done.

But the most perfect, active fly-trap among these plants is D. longifolia. In less than three hours a vigorous healthy leaf will fold completely around a struggling fly, and bits of raw beef will become so enfolded in the leaf as to be completely hidden from view. . .

Yours very respectfully
Mary Treat

In his reply dated August 12, 1873, Darwin acknowledges Mary Treat's findings but warns:

> If I were in your place I should be afraid to publish the statement about the Drosera bending towards flies or meat which they did not touch; unless I had tried the experiment many times, under the most rigorous precautions; for I am convinced that no botanist would believe the statement unless all the precautions taken were described in detail.

Things to talk about

Ask children what they think Mary Treat learnt from her experiments. Why did Darwin caution her to repeat the experiments? Talk about how repeating experiments makes the results more reliable. Reliable means that if other scientists repeat the experiments they will get the same or very similar results. Discuss the rigorous nature of Darwin's science. Criticism upset Darwin, which was perhaps reflected in the comments he made to Mary. Darwin would not publish the results of his experiments until he was convinced that other scientists could not find fault with them.

Drama: visit to Down House

Often Darwin's correspondents visited him at home to talk science and meet the family. Children imagine that they are scientists who corresponded with Darwin on the subject of earthworms. They have been invited to Down House to talk about their experiments and other things of interest about earthworms. Working in groups, children plan the drama which involves conversations between themselves, Darwin and members of his family.

Darwin's wife, Emma, often helped with his science by writing on his behalf and editing his work. The same can be said for his children, especially Henrietta, who wrote letters to many of his correspondents on his behalf. It can be imagined Emma and Henrietta would have been keen to welcome correspondents to the house, especially if they had exchanged letters with them. Children should include Emma and Henrietta and perhaps other members of the family in the drama.

The drama could be set in his garden or a room in the house. The drama should include a narrator who sets the scene for the meeting, introduces the main protagonists and comments on the conversation so the audience can make sense of it. The nature of the conversation between the protagonists should be one of collaboration, with each sharing and politely challenging each other's ideas in a shared quest for knowledge. The drama can be further developed by including key figures in Darwin's life such as John Henslow, Charles Lyell, Joseph Hooker, Thomas Huxley, Alfred Wallace and Asa Gray. Lots of background information can be found on the *Darwin Correspondence Project* website. Use the activity to assess children's progress towards the learning goals.

Chapter 7 Following in Darwin's footsteps

Following in Darwin's footsteps

Darwin loved collecting beetles. He created a very large collection when he was at Cambridge University. His enthusiasm for collecting beetles is reflected in this extract from his autobiography:

> But no pursuit at Cambridge was followed with nearly so much eagerness or gave me so much pleasure as collecting beetles. It was the mere passion for collecting; for I did not dissect them, and rarely compared their external characters with published descriptions, but got them named anyhow. I will give a proof of my zeal: one day, on tearing off some old bark, I saw two rare beetles, and seized one in each hand; then I saw a third and new kind, which I could not bear to lose, so that I popped the one which I held in my right hand into my mouth. Alas! it ejected some intensely acrid fluid, which burnt my tongue so that I was forced to spit the beetle out, which was lost, as was the third one.
>
> (from an edition edited by Francis Darwin, 1887)

Children follow in Darwin's footsteps by going on a beetle hunt (survey) in a quest to discover and record the different types of beetles which live in their area. They will obviously *not* put one in their mouth! Prepare for the survey by talking about Darwin's fascination with beetles, and

use images from the web to explore the different kinds of UK beetles he was likely to have in his collection. There are hundreds of thousands of different kinds (species) of beetles worldwide and over 4,000 in the UK. Perhaps the most commonly known are ladybirds and stag beetles. Show children pictures of a ladybird and a stag beetle, and ask them to compare them. How would they tell the difference between them? What is similar about them? How do they differ from other insects such as bees and butterflies? Children use information sources to compare beetles with other kinds of insects and to learn which physical characteristics are used to classify them. Beetles can be distinguished from other types of insects by their front pair of wings, which are hard and ridged and, when not in use, form wing cases to protect the more delicate hind-wings underneath. The hind-wings are used for flying and swimming.

Use this opportunity to work on children's understanding of how animals are classified into broad groups by identifying similarities and differences between them. Talk about how classification puts the huge range of living things on our planet into some sort of order so that we can make sense of the natural world. Children use information sources to classify invertebrates commonly found in the school garden, park or woodland. They can be classified into three main groups: worms, molluscs and arthropods. To which group do beetles belong?

Beetle survey

While out exploring, Darwin used notebooks to jot down his thoughts and observations about the things he discovered. On his five-year expedition aboard the *Beagle*, Darwin filled 15 notebooks with comments, diagrams and sketches. Children follow in Darwin's footsteps by using notebooks to record their findings on their beetle hunt.

Start with the school grounds, where groups can survey different areas, including the compost heap. Beetles can be found in most habitats including under logs, in leaf litter, in the soil, on leaves, under the bark of a tree and in the school pond. For each beetle they find, children should describe in their notebook where they found it and what it looks like, including a sketch. Children collect beetles in specimen jars to observe them closely using magnifiers. They should describe their anatomy, including their legs, wings and head. Encourage children to speculate about what the beetles eat and how they keep safe where they live. Beetles should be returned to their habitats as soon as possible.

Based on their notes and sketches, children use information sources back in the classroom to identify the beetles which they discovered. Use children's findings to create a large map of the school grounds showing where the different types of beetles were found.

Darwin would never have been satisfied with just one survey. Children can follow up their survey of the school grounds by exploring the local park and other green areas in the neighbourhood. Compare the places where particular kinds of beetles are found. Are some beetles only found in particular habitats, or are they not fussy about where they live? Talk about how the beetles are adapted to their habitats.

Beetle brigade

Darwin's enthusiasm for beetles was so infectious that while at Cambridge University he persuaded some of his friends to form a 'beetle brigade', who spent their time collecting beetles. Following in Darwin's footsteps, children could form their own beetle brigade and encourage children from other schools to join. Instead of collecting specimens, children can collect drawings and photographs of the different species which they discover. The brigade can invite expert entomologists to the school to talk about these fascinating creatures. Visit the STEM Learning website to find an expert in your area.

Botanical art

During Darwin's time, the best way to record a plant or animal was to draw it as carefully and accurately as possible. Taking a photograph was not an option. Darwin sent specimens of different types of animals and plants to artists who recorded accurate drawings and paintings of them.

Botanical art combines science and art, using tools such as pencil, ink and watercolour. Children can create botanical drawings of different kinds of beetles and use them to illustrate a book entitled *Beetle Mania*. The foreword to the book could include an account of Darwin's enthusiasm for collecting beetles, with each of the chapters providing detailed information and accurate illustrations of different kinds of beetles and their habitats.

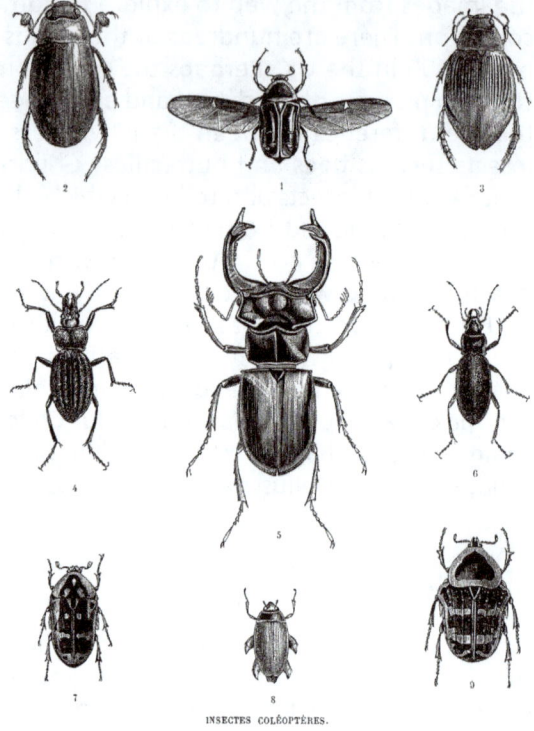

Visit to a botanical garden

Children can follow in Darwin's footsteps by visiting a botanical garden nearest your school. These gardens are places where children can enjoy a rich diversity of plants which originate from all corners of the world. Botanical gardens are also places where scientists study plants, and in some cases carry on work started by Darwin and other botanists of his time. During Darwin's time, his great friend Joseph Hooker was the director of Kew Gardens. Under his directorship, Kew grew to become a world-renowned centre for the study of plants.

Kew and other botanical gardens provide the perfect settings for outdoor learning. To help plan children's learning, botanical gardens often provide pre-visit planning passes which enable teachers to look around and talk to staff from the education centre. Botanical gardens can also offer hands-on curriculum-linked activities led by trained teachers. Ensure your visit provides opportunities for children to ask questions about the research carried out by plant scientists and how it links to work done by Darwin and other Victorian scientists.

Information sources

- Beetles: https://animalcorner.co.uk/beetle-anatomy/
- Beetles: www.naturespot.org.uk/taxonomy/term/19338?page=2
- Birmingham Botanical Gardens: www.birminghambotanicalgardens.org.uk/education/primary/

- Botanical artists: www.botanicalartandartists.com/famous-botanical-artists.html
- Bug Life: www.buglife.org.uk/
- Cambridge Botanical Gardens: www.botanic.cam.ac.uk/education-learning/educational-visits/
- Darwin's experiments: www.darwinproject.ac.uk/learning/11-14/doing-darwins-experiments
- Kew Gardens: www.kew.org/kew-gardens/school-visits
- Royal Botanic Garden Edinburgh: www.rbge.org.uk/
- STEM Learning: www.stem.org.uk/stem-ambassadors
- The National Botanic Garden of Wales: https://botanicgarden.wales/

The bigger picture

Start this part by talking about Darwin's theory of evolution. As an example, use the theory about how the giraffe evolved its long neck. Compare Lamarck's theory, presented in Part 1, with an explanation based on Darwin's theory.

Using Darwin's theory, giraffes evolved their long necks as a result of competition for food. When food was short, those giraffes with slightly longer necks would be able to reach slightly higher into the trees to reach the last of the leaves. This means that those longer-necked giraffes were more likely to survive and pass their advantageous trait to the next generation. Shorter-necked giraffes who could not compete for the available food were likely to die before reproducing. Hence the next generation of giraffes would have longer necks on average. If this continued, future generations of giraffes would gradually develop longer necks. Also, a long neck gives a male giraffe an advantage when fighting another male to attract a mate. This provides another reason for why shorter-necked giraffes are less likely to reproduce.

Things to talk about

Which of the theories do children think is most convincing? Encourage them to talk about whether it is possible to collect evidence to support either of the theories. What sort of evidence would Darwin need to collect to prove his theory?

Darwin's pigeons

Darwin was fascinated by the variety of shapes, sizes and colours of the pigeons that breeders were able to produce, and realised that he could use pigeon breeding as a model to help explain how evolution happens in nature.

Darwin bred pigeons for over 20 years and gathered a great deal of scientific evidence and kept rigorous notes on his work. By crossing birds with different traits, he could generate off-spring that were different from their parents. Some birds he used had white feathers, others were brown. Some had long necks, others very short beaks. By artificially selecting, he gathered valuable evidence for his theory of evolution. Using pigeon breeding as a model, Darwin imagined that if animals can be artificially changed by selective breeding, then perhaps they could also be changed through natural selection, in which nature acts to select favourable traits.

Charles Darwin was not the first person to suggest that animals naturally evolve. However, he was the first person to offer a scientifically plausible account of the causes of evolution based on reliable evidence. He published his ideas in his famous book *On the Origins of Species by Means of Natural Selection*.

Pigeon breeding

It is believed that today's rich variety of domesticated pigeons are all descendants of the wild rock dove, which can still be found along the coasts of Scotland and Northern Ireland. People have bred pigeons in many parts of the world for about 10,000 years, and in that time they have substantially changed the physical appearance and the behaviour of the domesticated descendants of the rock dove.

Children use information and images from the web to compare the wild rock dove with different breeds of domesticated pigeons to study how 10,000 years of selective breeding has changed the bird. Groups identify the physical characteristics and behaviours that have been most changed and those which have remained the same. Which of today's domesticated birds are most similar to their wild ancestor?

Bird spotting survey

The three most common kinds of pigeons in the UK are the feral pigeon, the wood pigeon and the stock dove. Feral pigeons are the same species as the rock doves. Other common birds include the blue tit, great tit, long-tailed tit, common blackbird, chaffinch, goldfinch, starling, robin and house sparrow. The RSPB's annual Big Garden Birdwatch 2019 found that the house sparrow was the most common garden bird.

To prepare for the survey, children use information sources to learn to identify birds which they are likely to find in their area. They can compare characteristics of different kinds of birds, and use similarities and differences to classify them into families. Encourage children to justify the way they group the birds, and compare with official classifications.

Start the survey in the school grounds, then move on to the local park and other green areas near your school. Groups will need binoculars and their field notebooks. When they spot a bird, children describe its main features in their notebook and make a note of the habitat in which it was found. If they are not sure of the species, they can use their notes back in the classroom to help identify it. Groups should also make a tally of the number of birds they see, taking care not to record the same bird more than once.

Following in Darwin's footsteps

Back in the classroom, groups can use the RSPB identifier or other resources to identify the birds they surveyed. Display children's results, and make a list of the birds which live in your area. Which are the most common? Which are the rarest? How do these compare to the RSPB surveys?

During Darwin's time, the best way to record a plant or animal was to draw it as carefully and accurately as possible. Children use images from the web to paint accurate illustrations of birds from their survey. Use the illustrations to create a display of the different birds which live in your area.

Dog breeding

From a teacup-size chihuahua to a great dane, there is an incredible amount of variety among dog breeds. Although there is such a rich variety of breeds, they are all thought to have originated from a single species. Research suggests that domestic dogs evolved from a group of wolves that came into contact with European hunter-gatherers thousands of years ago. Following in Darwin's footsteps, scientists continue to study the breeds to better understand the workings of evolution and how such great variation could have arisen within one group. Display photographs of dogs owned by the children, and discuss their similarities and differences.

Children imagine they are dog breeders who want to breed a working dog with particular characteristics. Working dogs are used for a purpose, such as sheep dogs, guide dogs, police dogs, therapy dogs and rescue dogs. Working in groups, children consider the characteristics a working dog would need for a particular purpose. Encourage the children to use their imagination when choosing the purpose, which could include working in disaster areas and war zones to help rescue people trapped in collapsed buildings. Having chosen the work, children search images of different breeds on the web to find two types of dog which can be crossbred to produce offspring which would be suited to the work. Children combine characteristics from the two types of dogs to create drawings of the dog which they want to breed.

Groups present and justify their ideas to the rest of the class. Talk about the problems involved in crossbreeding dogs. Can breeders be sure that offspring will inherit the traits which the breeders want? There are ethical issues related to breeding designer dogs. Groups can research the issues on the web and debate them. The class endeavours to come to some agreement on the rights and wrongs of artificial selection.

Information sources

- Bird watch results: www.rspb.org.uk/get-involved/activities/birdwatch/results/
- Darwin Correspondence Project: www.darwinproject.ac.uk/
- Darwin's pigeons: http://darwinspigeons.com/
- Dog breeding: www.onegreenplanet.org/animalsandnature/why-breeding-dogs-is-a-problem-even-if-the-breeder-is-reputable/
- Dog breeding: shttps://thenorthernquota.org/campaigns/animal-welfare-organisations-rspca-and-dog's-trust-back-new-breeding-regulation
- Identifying pigeons: www.bto.org/develop-your-skills/bird-identification/videos/bto-bird-id-pigeons
- Identify a bird: www.rspb.org.uk/birds-and-wildlife/wildlife-guides/identify-a-bird/
- Rock dove: http://darwinspigeons.com/rock-dove/4532819347
- Rock dove: www.rspb.org.uk/birds-and-wildlife/wildlife-guides/bird-a-z/rock-dove#DjkFyqJi3LOJKkJG.99

Further reading

Websites

- Darwin Correspondence Project: www.darwinproject.ac.uk/
- Darwin Correspondents: www.darwinproject.ac.uk/commentary/key-correspondents
- Darwin Online: http://darwin-online.org.uk/
- Darwin's Scientific Women: www.darwinproject.ac.uk/learning/11-14/darwins-scientific-women
- Gloriana Online: http://digital.library.upenn.edu/women/dixie/gloriana/gloriana.html

Books

- Boulter, M. (2008) *Darwin's Garden: Down House and the Origin of Species*, London: Constable.
- Dixie, F. (1890) *Gloriana or, the Revolution of 1900*, London: Henry and Company.
- Hesse, A. (2015) *Charles Darwin and the Theory of Natural Selection*, Stafford: Millgate House Publishers.
- Hopkinson, D. (2005) *Who Was Charles Darwin?* New York: Grosset and Dunlap.
- Loxley, P., Dawes, L., Nicholls, L. and Dawes, B. (2018) *Teaching Primary Science: Promoting Enjoyment and Developing Understanding*, Abingdon: Routledge.
- Manning, N. (2009) *What Mr Darwin Saw*, London: Frances Lincoln.
- Radeva, S. (2019) *Charles Darwin's On the Origin of Species*, London: Puffin.

ASE Journals

- Primary Science 107 (March–April 2009) This issue of the journal is devoted to Darwin's Legacy.
- Primary Science 141 (January–February 2016) *Darwin's Doodles* by Robbie Kirkman.
- Primary Science 151 (January–February 2018) *Relating School Science to Real-World Scientists* by Helen Spring.
- Primary Science 151 (January–February 2018) *The 'Mighty Women of Science' Make an Impact in a Primary School* by Agnieszka Barden.
- Primary Science 151 (January–February 2018) *Standing on the Shoulders of Giants: Contemporary Scientists Bringing Your Science Curriculum to Life* by Alex Sinclair and Amy Strachan.

Chapter 7 Following in Darwin's footsteps

Jane Goodall   Jennifer Doudna   Rachel Carson

Rosalind Franklin   Kathleen Basford   Mary Leakey

Maria Sibylla Merian   Nora Lilian Alcock

Beatrix Potter   E K Janaki Ammal   Anne McLaren

Margaret Morse Nice   Irène Curie-Joliot

Barbara McClintock   Gertrude Elion   Vera Rubin

Mary Anning   Dorothy Hodgkin   Katherine Freese

Muriel Wheldale Onslow   Margaret Bryan Davis

Abbess Hildegard of Bingen   Caroline Herschel

Marie Curie-Skłodowska   Jane Cooke Wright

Rita Levi-Montalcini   Sau Lan Wu   Sara Seager

Maria Goeppert-Mayer   Tiera Guinn Fletcher

Alfred Russel Wallace   Joseph Dalton Hooker

Richard Owen   Henrietta Darwin   Francis Galton

George Robert Waterhouse   Leonard Jenyns

James Dwight Dana   Charles Cardale Babington

Thomas Henry Huxley   Hugh Edwin Strickland

Adam White   John Herschel   Herman Müller

Robert Chambers   George Brettingham Sowerby

John Burdon-Sanderson   William Lonsdale

Christian Gottfried Ehrenberg   Thomas Bell

William Darwin Fox   Francis Walker

Daniel Sharpe   Thomas Vernon Wollaston

Edward Forbes   John Gould   John Phillips

Samuel Pickworth Woodward   David Milne

William Jackson Hooker   Charles Lyell

Harriet Martineau   Asa Gray   Miles Joseph Berkeley

Vice-Admiral Robert Fitzroy   F W Hope

John Stevens Henslow   CharlesDarwin

CHAPTER 8
PROTECTING ECOSYSTEMS

Big idea: *We need nature and nature needs us. Nature is in serious trouble and it needs our help to recover.*

Part 1: Subject knowledge

This part sets out subject knowledge teachers require to support children's learning towards the big idea. The ideas relate to the impact human activity has had on the natural environment and provides insights into the actions schools can take to help conserve wildlife.

Topics include:
- Loss of biodiversity
- Farming, food and climate change
- What has biodiversity ever done for us?
- Ecosystem services
- Wildlife conservation
- Garden habitats
- Citizen science

Part 2: Working towards the big idea

Each topic aims to move children's understanding further towards the big idea. The journey starts when children engage with activities designed to protect wildlife and are encouraged to think of themselves as wildlife guardians. Children are introduced to the 'health services' nature provides and explore the benefits provided by bees and other pollinators. Children work on their understanding of ecosystem services and explore the damaging effects human activity can have on wildlife. Opportunities are provided for children to take practical action to contribute to wildlife conservation, including taking part in citizen science projects carried out by wildlife conservation trusts.

Chapter 8 Protecting ecosystems

The topics are:
- Wildlife guardians (5–7 years)
- Homes for bees (7–9 years)
- Protecting ecosystems (9–11 years)

Part 1: Subject knowledge

Loss of biodiversity

Sir David Attenborough, in his foreword to the *State of Nature Report 2016*, wrote:

> Our wonderful nature is in serious trouble and it needs our help as never before. We continue to lose the precious wildlife that enriches our lives and is essential to the health and wellbeing of those who live in the UK.

This is a big idea with a big message for us all, especially our children who will need to live with the consequences of climate change and the loss of biodiversity.

Global biodiversity has been in decline for thousands of years, ever since the development of agriculture led to large increases in the human population. To prevent malnutrition and starvation, increases in population require increases in food production. Through the years, more and more forests have been cut down to provide land for farming. As demands for food have increased, farming methods have become more intensive, often only growing huge amounts of particular cereal crops. The agricultural practice of producing a single crop or type of animal is called monoculture.

Farmers target and eradicate pests that damage their crops using pesticides. The use of pesticides can also have a damaging effect on pollinating insects, on which many other plants and our own wellbeing depend. Consequently, much of modern farming reduces biodiversity by creating environments suited to particular animals and plants which are harvested and sold as food, often in supermarkets. Human activity of this kind creates artificial ecosystems which limit biodiversity and result in the loss of precious landscapes and wildlife.

Chapter 8 **Protecting ecosystems**

Today, intensive farming, urbanisation and climate change continue to decimate biodiversity throughout the world. In recent years global biodiversity has fallen dramatically, with wildlife populations falling by 58% since 1970. In the UK, populations of plant and animal species have on average dropped by 13% since 1970. Butterflies and moths have been hit particularly hard, falling by 17% and 25% respectively. According to the *State of Nature Report 2019*, amongst the thousands of animal and plant species assessed, over 40% are in decline and 15% are at risk of being lost.

Farming, food and climate change

A major report published in 2019, by the Intergovernmental Panel on Climate Change (IPCC), called for a radical transformation of the food system. The report found that up to 37% of the world's total greenhouse gases come from the production of food and its refrigeration and transportation, and that about a third of the food is lost or wasted. Methane emitted from farm animals, especially cows, was found to be one of the major contributors to climate change.

The report calls for a reform of farming practices and the conservation and restoration of ecosystems and biodiversity. By reducing food waste, planting forests and restoring wildlife habitats, greenhouse gas emissions can be reduced and the decline in biodiversity can be addressed.

The report highlights how some dietary choices require more land and water and cause more emissions of heat-trapping gases than do others. The report recommends that people play their part in combatting global warming by adopting a balanced diet to improve our health and the health of the planet. It recommends that people eat a lot less meat, especially pork and beef, and eat more plant-based foods. Debra Roberts, co-chair of IPCC Working Group II, wrote:

> Balanced diets featuring plant-based foods, such as coarse grains, legumes, fruits and vegetables, and animal-sourced food produced sustainably in low greenhouse gas emission systems, present major opportunities for adaptation to and limiting climate change.

The changes which are thought necessary to combat global warming add up to a radical transformation in farming practices and people's diets. It means that many people will be asked to reduce their meat consumption by 77% and their consumption of dairy products by 40%. Clearly, saving the planet is not just about planting more trees and using less fossil fuels; it requires cultural changes which many people may be very reluctant to adopt.

What has biodiversity ever done for us?

Our wellbeing is dependent on the wellbeing of the living things with which we share the planet. As consumers we are directly or indirectly dependent on plants for our energy needs. Cereals and other staple crops which provide the majority of human foods are wind-pollinated or self-pollinated. However, at least one third of the crops grown around the world, including fruits, nuts, seeds, beans, coffee and oilseed rape, rely on insects to pollinate them. A wide variety of wildlife contribute to agriculture, including bats, bees, birds, dragonflies, ladybirds, nematodes and worms, among countless others.

When we get sick numerous medicines we need are derived from plants, many of which are only found in rain forests. In the fight against the antibiotic-resistant bacteria MRSA, scientists in the USA have discovered a chemical in the needles of the eastern red cedar which has proved to be effective. In addition, researchers found other chemicals in the tree which are able to kill skin cancer cells present in mice. Although both discoveries are a long way from commercial use, they demonstrate the value of conserving biodiversity. As the National Wildlife Federation points out:

> Every time a species goes extinct or genetic diversity lost, we will never know whether research would have given us a new vaccine or drug.

Ecosystem services

Food and medicine are just two of the many 'ecosystem services' which rely on conserving the earth's biodiversity. Biodiversity provides stable ecosystems that supply oxygen and clean the air we breathe. They also absorb carbon dioxide from the air, which helps prevent climate change. Forests, woodlands, grasslands, gardens and other green spaces absorb and clean water, reduce flooding and limit erosion.

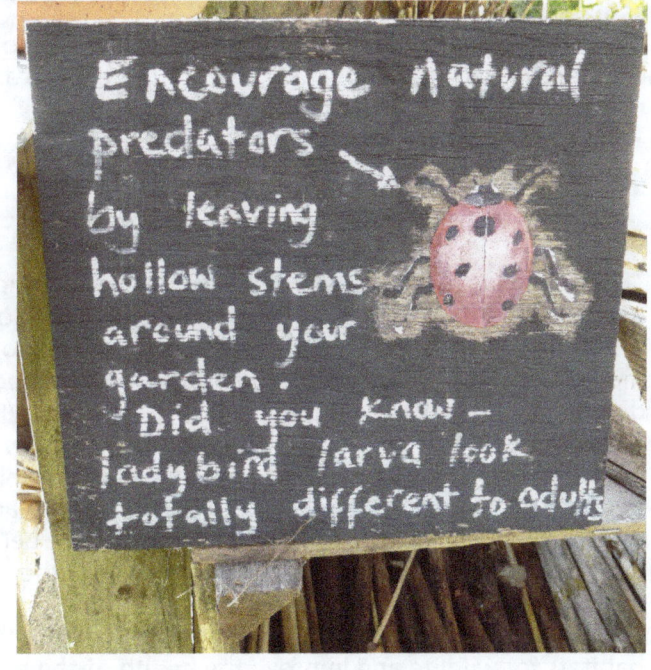

Another service which nature provides is pest control. Why use polluting chemicals in the garden to control pests like aphids, when predator insects and bug-eating birds will do the job for you? By managing habitats in ways which maintain a stable balance in the garden ecosystem, pests can be controlled, while at the same time enriching the biodiversity of the area.

Organic farms control pests by introducing natural predators, growing pest-resistant plants and planting mixed crops which can be rotated from year to year. The term 'agricultural biodiversity' refers to farming practices which make the most of what natural ecosystem services can provide. Increasing the number of crop varieties in an area can reduce the chances of pests finding the plant they feed on and increase the numbers and diversity of predators and parasites that feed on the pests. High levels of agricultural biodiversity can help reduce damage by pests and disease, and also provide a wider variety of food, not just countless tons of the same stuff!

An ecosystem which is species-rich is more resilient and adaptable to external stress, such as disease, than is one in which the range of species is limited. For example, imagine a woodland which only contains one kind of tree, such as elms. Elms are highly susceptible to Dutch elm disease, a fungal infection that could wipe out the majority of the trees in the woodland, and with them most of the wildlife that depend on them. In other words, this one disease could destroy the whole ecosystem. In woodland with a richer biodiversity, the loss of one species is less likely to have such a major effect on the stability of the system. If one species fails in an ecosystem supported by a wide variety of living things, then it is likely there will be other species which are able to keep energy flowing to maintain the system. Biodiversity allows for ecosystems to adjust to disturbances such as disease, fires and floods.

There is a wide range of cultural ecosystem services which are important for people's wellbeing. A biologically diverse environment can be very beautiful and utterly fascinating. Spending time in nature provides experiences and opportunities which can inspire us aesthetically, as well as improve our physical and mental health. All it takes is one step into a natural woodland or a walk through a landscape of wildflowers to makes us realise how lucky we are to be alive, and how much we owe to the great diversity of species with which we share the world.

Wildlife conservation

There is a wide range of national and local conservation groups that are committed to preserving natural habitats and maintaining the rich diversity of UK wildlife. Organisations including the Wildlife Trusts, the Woodland Trust and the Royal Society for the Protection of Birds (RSPB) are making a difference by restoring and protecting important habitats on which struggling species depend. In addition, the Royal Horticultural Society (RHS) are playing their part by campaigning to green up urban areas. The *Greening Grey Britain* campaign is designed to persuade households, schools and other institutions to grow more plants. For example, a quarter of urban gardens are paved over, often creating a barren, lifeless and uninviting feel to the front of the house.

According to the Royal Horticultural Society, the benefits of gardens go far beyond the pleasure they provide for their owners. No matter where they live, people in cities benefit from greening up the environment. Gardens not only brighten up the neighbourhood but also protect against flooding and extremes of temperatures. In addition they improve air quality, provide a source of habitats for wildlife and improve the health of the people who grow plants.

It is surprising how much space there is in our cities to grow plants. When added together garden spaces take up about 25% of the land in a city. A significant proportion of this green space belongs to schools. If all the garden spaces throughout the UK are added together, they cover an area about a fifth of the size of Wales. Think of the diverse range of plants which could be grown in an area this size and the variety of habitats it provides for animals and other living things.

Garden habitats

Gardens provide habitats for a huge variety of plants and animals, as well as other types of living things such as fungi and bacteria. Due to the numbers of different kinds of plants which are grown in close proximity, gardens can maintain a richer diversity of plants and animals than many natural habitats. No natural habitat manages to cram together so many different plants into such a small area, and consequently the richer plant diversity of gardens can lead to greater animal diversity.

One reason plant diversity in gardens tends to be richer than natural habitats is because gardeners often like to grow native and non-native plants. All around a garden a diverse range of micro-habitats are created by clumps of different types of plants, each with the potential to support various species of animals. Most herbivores have different food preferences and hence richer plant diversity naturally leads to greater animal diversity.

A detailed study of an ordinary suburban garden recorded 2,673 species of plants, insects and other invertebrates living there (WLGF online). In addition 54 species of birds, 7 species of mammals and 3 species of amphibians were identified. Even the briefest study of any garden is likely to reveal a diverse range of invertebrates and other animals living there. For example, most gardens provide habitats for worms, slugs, snails, butterflies, moths, bees, wasps, beetles, spiders and ants. These are just a few of the invertebrates commonly found in gardens. Other common animals include amphibians such as frogs and toads, mammals such as mice, bats, squirrels and hedgehogs and a large variety of birds. If you live in the right areas, you might find reptiles such as snakes and lizards also sharing your garden.

The use of non-native plants in a wildlife garden is perhaps controversial, but research has shown that many native and local animals thrive in gardens which contain an abundance of non-native plants. An animal's priority is simply to find accessible food as quickly and efficiently as possible. For some pollinators it doesn't matter whether a flowering plant is native or non-native; the only consideration is the accessibility to the food inside the flowers. In some cases, where non-native plants are bred to produce copious flowers, pollinating insects may prefer them to native plants because they provide a richer source of food.

While providing a rich variety of nectar sources will help adult pollinators to survive, producing the next generation requires providing food for their offspring. Bees take food back to their nest or hive to feed their offspring, but butterflies lay their eggs on the leaves of certain plants. Unlike the adults, the caterpillars of each species are very demanding about the plants they eat. For example, many species of caterpillars will only eat specific native plants, which are called host plants. The nettle is the host plant of a variety of caterpillars including the red admiral, peacock, small tortoiseshell and comma species. The stinging nettle is one of the most important native plants for wildlife in the UK. The nettle provides a habitat for over 40 species of insect which in turn provide food for blue tits and other woodland birds.

Whatever their size, gardens provide a variety of different habitats for wildlife. For example, just by allowing an area of grass to grow long provides a valuable habitat for all sorts of invertebrates, and consequently food for their predators. Long grass is like a mini jungle providing shelter, moisture and food for beetles, various species of caterpillars (moths and butterflies), grasshoppers and other animals. Predators include birds, bats, hedgehogs and small rodents.

Digging a vegetable patch and adding compost to the earth creates habitats for worms and other soil-dwelling creatures, not to mention those animals further up the food chain which prey on them. You will attract herbivores and their predators which feed on the vegetables. If you make your own compost, you also provide a rich habitat for invertebrates, fungi and bacteria. No matter what you do in the garden your actions affect its biodiversity. Uprooting a hedge destroys a whole ecosystem, while planting a tree is the start of a whole new one.

Citizen science

Science education should be relevant to children's lives, and what could be more relevant than helping them take part in real scientific research. Citizen science lets children get involved by collecting or analysing existing data and uploading the results. The results contribute to the success of national and international research projects. Children benefit because they learn more scientific knowledge and skills, and at the same time gain the satisfaction of knowing they have been involved in real and important scientific research.

Mass participation projects enable scientists to collect huge amounts of data which, without the help of the public, would not be possible. For example, the Big Garden Birdwatch is a long-standing citizen science project which is organised by RSPB. The large size of the survey allows scientists to monitor the numbers of the different species of birds which visit our gardens and, by comparing them with previous years, to work out which birds are thriving and which are in decline. The project has been going since 1979, so scientists have a lot of data on which to draw conclusions about the wellbeing of our garden birds.

The 2018 results show that the most abundant bird in the UK and Northern Ireland was the house sparrow. Overall there was an increase in sightings of smaller birds such as goldfinches, long-tailed tits and coal tits from the previous year, but there was a drop in the numbers of blackbirds and robins. It was a good year for some smaller birds, but this has to be set against the enormous decline in numbers of some species over the last 39 years. For example, in 2018 there was a 5% rise in the numbers of greenfinches, but overall they have decreased by 60% since 1979. Outcomes of the Big Garden Birdwatch can be found on the RSPB website, including a list of the top 10 garden birds in the UK and Northern Ireland.

There is a whole spectrum of different types of citizen science activities, from weather monitoring to counting butterflies to recording changes in the shape of clouds. Over time, the scope of citizen science has continued to evolve, with volunteers taking a more active role in the initiation and planning of the projects.

Information sources

- Changing Climate: www.rhs.org.uk/science/pdf/RHS-Gardening-in-a-Changing-Climate-Report.pdf
- International Governmental Panel on Climate Change: www.ipcc.ch/
- Sheffield State of Nature 2018: www.wildsheffield.com/wildlife/wildlife-conservation/sheffield-state-of-nature/

- Species in decline: www.wired.co.uk/article/uk-wildlife-species-decline
- State of Nature Report 2019: www.bto.org/our-science/publications/state-nature-report/state-nature-report-2019
- State of Nature Report 2016: www.rspb.org.uk/our-work/stateofnature2016/Wildlife Gardening Forum (WLGF): http://wlgf.org/

Part 2: Working towards the big idea

Models of good practice

Topic: Wildlife guardians

Age group: 5–7 years

Learning goals

Children take a step towards the big idea by exploring some of the problems wildlife face to survive and by coming to think of themselves as wildlife guardians. Children create simple habitats in the school grounds to provide homes for wildlife, and monitor them to discover the variety of animals which live there. Children are introduced to the 'health services' nature provides by exploring some of the benefits trees provide in their local park. They are introduced to the bigger conservation picture by taking part in citizen science projects to monitor 'bug' and butterfly populations.

Working scientifically

In this topic children will:

- observe closely using simple equipment;
- use their observations and ideas to suggest answers to questions;
- gather and record data to answer questions.

Health and safety

Plan all gardening activities to include appropriately sized tools and equipment, as well as considerations of safety and hygiene. Children should wear protective gloves when handling plants and other materials. Safeguard children against irritant plants. Risk assess the use of plants in the classroom, as well as the outdoor activities. Refer to the relevant safety codes in the ASE publication *Be Safe!* (2011) when planning to teach the activities in this topic.

Chapter 8 Protecting ecosystems

Exploring children's ideas

Set the scene by talking about the need to protect wildlife. Show children a picture of a hedgehog and listen to what children know about them. Explain that they are in danger because many of the wild places where they live have been destroyed. Ask children whether they would like to help the hedgehogs by building a home which they can use in the school grounds. What other animals would they like to help?

Log homes

Piles of logs, branches and twigs can provide shelter for a wide range of wildlife, including hedgehogs, frogs and toads. They are likely to be inhabited by a variety of minibeasts, including beetles, which hedgehogs like to eat. Where you place the logs can make a difference to which creatures choose to use them. Place some in sun and some in shade, and others can be partly buried in the soil. Be creative when building log homes. You can either scatter the logs around a flower bed to create a 'log village' or pile the logs up to create a log 'stately mansion'. Alternately, you can plant different-sized logs vertically into the ground to create 'high-rise apartments' for stag beetles and other creatures. Information for attracting stag beetles can be found on the People's Trust for Endangered Species website.

Encourage children to predict the kinds of creatures that will use the log homes. Children test their predictions by monitoring the log piles at different times of the year. Try not to disturb the piles too often, especially in the winter months when frogs and hedgehogs may be hibernating. Children help design and put up signs explaining what the log homes are about. Use wildlife cameras to discover creatures which visit the log piles in search of food, especially during the night. Post photographs and information about the animals which use the log homes on the school website.

Rock homes

Creatures that are attracted to rock piles are not all the same as those that prefer logs. Rock piles provide dry habitats which attract spiders, solitary bees and perhaps, if you are lucky, the odd lizard or two. Use a range of sizes of stones, with the larger ones on the bottom dug into the soil. Allow plants (weeds) to colonise the rock piles. Children carefully monitor the creatures which use the rock homes, while trying not to disturb creatures that live there. Put up signs explaining what the rock homes are about. Use wildlife cameras over selected periods of time to discover the creatures which visit the rock piles in search of food. Post interesting images from the wildlife cameras on the school website.

Mini-ponds

Even the smallest pond can provide for the needs of an interesting variety of wildlife, including damsel and dragonflies, frogs and newts. It can also supply food and water for birds, hedgehogs and bats.

Build the pond at the beginning of the autumn term. With the help of adults, children can use washing-bowls or large containers to create a number of small ponds in selected places in the school grounds. Choose sheltered places where the bowls can be dug into the ground, providing animals with easy access. Otherwise, provide a ramp to help wildlife access the water.

Fill the ponds with rainwater, which is better for wildlife than tap water. Add one or two water-loving plants to the pond such as miniature waterlily or lesser spearwort. Grow different plants in the various ponds. Visit the *Wildlife Trust* website for more ideas. Allow plants to naturally grow around the ponds, and keep the water topped-up in warm weather.

Children regularly monitor their ponds throughout the year and record how they change from season to season. During the day children can look out for insects and amphibians, as well as birds. They can come to recognise a variety of insects and other creatures such as dragonflies, beetles, pond skaters, water boatmen, water snails, frogs and newts.

Teach children pond-dipping techniques and how to use magnifiers to study the smallest creatures in the pond. Children compare the types of creatures which they discover in the different ponds. Which pond is home to the greatest variety of animals? Which has the greatest numbers? Do the types of plants in the pond influence which animals live there? Does the surrounding vegetation make any difference? Children use their results to describe the characteristics of a pond which make it popular with wildlife.

The best way to monitor the wildlife that visit the ponds is to set up wildlife cameras. Children will be surprised by how many animals visit the ponds, especially after dark. Throughout the year take photographs of the ponds and their inhabitants, and use them to create a display which depicts the diversity of wildlife. Update the display each term to show how pond life changes from season to season.

Butterfly garden

Excite children's enthusiasm for nature by creating a stunning garden full of colourful, nectar-rich plants for butterflies and food for their caterpillars. Nothing is more fascinating than to watch strikingly beautiful butterflies fluttering this way and that amongst a host of multi-coloured flowers.

Start by contacting a branch of Butterfly Conservation in your area, and invite an expert into your school. Children can ask questions about how to attract butterflies to the school grounds. Arrange the content of the presentation in advance so it suits your children.

When attracting butterflies, the way to go is to go wild! Go wild by turning a sheltered, sunny corner of the garden into a wildlife area full of pollen-rich plants for adult butterflies and 'tasty' plants for their caterpillars. To provide a continual source of nectar make sure your plants do not all flower at the same time of the year. For example, plant primroses for early spring flowering, red campion for late spring into summer and verbena for summer into autumn. Plant in blocks, as butterflies like large patches of the same flower. If you have the budget, plant some butterfly (buddleia) bushes against a sunny wall or fence. For the caterpillars plant nasturtiums and common comfrey, and dare I suggest it, nettles. Plant the nettles out of reach of the children, and with their help design signs warning not to touch the leaves. Surround the area with a mixture of aromatic herbs such as lavender, thyme and marjoram. Leave nearby grassed areas to grow, and encourage wildflowers such as dandelions, daisies and buttercups. Organise a rota for regular watering and maintenance.

Children monitor the growth of the plants and the variety of wildlife that visit the habitat throughout the spring and summer terms. Take photographs and publish them week by week as part of a classroom display, so children can see how the habitat changes.

Information sources

- Log homes: https://ptes.org/wp-content/uploads/2016/11/Build-a-log-pile-for-stag-beetles.pdf
- Wildlife Trust: www.wildlifetrusts.org/actions/how-attract-butterflies-your-garden
- Woodland, pond and ditch habitats: www.bbc.com/bitesize/clips/zf6mhyc

Working on scientific understanding

The purpose of this part is to introduce children to some of the things that nature does for them. There are also opportunities for children to further their understanding of habitats.

Start by focussing on habitats. Find out what children know, and revisit some of the ideas from the science curriculum. Establish that habitats are places where animals and plants live and where animals find the food, water and shelter they need to survive. Talk about how the 'homes' which they set up in the school grounds to provide habitats for different kinds of animals. In all, how many different kinds of animals live in the habitats? List the animals for which the children are providing homes, and display the list prominently in the classroom.

What have trees ever done for us?

Take children to a wooded park on a warm summer's day. Measure the temperature outside the park and in areas where there are no trees. Take children on a tour of the park and ask them where they feel coolest, under the trees or out in the open? Compare the temperatures. Talk about how trees cool and clean the air on hot summer days. Discuss how the air in the park is cleaner than the air where there is lots of traffic. Encourage children to hug the trees, and talk about how the trees also provide homes (habitats) for different types of animals.

Ask children what they like about parks. How do parks make them feel? Compare how they feel in a noisy built-up area with a park. What can they do in a park that they cannot do in a built-up area? Ask children to imagine how they would feel if the park were destroyed and turned into a huge carpark. What would happen to all the wildlife that lives in the park?

In small supervised groups, children explore the park to find and identify plants, including trees, which they would want to save if the park were going to be turned into a carpark. Help them take photographs, and listen to their reasons for wanting to save the plants. Ask children to explain why saving the plants will also help save animals that live in the park.

Things to talk about

Back in the classroom, encourage children to talk about what they learnt from their visit to the park. Display their photographs, and together talk about some of the plants which they wanted to save. Focus their attention on the trees, and talk about how saving a tree also helps save the animals which use it for food and shelter. Discuss how planting trees in the school grounds would benefit the children by providing clean air and helping to keep them cool in summer, as well as providing a habitat for wildlife. With the children's help, choose an appropriate deciduous tree to plant in the school grounds which will provide a suitable habitat for local birds. Once planted, children monitor how it changes from season to season, and year to year. Measure its height when it is first planted, and then each term after that to discover how much it has grown. Keep a record of any birds and other animals which visit the tree. In subsequent years, the class can continue to monitor their tree and animals that use it. At different times of the year, set up a wildlife camera which focusses on the base of the tree to identify any after-dark visitors. Create a giant tree display in the classroom, and stick on pictures of animals that may use it.

What are the benefits of plants in the classroom?

Studies suggest that having plants in the workplace can have major benefits for people working in office environments. The benefits include a more attractive workspace, reduced stress levels, increases in productivity, better wellbeing and reduced sickness, cleaner air, reduced noise levels and a boost in creativity (CIPHR, 2018). The limited amount of research which has been done into having plants in the classroom suggest similar benefits, which include reduced absences and improved performance.

Plan your own study to find out what plants in the classroom can do for children's learning in your school. In the short term you could focus on children's attitudes to learning. Start by letting different groups choose and look after their own houseplants. Find out how children feel about the plants and whether they think they make the classroom a better place to learn. Do the plants make them more enthusiastic about learning and why? Monitor their attitudes to learning. Do they work better in groups? Is there less unproductive noise in the classroom? Over the long term you could plan a more objective study into the potential benefits classroom plants have for children's academic learning. Publish the outcomes of your studies in the ASE journal *Primary Science*.

Studies have shown that even pictures of trees and plants in hospitals have been found to have beneficial effects for patients. A similar study in the classroom provides an opportunity for research into the beneficial effects images of nature may have on children's learning.

Information sources

- Benefits of indoor plants: www.ciphr.com/advice/plants-in-the-office/
- Climate and woodlands: https://climate-woodlands.extension.org/trees-and-local-temperature/

The bigger picture

There is a wide range of citizen projects to which primary schools can contribute, with more being started every year. This part provides examples of projects which are suitable for this age group and active at the time of publication. All the projects can be carried out in the school grounds or the local park, and they will help enhance children's understanding of the requirements of the National Curriculum regarding living things and their habitats. To carry out the surveys children will need to rely on their teacher and support staff to help identify the different kinds of invertebrates involved. National surveys also provide opportunities for parents to take part.

OPAL Bugs Count Survey

The Open Air Laboratories (OPAL) network is a UK-wide citizen science initiative that encourages people of all ages to get involved with nature and its preservation, regardless of their background and level of ability. The OPAL Network is led by Imperial College London and includes leading museums, universities and environmental organisations across the UK. The *OPAL Bugs Count Survey* is just one of the many national citizen science surveys which they organise. Its purpose is to audit the variety of invertebrates which live in the built environment, and to compare their habitats in urban, suburban and rural areas. Visit the OPAL website to download all the relevant information, including the *Survey Booklet*, *Identification Guide* and other useful resources. Also download the *Species Quest Identification Guide*.

In addition to the main survey, the *Species Quest Survey* provides exciting opportunities for teachers and children to search for six particular bugs in which scientists have special interest. The bugs are the two-spot ladybird, a beetle called the devil's coach-horse, the small tortoiseshell butterfly, the green shield bug, the leopard slug and the tree bumblebee. Some of these creatures are relative newcomers to the UK, while others are in decline. Information collected by children and teachers can be sent to the research team using the online form on the OPAL website.

The Big Butterfly Count

The *Big Butterfly Count* is organised by Butterfly Conservation. It is a survey which helps researchers assess the health of our environment using butterflies as indicators. It was initially launched in 2010 and is now the world's biggest survey of butterflies and day-flying moths. The count usually takes place between July and August, so it is a nice activity which children can do at the end of the summer term.

All the information you need for children to carry out the survey can be downloaded from the Butterfly Conservation website. Resources include a useful butterfly identification chart, along with instructions about how to carry out the survey and how to submit your results. There is also a *Garden Butterfly Survey* which runs throughout the year, which may interest some schools.

Information sources

- Butterfly Conservation: www.bigbutterflycount.org/
- OPAL: www.opalexplorenature.org/bugscount

Chapter 8 **Protecting ecosystems**

Topic: Homes for bees

Age group: 7–9 years

Learning goals

In this topic, children take a step towards the big idea by focussing their attention on the eco-services provided by bees and other pollinators. They begin by exploring why bees need protecting and act by creating habitats in the school grounds for different types of bees. Children work on their understanding of different kinds of bees and the eco-services which they provide. Children further develop their understanding of conservation by contributing to national citizen science projects which focus on the welfare of bees.

Working scientifically

In this topic children will:

- ask questions and use scientific enquiries to answer them;
- gather, record, classify and present data in a variety of ways;
- report findings from enquiries in appropriate ways;
- use results to draw conclusions and make predictions.

Health and safety

Plan all activities to include appropriately sized tools and equipment, as well as considerations of safety and hygiene. Children should wear protective gloves when handling plants and other materials. Safeguard against irritant plants. Risk assess construction activities in the garden, as well as citizen science projects. When planning to teach the activities in this topic refer to the relevant safety codes in the ASE publication *Be Safe!* (2011).

Exploring children's ideas

Discuss children's attitudes to bees, and find out what they know about them. Do they know that bees around the world are disappearing? In the UK the bee population has declined by one third over the last decade. Is there anything children can do to help? Discuss their ideas and talk about the types of habitats which they can create for bees in the school grounds.

Solitary bees, bumblebees and honeybees

In the UK there are many kinds of bees. Some like the bumblebees and honeybees live in colonies, while others are solitary bees who work alone to build their nests and raise their young. Working in groups, children discuss what they know about the different types of bees. They can use information sources to research the life cycle of the solitary bee and compare it with the bumblebee and the honeybee. A good source of information is the Kew Gardens *Grow Wild* website. Groups produce posters which depict the differences and similarities between the bees.

Nesting sites for solitary bees

Out in the school grounds children can put the outcomes of their research into action by designing and creating nesting sites for different types of solitary bees. Roughly 70% of solitary bees nest in underground burrows. These are mining bees. Sites for mining bees can easily be created with mounds of loose soil. The mound should be big enough to allow the bees to create tunnels about 60 cm deep. It should also have a south-facing bank which catches lots of sunshine to warm up the nests.

Bee hotels are great for providing much-needed shelter to solitary bees that nest in tiny spaces above the ground. To build bee hotels children will need plenty of hollow stems of different diameters, between 3 to 5 mm. Reuse old broken bamboo sticks or buy new ones from your local garden centre. The sticks can be cut and securely tied together to form a nesting site which can be hung in a sunny, yet sheltered position. If you prefer, children can use metal cans or make wooden frames to house their stems. Nesting sites can also be created by drilling holes in old wooden logs, and any other substantial piece of timber you have hanging around.

Nesting sites for bumblebees

Bumblebees require nesting and hibernation sites. In spring the queen emerges from where she has been hibernating in the winter, which may have been a hole in the ground or in a compost heap. This is a dangerous time for the queen because she needs to find food quickly or she will not survive. Queens that are fortunate enough to find enough food go in search of a nest site to lay their eggs and establish a colony. Queens look for a site which is sheltered and near to plants with a good supply of nectar and pollen. Different species prefer different sites. Some like to nest underground, using old mice and vole burrows, while others prefer to nest in undisturbed areas of long grass. Tree bumblebees, as their name implies, like to nest in trees or they may choose an old bird box or an area under a roof.

To add to the number of natural nesting sites in the school grounds, children can do a variety of things. For example, choose a patch of ground and simply let the grass grow wild, including any weeds that appear. They can create a compost heap from piles of leaf litter and grass cuttings, which bees can use as a nesting site and a warm place to hibernate in the winter. For those bees that prefer to nest in trees, children can mimic their habitats by using simple nest boxes lined with leaves. Visit the Bumblebee Conservation Trust website for more ideas.

Things to talk about

Talk about how bees of all kinds feed on nectar and pollen, which attracts them to flowering plants. From this point of view, bees are not fussy eaters. However, different kinds of bees have their own physical characteristics which can make them more suited to feeding from particular types of plants. For example, long-tongued bumblebees are attracted to herbs with deep tubular flowers, while bees with relatively shorter tongues require more open flowers where the nectar is easier to reach. Ask children to talk about how these different requirements influence the design of a bee garden. Children will need to grow a wide range of flowering plants to accommodate

Chapter 8 Protecting ecosystems

different kinds of bees, and also choose a range of plants that will provide flowers for bees from spring through to autumn.

Common garden plants such as lungwort, hellebores, aquilegia, foxgloves, geraniums, cosmos, verbena and sunflowers, grown in the right conditions, will provide continuous sources of nectar and pollen while the bees are active. Also a wide variety of herbs, vegetables and fruit trees produce flowers which are good sources of food. There is lots of information on the web about creating bee-friendly gardens.

Make a herb garden

Planting a herb garden is a sure-fire way of attracting pollinators like bees and butterflies into the school grounds. No matter the size of your school grounds, it is easy to set up a herb garden in raised beds, borders, large containers, hanging baskets or terracotta pots. Buy ready-grown plants in spring, and plant a range of different herbs in the same beds or in containers grouped together. A wider variety of plants is likely to attract a larger range of pollinators. According to the Wildlife Trust, the top 10 wildlife-friendly herbs are rosemary, caraway, hyssop, English lavender, common sage, wild thyme, fennel, chives, common mint and wild marjoram. Mint can be invasive, so it may be a good idea to plant it in its own container.

Bee active

From spring into summer, children monitor and record the different types of bees and other pollinators which feed on the herbs and the use of the nesting sites. They use their findings to identify the types of herbs which are most popular and to find out which kind of herbs different bees prefer. Take photographs and enable children to present their findings in a school assembly.

Information sources

- Bumblebee Conservation Trust: www.bumblebeeconservation.org/about-bees/
- Friends of the Earth: www.friendsoftheearth.uk/bees/bee-hotels-solitary-bees-simple-guide
- GrowWild:www.growwilduk.com/wildflowers/bees-pollinators/take-crash-course-solitary-bees
- Royal Botanical Gardens Kew: www.kew.org/search?textsearch=Bees+
- Solitary bees: www.wlgf.org/wildlife/solitary_bees.html
- Wildlife Trusts: www.wildlifetrusts.org/blog/ryan-clark/guide-solitary-bees-britain

Working on scientific understanding

Start this part by posing the question: what has nature ever done for us? Working in groups, children collaborate to construct arguments for whether the natural world has any relevance to their lives. It is an interesting question to ask young children, and I expect their responses will be both unpredictable and thought provoking. Groups present their arguments and explain their reasoning. Together the class decide whether nature significantly benefits their lives.

What have herbs ever done for us?

Talk about the herbs grown in the school garden. How successfully did they attract pollinators? Encourage children to talk about the things they liked about the herbs. Ask them whether they think herbs have any practical use. Listen to children's ideas, and encourage them to describe how they are used in their homes. Show children a range of lavender products, alongside a potted lavender plant from the school garden or a garden centre. Talk about how the products are used and the purpose of using lavender in the products.

People have used herbs for a wide range of purposes for thousands of years. It is thought that people were using herbs for medicinal purposes as early at 7000 BC. Groups use information sources to research the variety of ways herbs have been used throughout history. Children can focus their research on the use of the herbs grown in the school garden. Prominently display the ways herbs have been used from the time of the ancient Greeks until the present day. Characterise their uses in terms of food flavouring, fragrances and medicinal purposes. Use herbs from the school garden to flavour a summer salad, which children can share while they are doing their research.

Sensory and therapy gardens

Herbs are used to help create sensory gardens in hospital grounds and other care institutions where they can have an impact on the health and wellbeing of patients, staff and visitors. Children can redesign the herb garden to stimulate all the senses. Discuss how the garden will cater for each of the senses. Arrange for a guided tour of a therapy garden in a hospital near you. Visit the *Horatio's Garden* website to discover more about therapy gardens and how they are used to support patients with spinal injuries. Children use information sources to explore gardens around the UK designed to support people with physical and mental disabilities.

What have pollinators ever done for us?

Start by asking children to speculate about whether herbs would exist without the pollinators. Encourage them to justify their ideas. This is an opportunity to revisit some of the ideas about pollination from the science curriculum. Discuss the part pollinators play in the life cycle of flowering plants. Describe how flowers provide food for the pollinators, and how in return the pollinators help the plants reproduce. Talk about what would happen to our plant life if pollinators became extinct.

Talking points: true, false or not sure?

- Bees pollinate all our flowers.
- There are lots of different types of pollinators.
- Flowering plants would not survive without pollinators.
- Pollinators would not survive without flowering plants.
- Pollinators are working for us.
- Pollinators are working for themselves.
- Pollinators are working for nature.

Working in groups, children discuss the talking points and try to reach agreement on their responses. Groups then share their ideas with the rest of the class. Focus discussion on the reasons for their responses. Establish that we get a lot of our fruit and vegetables from flowering plants which are pollinated by insects. Children use information sources to discover the fruit and vegetables which rely on pollinators. Draw children's attention to the fact that at least one third of the crops grown around the world rely on insects to pollinate them. Create a roll of honour for the pollinators which help produce our food. Display it prominently in the classroom.

What have honeybees ever done for us?

Start by asking children what they think honeybees have ever done for them. Listen to their ideas, and find out whether any of the children have experience of beekeeping. If so, give them time to share their experiences with the class. Talk about how, in addition to helping produce fruit and vegetables, honeybees also produce honey and wax. Honey is a nutritious food which is high in carbohydrates (sugar), with very little fat. It is also high in antioxidants which can produce health benefits. Honey is also widely used in the skin care industry. Beeswax has long been used as polish, for both furniture and shoes. It is also used for making candles and in the production of food and cosmetics. So, honeybees are really quite helpful to us!

Beekeeping

Invite a local beekeeper from the British Beekeepers Association (BBKA) to visit your school. Information about how to contact your local branch can be found on their website. To prepare, children discuss what they know and what they would like to find out about honeybees. Compile a list of questions which can be shared with the beekeeper prior to the visit. Things children might want to know include:

- How many bees live in a hive and how is the hive organised?
- How do bees find nectar-rich flowers?
- How do bees make honey?
- How many journeys does it take to make a teaspoon of honey?
- Do bees communicate with each other?
- Why do bees do the waggle dance? (There are video clips on the web.)
- How long do bees live?

- Do bees have any predators?
- Why do bees swarm?

It may be possible to organise a trip to see a beekeeper's hives in action and to talk about setting up a hive in your school grounds. Visit the BBKA website to discover the benefits children can gain from keeping honeybees, and download some of their school resources.

Information sources

- Bees in the curriculum: https:www.beesinthecurriculum.com/
- Beekeeping in schools: www.bbka.org.uk/project-bees-in-schools
- Find a beekeeper near you: www.bbka.org.uk/find-beekeeping-near-you
- Horatio's Garden: www.horatiosgarden.org.uk/
- The Bee Centre: https://thebeecentre.org/get-involved/schools-and-groups/
- The British Beekeepers Association: www.bbka.org.uk/project-bees-in-schools
- Thrive: using gardening to change lives: www.thrive.org.uk/

The bigger picture

Citizen science projects help children to become aware of the role science plays in the conservation of wildlife. This part of the topic enables children to contribute to surveys aimed at monitoring bee populations and reducing their decline. Children gain satisfaction from knowing that the work they are doing is valued and meaningful.

Bee Walk Project

Bumblebees are in trouble. By contributing to the Bumblebee Conservation Trust's *Bee Walk Project*, children collect data which can be used to help reduce their decline. The Bee Walk is a national recording scheme to monitor the numbers of bumblebees across the UK. They are asking volunteers to identify and count the bumblebees they see on an hour's walk each month from March to October. All the data collected contributes to the long-term monitoring of changes to bumblebee populations due to climate change and changes in land use. It will allow the Trust to detect early warning signs of decline in populations.

To take part in the survey children need some basic knowledge about how to identify different types of bumblebees. It may be difficult to organise this as a whole-class activity, but it may provide an opportunity to create a Bumblebee Society in the school to take on this important work. Full details and resources for the project can be found on the Trust's website.

Polli:Nation Survey

The *Polli:Nation* survey is an OPAL project that will provide answers to important research questions about the health and status of pollinating insects across the UK. Children can contribute to this research by surveying the school grounds or the local park.

The *Survey Booklet* and the *Habitat, Plant and Pollinator Guide* can be downloaded from the OPAL website. This is an ideal project for primary schools. It has been designed for people of all ages, backgrounds and levels of experience and is compatible with the requirements of the National Curriculum. Children's findings can be submitted on the OPAL website and published in the school science magazine or on the school website.

The Great British Bee Count

In 2018, Friends of the Earth launched the *Great British Bee Count* to identify how many species of bee are still present in the UK. The results of the survey are available on the Friends of the Earth website. In total, more than 480,000 bees were identified and recorded from 50 different species. The data contributes to the national *Pollinator Monitoring Scheme*, which is the first comprehensive health check of Britain's bees and other pollinators. Children can carry out their own bee surveys and compare their results with the outcomes of the national survey. Downloadable apps from the project can still be used for identification and recording.

The Big Butterfly Count

Butterflies are also important pollinators, and the children can collaborate with other age groups to take part in the *Big Butterfly Count*. Details of the project are set out earlier in this chapter. All the information you need for children to carry out the survey can be downloaded from the Butterfly Conservation website.

Conker tree science

Our conker trees are under attack by 'alien' invaders! The leaf-mining moth is invading the UK and damaging our conker trees. The moth's caterpillars eat the leaves of horse chestnut trees from the inside. The infected trees are weakened and produce smaller conkers. Children can help scientists at Newcastle University monitor the damage being caused by the moths. Visit the *Conker Tree Science* website for details of how to get involved.

Information sources

- Beewalk project: www.bumblebeeconservation.org/beewalk/
- Butterfly Conservation: www.bigbutterflycount.org/
- Conker Tree Science: www.conkertreescience.org.uk/home
- Friends of the Earth Great British Bee Count: https://friendsoftheearth.uk/bee-count
- Polli:Nation: http://polli-nation.co.uk/

Chapter 8 Protecting ecosystems

Topic: Protecting ecosystems

Age group: 9–11 years

Learning goals

In this topic, children make progress towards the big idea by exploring the eco-services provided by trees, hedges and woodlands. They begin by discussing the loss of woodland habitat due to agriculture and urbanisation. To contribute to wildlife conservation, children design and create habitats which replicate features of the woodland in the school grounds. Subsequently, children work on their understanding of ecosystem services and explore the damaging effects human activity can have on them. Opportunities are provided for children to explore what is being done to protect ecosystems by engaging with work carried out by wildlife conservation trusts. Children further develop their understanding of conservation by collecting data for citizen science projects concerning the effects human activity has had on UK wildlife.

Working scientifically

In this topic children will:

- engage in scientific enquiry to answer questions;
- record data appropriately according to the nature of the enquiry;
- analyse results of enquiries to draw conclusions and make predictions;
- report and present findings from enquiries in oral and written forms;
- communicate and disseminate outcomes of enquiries to a range of audiences.

Health and safety

Plan all activities to include appropriately sized tools and equipment, as well as considerations of safety and hygiene. Children should wear protective gloves when handling plants and other materials. Safeguard against irritant plants. Risk assess construction activities in the garden, as well as citizen science projects. When planning to teach the activities in this topic refer to the relevant safety codes in the ASE publication *Be Safe!* (2011).

Exploring children's ideas

Start this topic by quoting the words of Sir David Attenborough:

> Our wonderful nature is in serious trouble and it needs our help as never before. We continue to lose the precious wildlife that enriches our lives and is essential to the health and wellbeing of those who live in the UK.

Talk about the reasons for the decline in wildlife, and focus children's attention on the loss of habitat due to modern agricultural practices and urbanisation. Groups use information sources to discover the reasons why the UK is amongst the most nature-depleted countries in the world. Groups present their findings to the class and discuss whether they think nature needs saving. Talk about the evidence on which their views are based. Ask children what *they* are prepared to do to save nature. Make a large display of all the things they suggest, and create a wish list.

A woodland edge habitat

Propose building a wild area in the school grounds which replicates some of the habitats which have been destroyed by human activity. Suggest that a woodland edge habitat will attract a wide variety of animals into the garden.

In spring, when the trees have grown their leaves, organise a visit to a local area of woodland so children can see what a woodland edge habitat looks like. Encourage children to listen carefully to the sounds of the woodland, both at the edge and deeper inside. Take recorders to compare sounds. Children compare the biodiversity of the edge to further inside the woodland. Compare both flora and fauna, including the variety of wildflowers and invertebrates. Search for signs of larger animals such as frogs, toads, mice, hedgehogs, birds etc. Speculate about what animals might eat in different parts of the woodland, and identify places where they might shelter. Children record their results by taking photographs, making sketches and taking notes. Take photographs of the different levels of vegetation at the woodland edge.

Talk about how woodland edge habitats generally gain more sun than those under the trees further inside the woodland, and hence plants that prefer more sun are often able to grow there. Being open to higher levels of light and rainfall, woodland edge habitats can be more diverse than those deeper inside the woodland. In fact, the majority of plants and animals that inhabit a woodland can be found within a short distance from its boundary or edge.

Creating a woodland edge habitat

Back in the classroom, children analyse their results and draw conclusions about which area of the woodland has the greatest biodiversity. Children use their photographs, sketches and information sources to create a display depicting the biodiversity of the woodland edge. An important feature of a woodland edge is that it is made up of different levels. At the top is the tree canopy formed by the tallest trees, directly below the next level is made up of younger trees, shrubs and bushes, and at the bottom is the ground level which is covered in plants, logs, leaf litter and other rotting vegetation.

To build the habitat in the school garden, you will need a native tree or two to form the backbone of your woodland edge. Purchase deciduous trees to suit the space you have. Just a few metres of ground is enough to establish a dynamic habitat that will support a wide range of creatures. Choose a sunny position.

Plant the trees first; the children can then design the rest of the area. Based on the photographs they took of the woodland edge, groups visualise how the space available to them can be turned into a woodland habitat. Using information sources, they choose wildlife-friendly shrubs, bushes, herbaceous plants and bulbs to create the layers of vegetation found in the woodland. Groups present and justify their designs to the rest of the class. The class collaboratively come to an agreement on a final design, and then they can set about creating it true to nature.

Monitoring the habitat

Children monitor the biodiversity of the habitat at regular intervals throughout the year and for years to come. Use wildlife cameras to record the comings and goings of birds and mammals. Records should be kept which show how the biodiversity responds to seasonal changes and to the introduction of new species of plants. Organic debris such as logs and leaf litter can be added in the early stages to encourage decomposers. Create food webs for the habitat which illustrate the feeding relationships within the woodland edge ecosystem. Children publish their findings in the school science magazine or on the school website.

Add a pond to the woodland edge habitat

Garden ponds play an important role in the conservation of wildlife, as they provide a source of water for a wide variety of living things. As large ponds continue to disappear from our towns and countryside, garden ponds become increasingly important for the survival of the local wildlife. Frogs, for example, are now thought to be more common in garden ponds than in the countryside.

If you are thinking of building your own wildlife pond, there is lots of information available from gardening books or from the web. Otherwise it is just a small job for a local builder or adult volunteers. Choose a site which is open and sunny and not overhung by trees. Make sure the pond is fenced with a locked gate to ensure children's safety when not supervised.

Children should keep a record of how life in the pond changes from season to season, and create a giant food web display which depicts how the ecology of the pond changes over time. Children can publish the results of their findings on the school's blogging platform or in the school science magazine.

Hedgerow habitat

Children are familiar with hedgerows, as they are often found lining roads and footpaths, bordering fields and gardens and on the coast. Hedges come in all shapes and sizes, ranging from neatly trimmed bushes to thick overgrown bushes tangled with dog rose, bramble, honeysuckle and bindweed.

According to the Wildlife Trust, hedgerows provide valuable services for a wide range of wildlife, including:

> song posts, shelter and nesting opportunities for both woodland and farmland birds such as yellowhammer, whitethroat, blue tit and great tit, while nectar, berries, nuts and leaves provide food for an assortment of invertebrates, mammals and birds. In addition to providing excellent wildlife habitats, hedges can help reduce soil erosion and water run-off on arable land.

Hedgerows also provide 'wildlife corridors' which enable small mammals such as hedgehogs to travel safely from one wildlife area to another in search of food.

If you only have a narrow space in which to create a wildlife habitat, then grow hedging from hawthorn, field maple, blackthorn, beech, hornbeam and holly. In the same bed, plant shrubs and herbaceous flowers to provide food for pollinators and other creatures. Plant bare-rooted hedge plants in winter, and stock the bed with shrubs and herbaceous plants that attract the pollinators in spring. Monitor the habitat in similar ways to the woodland edge habitat.

Get the community involved

Projects such as creating a woodland edge habitat, a pond and a hedgerow habitat provide opportunities for parents and other members of the school community to get involved. Take advantage of local expertise and skills. Also take advantage of funds made available to schools by local charities, companies and supermarkets.

Information sources

- Garden ponds: www.rhs.org.uk/advice/profile?PID=622
- RHS wild about gardens: http://wildaboutgardens.org.uk/
- RHS wildlife gardens: www.rhs.org.uk/advice/wildlife-garden
- Woodland edge garden: www.wildlifetrusts.org/actions/how-make-woodland-edge-garden-wildlife
- Woodland, pond and ditch habitats: www.bbc.com/bitesize/clips/zf6mhyc
- Wildlife Trust: www.wildlifetrusts.org/actions

Working on scientific understanding

This part provides opportunities for children to explore the benefits ecosystems provide for their own wellbeing and the health of the planet. They also work on their understanding of the effects human activity can have on ecosystems and what conservation trusts are doing to protect wildlife.

Things to talk about

Talk about how ecosystems provide services which are vital for our wellbeing. As an example, point out that woodlands provide oxygen to breathe, clean the air, reduce climate change by absorbing carbon dioxide and help prevent flooding. Children can discover more about the eco-services provided by woodlands using information sources.

To start to develop the bigger picture, tell children the story of the eco-services provided by vultures in India. For centuries, India's vultures performed an essential cleaning purpose by eating the flesh of the many dead animals that littered the countryside. When the vultures disappeared due to eating toxic farm chemicals, the putrefying fly-ridden corpses were left to be eaten by wild, rabid dogs. As a result the population of dogs

increased rapidly, which led to more and more attacks on local people. The diseased animals killed tens of thousands of people, at a cost of billions of pounds to the Indian economy. This is an example of how human activity can have damaging effects on an ecosystem. The full story and a lot more about ecosystem services can be found in Tony Juniper's book entitled *What Has Nature Ever Done for Us?*

Talking points: true, false, not sure?

- Nature makes our lives better.
- Nature provides our food.
- Nature provides us with clean air to breathe.
- Nature provides us with medicines.
- Nature keeps us warm in winter.
- Nature provides our clothes.
- Nature provides clean drinking water.
- Nature provides materials to build our homes.
- Nature cleans up our pollution.

Groups collaborate to respond to the talking points. Focus class discussion on the reasons for their responses, and encourage children to use information sources to provide examples. Discuss and expand children's ideas to develop their understanding of the wide range of eco-services nature provides.

What has nature ever done for me?

There are lots of different types of services provided by nature which we take for granted. Nature not only provides our food, cleans our air, cleans up the environment and provides clean water, it also looks after our health, provides us with leisure activities, inspires our art and stimulates us emotionally and creatively. Children tell their own stories of what ecosystem services have done for them. They can use their own experiences and information sources to help develop their narratives. Stories can be published in the form of a book of short stories entitled *What Has Nature Ever Done for Me?*

Things to talk about

Focus children's attention on the harmful effects human activity can have on ecosystem services. Use information presented at the beginning of the chapter to discuss how human activity has destroyed ecosystems, and the effect the destruction has had on biodiversity and climate change.

Talk about how 53% of wildlife species in the UK declined between 2002 and 2013, while the rest of the species were increasing. If that trend carries on into the future, we will soon be left with less than half of the species we have today. Choose parts of the *State of Nature Report 2019* to share with the children.

What is being done in the UK to protect wildlife?

To find out what is being done in the UK to protect wildlife, children explore the websites of the main conservation trusts. Groups choose a trust to research and produce posters which depict their work. Trusts and societies which work in the UK include Wildlife Trusts, Woodland Trust, National Trust, Royal Society for the Protection of Birds, World Wildlife Fund, Royal Horticultural Society, Plantlife, Bumblebee Conservation Trust, Bat Conservation Trust, Butterfly Conservation Trust, Freshwater Habitats Trust and the British Trust for Ornithology.

Most of the conservation trusts provide activities for schools. They are designed to encourage children to explore, appreciate and enjoy the natural world. Trusts also provide opportunities to support their work by taking part in award schemes, volunteering and citizen science projects.

Woodland Trust

The Woodland Trust runs the *Green Tree Schools Award*. The scheme rewards schools for completing environmental projects and encourages outdoor learning. Activities include planting trees, visits to the local woodland, becoming tree champions, recycling in school, the diamond photography challenge, the platinum award challenge and reducing carbon dioxide emissions.

The activities enable children to get to know their local woodland and to become a voice for conserving trees and woodland in their area. The award encourages children to share their experience of the woodland with other children, teachers and parents. It is suggested they put on a play, an assembly or a presentation for the whole school, including parents. Children may want to link up with another school to share their experiences. They can also publish on the school's website, in the newsletter or on the school's blogging platform.

Wildlife Trusts

Join your local Wildlife Trust and take action for wildlife by taking part in organised events, fundraising, campaigns, wildlife gardening and photography competitions and by organising regular visits to the local nature reserves. There are lots of things children can do, including caring for nature reserves, community gardening, planting trees, identifying plants, surveying species or forming a school Wildlife Watch group. Watch groups are organised by volunteer leaders who know about local places and wildlife. Groups work with local experts to organise all kinds of wildlife and environmental activities such as badger watching, bat detecting, pond dipping, wildlife campaigns, wildlife gardening, minibeast surveys, arts and crafts, environmental games, tree health surveys, composting, woodland wanders, and much, much more! Contact your local Wildlife Trust for details.

The Royal Society for the Protection of Birds

The RSPB website provides a rich source of ideas, activities and resources for schools to engage with and support wildlife. The *Schools Wild Challenge* provides opportunities for children to help wildlife, explore nature and work towards awards by taking part in a range of outdoor activities.

The RSPB offers outreach visits to primary schools by trained educators which are designed to inspire children's interest in nature. They also arrange visits to local RSPB reserves where children explore the wildlife and discover the delights nature has to offer. Not surprisingly, the RSPB has lots of useful information about supporting birds. The activities focus on helping birds with their basic needs, such as providing the right food, building nesting boxes and providing bathing and drinking water, and give other advice about how children can support the welfare of birds in their school, at home and in the surrounding areas.

World Wildlife Fund (WWF-UK)

In recent years, scientists have identified livestock farming as one of the main producers of greenhouse gases that contribute to global warming. One of the ways the WWF is tackling the problem is through their *Plant2Plate Campaign for Schools*, which focusses on what can be done to produce and consume food in a sustainable way that is less harmful to the planet and healthier for the children. Full details of the campaign, with lots of resources for schools, can be found on their Plant2Plate web pages.

The schools campaign is part of their *Livewell for Life* initiative, which addresses the changes needed in food production and diets to keep global temperature rise below 2 degrees. The work has produced a diet that is environmentally sustainable, affordable and consistent with national nutritional guidelines and food preferences in the UK. The *Livewell Plate* is a visual presentation of a healthy and sustainable diet, which illustrates the types and portions of food an average adult needs.

Children can visit the Livewell web pages to discover the changes needed in food production and diet to limit climate change. Using the Livewell Plate as a guide, they can plan their own sustainable diet and compare it with what they presently eat. Children discuss whether they eat both healthily and sustainably. What changes do they need to make to their diet to help limit climate change?

Working in groups, children discuss the six Livewell principles for healthy and sustainable food. Do they normally think about their health and the wellbeing of the planet when they choose what to eat? What normally influences their choices? Could children of their age be persuaded to adopt a sustainable diet? Talk about the practical problems. Groups discuss the questions and produce posters designed to inform and persuade children of their age to adopt a sustainable diet.

Six Livewell principles for healthy and sustainable food

1. Eat more plants – enjoy vegetables and wholegrains.
2. Eat a variety of foods – have a colourful plate.
3. Waste less food – one third of food produced for human consumption is lost or wasted.
4. Moderate your meat consumption, red and white – enjoy other sources of proteins such as peas, beans and nuts.
5. Buy food that meets a credible certified standard – such as the Marine Stewardship Council (MSC), free-range and fair trade.
6. Eat fewer foods high in fat, salt and sugar – keep food such as cakes, sweets and chocolate as well as cured meat, fries and crisps to an occasional treat. Choose water, avoid sugary drinks and remember that juices only count as one of your five a day, however much you drink.

(WWF Livewell website, 2019)

Information sources

- It's time to reconsider our food system: www.wwf.org.uk/what-we-do/area-of-work/food
- Livewell: www.wwf.org.uk/what-we-do/area-of-work/livewell
- Plant2plate: www.wwf.org.uk/get-involved/schools/school-campaigns/plant2plate
- Plant2plate resources: www.wwf.org.uk/get-involved/schools/resources/plant2plate-resources
- RSPB Birdwatch: www.rspb.org.uk/get-involved/activities/birdwatch/
- RSPB Birdwatch results: www.rspb.org.uk/get-involved/activities/birdwatch/results/
- Woodland Trust: www.woodlandtrust.org.uk/get-involved/schools/green-tree-school-award/
- RSPB: www.rspb.org.uk/fun-and-learning/for-teachers/schools-wild-challenge/

The bigger picture

Citizen science provides opportunities for children to engage in real-life science projects designed to help address the decline in UK wildlife, and also to contribute to science's understanding of the effects of climate change on the behaviour of wildlife. Citizen science projects can present global issues in a way that is locally relevant and provides motivation to get involved. Projects can also bring together the community, parents, experts and children in a quest to help save our wonderful wildlife.

Nature's Calendar

Nature's Calendar is a citizen science project organised by the Woodland Trust to track the effects of weather and climate change on wildlife. By creating a woodland edge garden in the school grounds children are contributing to the conservation of wildlife, and by taking part in this project they can use the garden to help scientists monitor the effects climate change is having on wildlife behaviour in the UK.

Chapter 8 Protecting ecosystems

The project involves looking out for signs of the changing seasons. For example, they log when certain leaf buds burst, when children see the season's first butterfly, when certain birds start to build their nests, when certain trees start to drop their leaves and when fruit starts to ripen on particular plants. By collecting and submitting the data, children will be contributing to a long biological record that dates back as far as 1736.

Information about the project can be found on the Woodland Trust website, with details of all the different animals and plants which children choose to record. They also provide a quick guide to recording which includes the following steps:

1. Choose the species and events children want to record.

Children choose from a wide range of animals and plants those they expect to be able to monitor in the school garden. At certain times of the year, children will need to check for specific events at least twice a week. For example, if they choose to monitor blue tits, children will be required to record when they first start building their nests and when they first start feeding their young.

Recording starts in February and may continue until June. The Trust provides a calendar which lists all the wildlife which could be monitored and the times of the year when children need to record specific events.

2. Choose recording locations.

Identify recording locations in the school grounds where children will be able to observe their chosen plants and animals. Areas like the woodland edge garden, the hedge habitat and the pond are likely to provide a range of wildlife for children to observe. Visit the Woodland Trust website for further ideas about where children can monitor wildlife.

3. Record observations.

At least twice a week, children look out for the seasonal events that they want to record. They should record the date when they first see each event, and take photographs to add to the record. They submit the record as soon as possible on the Woodland Trust website. Children are encouraged to continue taking records in the same location each year to add to the database.

The Woodland Trust uses the records to create live maps of the locations and dates, where and when seasonal events took place in the UK. Children use the maps to analyse how animals and plants behave in different parts of the UK. For example, do blue tits build their nests at the same time of the year in each part of the UK? If not, children can look for a pattern which can be used to predict in which part of the country they will nest first. Encourage children to speculate about the reasons for the patterns.

Biodiversity Survey

This is a project which is organised by the Open Air Laboratories network. OPAL is a UK-wide citizen science initiative that allows people of all ages to get hands-on with nature, whatever their background and ability. Take part in the *OPAL Biodiversity Survey* and uncover the diverse range of wildlife in hedges around the school or the local park. This project enables children to contribute to important research and further develop their understanding of habitats and ecosystems.

Hedges support a wide variety of animals by providing food and shelter. Berries and seeds are food for birds, while holes beneath the hedge are often home to small mammals. Also, children will find different kinds of invertebrates living among the leaves. By recording the wildlife they discover in the hedge and submitting their findings on the OPAL website, children can learn about the condition of the hedge and how to improve it. The best time to do this survey is from April to November.

Download the *Biodiversity Survey Booklet*, the *Hedgerow Identification Guide* and the *Invertebrate Identification Guide* from the OPAL website. Full details of how to carry out the survey and how to submit the results can be found in the guides and on the website.

Air Survey

OPAL is running activities for schools which help scientists learn more about how the natural environment is affected by air pollution. This project asks children to collect data on lichens on tree bark and tar spot fungus on sycamore leaves, both of which are indicators of air quality in the surrounding area. Lichens are fascinating because they are two types of organisms living together, a fungus and an alga. The fungus forms the body that protects the alga, while the alga in return provides food for the fungus. How wonderful is that! The project is well supported with a wide range of information and identification sheets to download. The data already collected is available for children to analyse. For more information, visit the OPAL surveys website where you can find a wide range of citizen science projects.

Tree Health Survey

Like much of our wildlife trees are under threat, not only from human activity, but also from attacks by pests and diseases which have increased in the last few years.

Children can help protect trees by taking part in the OPAL *Tree Health Survey*. By doing so they will contribute to an important national science project and develop their knowledge of ecosystems by exploring the pests and diseases which affect local trees. Children visit the OPAL website and download the survey pack which includes a *Tree Health Survey Booklet*, a *Tree Identification Guide* and a *Tree Pest and Disease Identification Guide*. Full details of how to carry out the survey and how to submit the results can be found in the guides and on the website.

Information sources

- Citizen science projects: https://blog.rsb.org.uk/everyones-a-scientist-and-here-are-some-places-to-start/
- OPAL Air Survey: www.opalexplorenature.org/airsurvey
- OPAL Biodiversity Survey: www.opalexplorenature.org/biodiversitysurvey
- OPAL Surveys: www.opalexplorenature.org/surveys
- OPAL Tree Survey: www.opalexplorenature.org/treesurvey
- Woodland Trust: https://naturescalendar.woodlandtrust.org.uk/

Further reading

Books

- Ikin, E. (2016) *Garden Friends*, London: National Trust.
- Juniper, T. (2013) *What Has Nature Ever Done for Us?* London: Profile Books.
- Titchmarsh, A. (2011) *Wildlife Gardening*, London: BBC Books.

Chapter 8 Protecting ecosystems

Extinction   Melting ice-caps   Carbon emissions
Rewilding   Deforestation   Recycling   Zero waste
Food miles   Renewable energy sources   Pollution
Greenhouse gasses   Sustainable production
Climate change   Carbon neutrality   Planting trees
Micro plastics   Up-cycling   Rising sea levels
Loss of habitat   Energy efficiency   Reforesting
Global eco-systems   Sustainable development
Single use plastic   Global warming
Eco-warriors   Recovering precious metals
Waste management   Green economy   Bug hotels
Plastic bag tax   Mob-hedging   Seed banks
Wildlife corridors   Urban greening   Pesticides
Endangered species   Biosphere reserves
National parks   Conservation   Agro-ecology
Edible playgrounds   Habitat fragmentation
Particulate capture   Living roofs & vertical greening
Forest bathing   The web of life   Nature reserve
Eco-school   Community gardens   Heirloom planting

Chapter 8 Protecting ecosystems

THE SHINING RAM'S-HORN – 80% EYED LONGHORN BEETLE – 90% WRYNECK – EXTINCT. THIN WEBLET – 84% COD – 87% HADDOCK – 99% GREY PARTRIDGE – 92% WILLOW WARBLER – 44% SMALL SKIPPER – 75% WHITE ERMINE – 70% SAND RUNNING SPIDER – 61% LING – 96% BLACK GROUSE – 80% HAIRY STONECROP – 45% TREE PIPIT – 69% APPLE BUMBLEBEE – EXTINCT. SONG THRUSH – 50% LAGOON SANDWORM – 50% CONGER EEL – 89% WHITE STORK – EXTINCT. WHIMBREL – 50% SMALL COPPER – 46% ROSEATE TERN – 52% JUNIPER – 15% WHITE LETTER HAIRSTREAK – 93% TAWNY OWL – 37% WESTERN WOOD-VASE HOVERFLY – 66% COMMON SANDPIPER – 46% CARLINE THISTLE LEAFHOPPER – 66% HOUSE SPARROW – 66% ROUND-FRUITED RUSH – 46% SPREADING HEDGE PARSLEY – 54% PINTAIL – 38% CALLUM'S BUMBLEBEE – EXTINCT. KINGFISHER – 17% FROSTED YELLOW MOTH – EXTINCT. BASTARD PALM – 37% LAPWING – 64% PURPLE EMPEROR – 61% LAGOON SANDSHRIMP –20% HIGH BROWN FRITILLARY – 67% SPOTTED FLYCATCHER – 85% RUFF – 72% GREATER WATER-PARSNIP – 65% PLAICE – 97% GLUTINOUS SNAIL – 50% SHAG – 45% FLOWERING RUSH WEEVIL – 90% LINNET – 55% EURASIAN LYNX – EXTINCT. TURBOT – 85% HARBOUR SEAL – 23% CORN BUNTING –89% BLACK VEINED WHITE BUTTERFLY – EXTINCT.

(Endangered species taken from A Peoples Manifesto for Wildlife: http://www.chrispackham.co.uk/a-peoples-manifesto-for-wildlife)

INDEX

acorns 121, 122
adaptation 3, 4, 65, 66, 67, 79, 82, 85, 89, 91, 95, 99; birds 83, 84; dinosaurs 90; wildflowers 140; woodland invertebrates 86; woodland vertebrates 87
agricultural biodiversity 181
anthers 109, 127
aphids 26
archaeopteryx 90
arthropods 87, 169
artwork 42; botanical 129–130, 138, 162, 170; creating woodland paintings 60; tulips 133
asexual reproduction 111, 135
Association for Science Education (ASE), *Be Safe!* 20, 29, 37, 48, 71, 80, 89, 113, 119, 131, 151, 156, 162, 185, 200
Attenborough, D. 179, 200
autumn 114, 120

bacteria 52, 54, 55, 182, 184
Barber, M. E. 150
bat boxes 35
BBC (British Broadcasting Corporation), *Blue Peter* 80
Beaty, A., *Ada Twist* 151
Becker, L. 150
beekeeping 197, 198
bees 1, 2, 85, 108–109, 110, 126, 127, 178, 183, 192, 195, 197–198; interdependence 2, 3; nesting sites 193; pollination 2, 3
Beetle Mania 170
beetles 162, 168, 169, 170
behaviour of earthworms 163–164
binoculars 9
BioBlitz 102, 103
biodiversity 8, 28, 70, 102, 181, 182; agricultural 181; conservation 179–180; loss of 179, 180; plants 183

birds 34, 59, 71, 86, 87, 89, 93, 94, 162, 184; adaptation 67, 68, 83, 84; evolution 90; finches 97; and the great extinction 90–91, 92; habitats 80, 81, 82; identifying 172–173; mating rituals 58; natural selection 68; nests 93; perching 66, 84; pigeons 172; vultures 204
Blackwell, A. 150
blogs 19, 59, 92, 94
botanical art 129–130, 138, 162, 170
botanical gardens 170
brachiosaurus 99
British Hedgehog Preservation Society (BHPS), *Hedgehog Street* 88
bulbs 132–133
Bumblebee Conservation Trust, *Bee Walk Project* 198
bumblebees 128, 192; nesting sites 193
burdock 109, 110
butterflies 75, 126, 127, 149; attracting 188; life cycle 76; probiscis 78; searching for 76, 77
Butterfly Conservation 76; *Big Butterfly Count* 191

carbon dioxide 25, 204; *see also* photosynthesis
carnivores 34, 58; Venus flytrap 25, 138
caterpillars 75, 76, 78, 93; searching for 77
catkins 126
children's learning 39; effective talk 18; indicators of good practice 16; re-describing stage 15; scientific inquiry 16; story-telling 16, 17; talking points 18
citizen science 178, 184, 185, 191, 198, 207
classification 82
classroom learning 7, 8, 86–87, 153, 189–190; connecting with outdoor learning 8–9; talking points 18

Index

climate change 180
cloning 111–112
collaboration 18, 19, 41, 74, 124, 152, 156, 161
collecting plants 153, 154
community gardens 9, 30, 47
companion crops 46–47
competition for resources 26, 27, 28
compost 39, 56; ecology of 49–50; testing 51
conkers 121, 122, 127, 199
conservation 182, 185
conservation trusts 205
consumers 47
cross-pollination 134

dandelion 124
Darwin, C. 1, 15, 19, 96, 97, 138, 144, 152, 153, 155, 157, 162, 163, 173; collection of beetle specimens 168, 169, 170; correspondents 148, 149, 150, 165, 166, 167; family life 145, 146, 156; *On the Origin of Species* 146, 158, 172; *The Origin of Species* 97; theory of evolution 70, 146, 147–148, 171; theory of natural selection 68, 69; tree of life 102; weed garden experiments 159–161; *see also* adaptation; evolution
Darwin, W. 146
Darwin Correspondence Project website 148, 150, 161, 165, 167
decomposers 3, 15, 47, 48, 52, 57; bacteria 55; detritivores 49; fungi 55; mould 54; mushrooms 53, 54
detritivores 48, 49, 50, 57
digital cameras 9
dinosaurs 89, 95, 98, 101–102, 110; archaeopteryx 90; brachiosaurus 99; fossil record 99; mass extinction 90, 91, 92, 95, 96, 100; triceratops 96; tyrannosaurus rex 96
discovery gardens 8–9
diversity 110
Dixie, F. 150; *Gloriana* 149
dog breeding 173, 174
Drosera filiformis 166
Dutch elm disease 181, 182

earthworms 150, 151, 152, 162, 165, 167; experiments 163–164
ecology 44; of a compost heap 49–50, 51
ecosystem services 181

ecosystems 3, 8, 23, 26, 47, 56, 178, 179, 203, 204, 205; biodiversity 28; competition for resources 26, 27, 28, 58; decomposers 3, 15, 47, 48, 52, 53, 54; primary consumers 3, 26; primary producers 3, 26, 41; *UK Ladybird Survey* 59, 60; woodlands 57
effective talk 18, 152
endangered species 100–101
erosion 181
evolution 3, 4, 67, 89, 96, 98, 99, 107, 110, 136, 146, 147–148, 162, 171; birds 90; Lamarck, J.-B. 148; mammals 100; natural selection 68, 69, 70; in the school garden 97; tree of life 102; *see also* Darwin, C.
experiments 154, 155, 157, 162; Darwin's weed garden 159–161; earthworms 163, 164, 165, 167
extinction 7, 66, 88; of dinosaurs 90, 91, 92, 95, 96

farm animals 112, 117, 118
farming 179, 180; and climate change 180; organic 181
feeding, plants 25
feeding relationships 23, 24
fertilisation 109
fertiliser 38, 39, 42, 52
figurative language 15
finches 96, 97; Darwin's theory of natural selection 68, 69; *see also* birds
first-hand experience 108
flowers 108, 123, 127; botanical art 129–130; comparing structures of 115, 116; floral formulae 129; growing from seeds 116; interdependence 2, 3; orchids 110; pollination 1, 2, 3, 109, 110; tulips 111, 131, 132–133
flying insects, searching for 76, 77
food chains 3, 34, 36, 43, 45
food production 179; and climate change 180; sustainable 206
food webs 45
formative assessment 19
fossil record 99
Friends of the Earth, *Great British Bee Count* 199
fruit 109, 119, 121, 122
fungi 52, 55, 102, 182, 184

Index

Galapagos Islands 69, 96, 97, 152
games: copycat 136, 137; hot seating 44, 83, 84; role play 71, 72; snap 31; sultana 120–121
gametes 109
gardens 7, 24, 29, 60–61, 70, 182–183, 184; bird-friendly 81, 82; butterfly 188; choosing vegetables to grow 38; companion crops 46–47; compost 39; creating wildlife habitats 60; decomposers 48, 52; discovery 8; fertiliser 38, 39, 42, 43; growing sugar snap peas 51–52; Harvest Festival 40; herb 195, 196; insects 48; keeping a garden journal 39; minibeasts 71, 72, 73; mushrooms 55; pests 44, 45, 46; seeds 37; sensory 196; soil testing 37–38; suburban 183; testing commercial compost 51; weeding 116, 117, 137–138; see also outdoor learning
Garrett, E. 150
germination 24–25, 123, 124, 125, 127
glucose 25
Grant, P. 69, 97
Grant, R. 69, 97
Gray, A. 167
Great British Wildflower Hunt (GBWH) 139–140
group discussion 43, 74, 83; collaboration 41; talking points 18, 29–30
growing: acorns and conkers 121, 122; edible plants 36; flowering plants from seeds 116; heirloom tulips 135; microgreens 32; mould 54; sunflowers 33, 34; tulips 131; vegetables 38; wildflowers 140
Guide to Running a BioBlitz 102–103

habitats 70, 71, 74, 75, 77, 78, 80, 185; bird 80, 81, 93, 94; butterfly 188; hedgerows 202, 203; log homes 186; loss of 66, 88; mammal 100; mini-ponds 187, 188; rock piles 187; trees 92, 93; wildflower meadows 128, 129; woodland edge 201; woodlands 66, 67, 83, 85, 86; see also woodlands
Harlen, W. 14; *Working with Big Ideas of Science Education* 16
Harlequin 59
health and safety, 19
hedgehogs 87, 88, 94, 100
Hedgehog Street 88

hedgerows 202, 203
heirloom tulips 135
Henslow, J. 146, 167
herb gardens 195, 196
herbivores 34, 58, 183, 184
HMS *Beagle* 146, 148, 152, 153, 157
honeybees 192–193, 197
Hooker, J. 159, 160, 167, 170
hornets 92
hot seating 44, 83, 84
Huxley, T.H. 97, 167
hybridisation 111
hyphae 52–53

identification apps 9
indicators of good practice 16; effective talk 18; formative assessment 19; health and safety 19–20; publishing 18–19; talking points 18
inheritance 3, 4, 107, 110, 117, 134, 139; selective breeding 111; see also evolution
insects 48, 72, 93, 126, 138; butterflies 75, 76; hornets 92; pollination 108–109; searching for 76, 77
interdependence 2, 3, 4, 26; pollinators 25; subject knowledge 23
invertebrates 49, 50, 67, 71, 85, 93, 102, 153, 183; arthropods 87; beetles 168, 169; hornets 92; woodland 86; see also insects

Juniper, T., *What Has Nature Ever Done for Us?* 204, 205

keeping a garden journal 39
Kew Gardens 170

ladybirds 59, 60
Lamarck, J.-B. 148, 171
learning 15, 112; collaboration 18; from first-hand experience 108; indicators of good practice 16; through experience 24; see also classroom learning; outdoor learning
leaves 41, 42, 113; compost 49–50
lichens 55
life cycle 139; of bumblebees 128; of butterflies 76
Loxley, P. 15
Lyell, C. 167

mammals: evolution 100; giant 99
marigolds 47
mass extinction of dinosaurs 90, 98, 100, 101–102
mating rituals 58
meadows 1, 128, 129
microgreens 32
minibeasts 71, 72, 73, 74, 150, 151, 153; butterflies 75, 76; searching for 76, 77; woodlice 74–75; *see also* insects; invertebrates
models of good practice 14, 15; formative assessment 19; indicators 16
molluscs 169
monoculture 179
Morris, W. 42
mould 54
mushrooms 52, 53, 54, 55

narrative 14
National Trust 11
natural selection 3, 68, 69, 70, 146, 147, 148; *see also* evolution
nature conservation 14
nature reserves 10–11
nectar 78, 127, 183, 188, 193; sources of 195
nettles 76, 183
North, M. 150
nutrients 42, 43, 45
nuts 121; growing acorns and conkers 121, 122

omnivores 34, 57, 58
OPAL website 164
Open Air Laboratories (OPAL) 9; air survey 209–210; *Biodiversity Survey* 209; *Bugs Count Survey* 191; Polli:Nation survey 199; *Tree Health Survey* 210
orchids 110
organic farms 180
outdoor learning 6, 7; and affection for nature 7–8; community gardens 9; connecting with classroom learning 8–9; food chains 35; growing sunflowers 33; health and safety 19–20; models of good practice 14; nature reserves 10–11; parks 9; science 7; support from experts 11; and technology 9; thinking and talking with scientific ideas 108–109; woodlands 10–11; writing about 19; *see also* children's learning; classroom learning; indicators of good practice
oxygen 25, 203; *see also* photosynthesis

Packham, C. 80
parks 9, 112, 113, 127, 172, 189, 191; seasonal changes 114; visiting 153, 154
Peoples Manifesto for Wildlife 8
People's Trust for Endangered Species (PTES) 100–101
pesticides 179
pests 44, 45, 181; controlling in the garden 45–46
pH testing 37, 51
photosynthesis 3, 24–25, 41
pigeon breeding 172
Places of Poetry 87
plants 3, 24, 29, 36, 39, 41, 70, 102, 108, 112, 113, 117, 122, 123, 124, 125, 127, 134, 136, 146, 153, 157, 162; asexual reproduction 111–112, 135; burdock 109, 110; in the classroom 190; cloning 111–112; collecting 153, 154; companion crops 46–47; competition for resources 26, 27, 28; dandelion 124; defences 58–59; feeding 25; formulae 129; germination 24–25; growing from seeds 116; interdependence 25, 26; leaves 41, 113; life cycle 119; medicinal 180–181; microgreens 32; nutrients 42–43, 45; photosynthesis 3, 25; pollination 109; roots 67; scientific drawings 42; seeds 109, 110; selective breeding 111; stinging nettles 59; stomata 25; Venus flytrap 138; wildflowers 138, 139; xylem tubes 25; *see also* flowers; gardens; seeds
pollen 127, 193
pollination 1, 2, 3, 107, 108–109, 109, 110, 126; wind 127–128
Pollinator Monitoring Scheme 199
pollinators 1, 2, 25, 27, 33, 34, 126, 139, 183, 192, 196; *see also* gardens
ponds 46, 187, 188; adding to a woodland edge habitat 202
Potter, B. 55
predators 34, 35, 44, 46, 58, 184
primary consumers 3, 26
primary producers 26
producers 36, 47; nutrients 45
publishing 18–19, 39, 51

Quadblogging 19

recyclers 15
reproduction 1, 2, 3, 67, 70, 107, 108, 110, 117, 126, 130, 148; asexual 111, 135; gametes 109
Roberts, D. 180
rock piles 187
role play 71, 72
Royal Horticulture Society (RHS) 7, 8, 11, 44; *Gardening in a Changing Climate* 60–61; *Greening Grey Britain* 182
Royal Society for the Protection of Birds (RSPB) 7–8, 91, 92, 93, 173, 182; *Big Garden Birdwatch* 80, 82, 184; *Schools Wild Challenge* 206
Royer, C. 150

scaffolding 14
school gardens 78; detritivores 49; health and safety 29; monitoring wildlife 79; vegetables 24
science 14, 165; citizen 184, 185, 191, 198, 207; *see also* experiments
science learning 7
science, technology, engineering and mathematics (STEM) 11
scientific explanations 144, 145
scientific ideas 15, 66; thinking and talking with 108–109
scientific inquiry 16; story-telling 16, 17
seasonal changes 114; autumn 120; spring 126
seeds 37, 109, 110, 121, 122, 123, 125, 141, 157; bulbs 132–133; buoyancy 157; dandelion 124; effect of saltwater on 157; growing flowering plants from 116; health and safety 48, 112–113
selective breeding 111, 134, 136
sensory gardens 196
sexual reproduction 109
shrews 99, 100
smartphone identification apps 9
snails, survival of mass extinction 101–102
snap 31
Social Farms and Gardens 9
soil 36, 41, 48; composting 49–50, 51; and earthworms 164–165; nutrients 42; testing 37–38
species 70
spring 126

squirrels 121
State of Nature 2016 report 179
State of Nature 2019 report 7, 180, 205
stigma 109, 127
stinging nettles 59
stomata 25, 41
story-telling 16, 17, 56, 58, 59, 71
sugar snap peas, growing 51–52
sultana game 120–121
sunflowers 32; growing 33, 34; *see also* plants
support from experts 11
sustainability 206

talking points 18, 19, 29–30, 40, 43, 48, 74, 83, 98; mushrooms 54
testing, commercial compost 51
Treat, M. 138, 149, 150, 162, 166, 167
tree of life 102
trees 92, 112, 113, 127, 189; autumn colours 114; Dutch elm disease 181, 182; elm 181; roots 67
triceratops 96
trusts 11, 205
tulips 131, 132–133, 136; heirloom 135; hybrids 135; Paul Scherer 134; *see also* flowers
tyrannosaurus rex 96

UK Ladybird Survey 59, 60
Understanding the size of bacteria 55
United Kingdom 24, 55, 201; 'biodiversity intactness' 7–8; British Beekeepers Association (BBKA) 197; Butterfly Conservation 76; National Curriculum 65, 107, 144; nature reserves 11; pigeons 172; population survey of British wildflowers 138, 139; trusts 11, 92, 205; Wildlife Trust 182; Woodland Trust 120, 182
urban areas: green space 182; nature reserves 11

vegetables 24, 29, 30, 41, 121, 184; growing 38; growing sugar snap peas 51–52; nutrients 42, 43; talking points 30–31; *see also* fruit; plants
Venus flytrap 25, 138
vertebrates 83, 85, 87, 88
vultures 204

Wallace, A. 167
Wedgwood, E. 145, 157

weeding 137–138
wheelbarrow gardening 116
wildflowers 138, 139, 141; adaptation 140; growing 140
wildlife cameras 9
wildlife conservation 178, 182
Wildlife Trust 11
wind pollination 127–128
winter 11
woodland edge habitat: adding a pond 202; creating 201; monitoring 202
woodlands 10–11, 56, 57, 66, 67, 83, 85, 127, 201; canopy 67, 86; comparison with school grounds 95; first floor 85, 86; ground floor 85; invertebrates 86; painting 60; trees 67, 92, 93; underground 85; vertebrates 87
Woodland Trust 11, 92; *Green Tree Schools Award* 205; *Nature's Calendar Project* 94, 207, 208, 209
woodlice 74, 75, 76
World Wildlife Fund (WWF): *Livewell for Life* initiative 206, 207; *Plant2Plate Campaign for Schools* 206
worms 15, 76, 150, 163, 169; *see also* earthworms; invertebrates
writing about outdoor learning 19

xylem tubes 25